SUBLIME SURRENDER

CORNELL STUDIES IN THE HISTORY OF PSYCHIATRY

A Series Edited by Sander L. Gilman and George J. Makari

SUBLIME SURRENDER

MALE MASOCHISM AT THE FIN-DE-SIÈCLE

Suzanne R. Stewart

CORNELL UNIVERSITY PRESS

ITHACA AND LONDON

First published 1998 by Cornell University Press
First printing, Cornell Paperbacks, 1998

Printed in the United States of America

Library of Congress Cataloging-in-Publication Data

Stewart, Suzanne R.
Sublime surrender : male masochism at the fin-de-siècle / Suzanne R. Stewart.
p.   cm. — (Cornell studies in the history of psychiatry)
Several chapters of this book were read at a colloquium and a seminar.
Includes bibliographical references and index.
ISBN 0-8014-3434-3 (alk. paper). — ISBN 0-8014-8450-2 (pbk. : alk. paper)
1. Masochism.   2. Sexual dominance and submission.   3. Masochism in literature.
4. Sex in opera.   I. Title.   II. Series.
HQ79s823   1998
306.77'6—dc21   98-15731

Cornell University Press strives to use environmentally responsible suppliers and materials to the fullest extent possible in the publishing of its books. Such materials include vegetable-based, low-VOC inks and acid-free papers that are also recycled, totally chlorine-free, or partly composed of nonwood fibers.

Cloth printing   10   9   8   7   6   5   4   3   2   1
Paperback printing   10   9   8   7   6   5   4   3   2   1

Siehst du denn nicht, daß ich
keine Arme habe und also nicht
helfen kann?

—Heinrich Heine

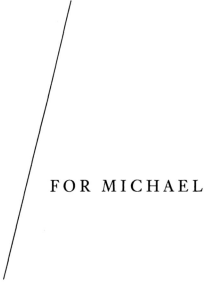

FOR MICHAEL

CONTENTS

ACKNOWLEDGMENTS

Much help and support stand behind the following pages, from both individuals and institutions. First and foremost, I thank Sander Gilman
and Dominick LaCapra for their continuous support, suggestions, and
criticisms over the past years. Without Sander Gilman's constant en-
couragement and Dominick LaCapra's wise exhortations against "wild
theory," this book would never have been written.

Various drafts of the following chapters were read by members of the
German Studies Reading Group and by participants in the German
Studies Colloquium conducted by Peter Hohendahl under the auspices
of the Institute for German Cultural Studies at Cornell University. As a
Mellon Fellow in Cornell's Department of Government in 1994/5, I was
able to try out some of my emerging ideas on the relationship between
the crisis of liberalism and male subjectivity in a seminar on politics and
masochism. The members of the NEH Summer Seminar on masochism
led by Sander Gilman also read significant portions of the manuscript
and offered many valuable suggestions. I thank as well the Department
of Modern Languages at Cornell University for release time from my
duties there, particularly Carol Rosen and Pina Swenson for their support and friendship.

Many friends and colleagues have been critical and generous readers of the manuscript in progress. I thank in particular Nelly Furman, Sandor Goodhart, Rahel Hahn, Eva Kufner, and Judith Surkis. Carolyn Dean's reading allowed me to refine the book's attempt at bringing history and theory into a productive dialogue. At Cornell University Press, John Ackerman and Terence McKiernan transformed printout to book with rigor, patience, and humor. My son Jonah Stewart Sweet patiently traced down missing footnotes and bibliographical references. I thank him and his brother Ben for their sustained patience over the past years.

An earlier version of Chapter 3 was published in the *Musical Quarterly*. I thank the editors for permission to reprint that material here.

Finally, to him who is my companion in life and to whom I dedicate this book, I say: Várlak, Michael, várlak!

SUZANNE R. STEWART

Ithaca, New York

SUBLIME SURRENDER

INTRODUCTION

Struck down by illness, Heinrich Heine left his Paris sickbed for the last time—or so at least he claims—in May 1848. His destination was the Louvre, in order to bid farewell to the revered idols of past, happier times: "Only with difficulty," he narrates, "did I drag myself to the Louvre and I almost collapsed as I entered the sublime hall where the most blessed goddess of beauty, our beloved Lady of Milo, stands on her pedestal. For a long time I lay prostrate at her feet and wept so bitterly that a stone would have taken mercy on me. And indeed the goddess looked down on me with pity, yet at the same time so disconsolately, as if to say: Do you not see that I have no arms and therefore cannot help you?"[1]

Heine's prostration before the pitying but nevertheless cold image of the goddess of beauty was to become a recurring motif during the second half of the nineteenth century. Heine's final farewell inaugurates, in May 1848, what he and others perceived as a serious crisis: of Enlightenment thought generally, of liberal republicanism more specifically, of a coherent male subject-body most concretely. "Do I really exist?" Heine asks. "My body has become so shriveled that nothing is left but my voice."[2]

The materiality of Heine's subjection—the decay of his body—passes into the terrain of fantasy after 1848 and as liberal ambition enters into a crisis. This passage effects a kind of resurrection of the sick man: it is the voice of this shriveled male body at beauty's feet that is the subject of this book. It investigates the contours of a discourse by and about men that took hold in the German-speaking world between 1870 and 1930 and that articulated masculinity as and through its own marginalization. Male masochism, as it came to be called, the compulsive pleasure in consensual submission and the desire on men's part "to act like women," was certainly not the only way in which masculinity was understood in the context of the need to reformulate the parameters of the classical bourgeois subject; the hegemony of this new kind of man remained steadily contested by contemporary critics. Nonetheless, the impact of masochism was significant and gained momentum in response to the growing dominance of monopoly and consumer capitalism at the end of the century. In its initial formulation in the 1880s—and contrary to its currently more popular association with feminine, passive sexuality—masochism denoted a particularly male affliction: it described the condition of those men who fantasized being either physically tortured or psychologically humiliated by a powerful, dominating woman. Denigration was conceived as the prerequisite for pleasure—a pleasure based not in fulfillment but in suspense, in the staging or make-believe of torture, enslavement, and humiliation. Indeed, from the very beginning, masochism was understood as a highly aestheticized practice: bedroom scenes were always stylized and posed, enacting fantasies that took for their props references from the world at large, in particular scenes of political repression.

It is this theatrical aspect of masochism, as well as its reversal of gender roles and its explicit linking of sexuality with political power, that has contributed to the renewed interest in masochism today. Masochism as a theoretical construct has become a favorite object of analysis in gender and cultural studies and an object of consumption in both popular culture and so-called subcultural practices. What these different articulations share is a perception of masochism's critical power, its subversive position vis-à-vis mass culture and consumer capitalism. Paradoxically, however, such a critique is achieved precisely through a staging of those same commercial relationships, on the one hand, and the mass consumption of masochistic scenarios, on the other. The masochistic contract between slave and dominatrix is the most capitalist of all relations because the masochist insists on the right to sell himself. And as Barbara

Ehrenreich has commented, "from a strictly capitalist viewpoint, [sado-masochism] is the ideal sexual practice" because it requires both a heavy investment in costumes and equipment and, more important, the constant commercial publication or publicization on which its exhibitionistic narrativization depends.[3]

The 1969 publication in France of Gilles Deleuze's ground-breaking essay on masochism accompanying the reissue of Leopold von Sacher-Masoch's novella *Venus in Furs*, the urtext of the masochistic male, and the translation of both texts into English in 1989 have become the starting points for most theoretical work on masochism in recent years.[4] Indeed, Deleuze's text has exerted a certain hegemony over Sacher-Masoch's 1870 novella, both in the sense that Deleuze's interpretation has become the dominant one of Sacher-Masoch himself and in the sense that it has taken priority over *Venus in Furs* and thus made itself into a new urtext of masochism. Of primary importance to Deleuze's analysis is his formal separation of masochism from sadism. The unity of the two concepts in the form of sadomasochism has, he insists, done nothing but harm to Sacher-Masoch.[5] Deleuze separates masochism from sadism and does so by relying for his definition of masochism on a literary text and not on a directly psychoanalytic or psychological discourse. The consequences are important, for the grounding of masochism in a literary text not only justifies his radical distinction between sadism and masochism but also makes the masochistic phenomenon into an aesthetic or cultural event. Masochistic fantasy, or more accurately the masochistic aesthetic, is defined as a form of narrative that relies on suspense insofar as it is sexual pleasure as fulfillment that is eschewed. Sexual pleasure is endlessly postponed in favor of a privileged, incestuous relationship with a cruel oral mother who is simultaneously disavowed. The masochistic fantasy is gendered because it is defined, according to Deleuze, as the incestuous relationship between mother and son at the expense of the now banished father. The masochist uses a pedagogical language of persuasion in order to educate the woman into the position of the despot.[6] To ensure that he will be beaten and that the father will be permanently expelled from his fantasy, the masochist is compelled repeatedly to enter into a contractual alliance with the cruel woman. To become a man, for the masochist, does not then mean to take the father's place or to assume the father's symbolic mandate: instead, "it consists in obliterating his role and his likeness in order to generate the new man."[7] Masochistic fantasy thus opposes what Deleuze calls the sadistic, institutional superego in the name of a now liberated ego—an ego that is free, however, only to the extent that it may be willingly fettered by its contract with the pre-Oedipal, oral mother.

Although Deleuze founds his theory of masochism in Sacher-Masoch's writings—a move he shares with other theorists of masochism from the late nineteenth century—he nevertheless depends on a certain psychoanalytic discourse, in particular that of Jacques Lacan. Lacan has been immensely influential in current theories of masochism to the extent that it is the failure by the son to respond to the father's symbolic mandate, on the one hand, and his equally high degree of acculturation in the social order, on the other, that has marked masochism in contemporary theory as a crisis or trauma of the male subject, a crisis that is deemed constitutive ultimately of all subjectivity. Through the category of masochism, the crisis of the subject is refined into a critical practice: the masochist triumphantly flaunts and exhibits the crisis of failed patriarchal symbolization; he points to the general fact that it takes trauma to be a real man. Masochism demonstrates the perverse nature of subjectivity; as Kaja Silverman has put it, the masochist substitutes "perversion for the *père-version* of exemplary male subjectivity."[8] In its modern theoretical elaborations, the concept of masochism thus bears a double burden: it functions as a critical position vis-à-vis the dominant ideology of "true masculinity," and it lays bare the mechanisms by which all subjectivity is constituted. Masochism is thus both exceptional or historically determined and general or universal.

This requirement to function both as a critical tool and as a general theory of subjectivity creates irresolvable tensions in the articulation of modern masculinity. Kaja Silverman, for example, seeks to "isolate a historical moment [in her analysis the post–World War II period] at which the equation of the male sexual organ with the phallus could no longer be sustained"—a moment, that is, when such a disjuncture leads to the collapse of the dominant ideology.[9] At the same time, she follows Lacan in claiming it is this gap between the phallic signifier and empirical masculinity that makes masculinity possible in all its historical forms. In order to avert the resultant collapse of trauma, crisis, and masochism (terms that are themselves difficult to distinguish in her text) into history in general, she is forced into a series of binary oppositions that the text cannot ultimately sustain without undermining her historical argument. For instance, Silverman distinguishes between two forms of identification: one that supports conventional masculinity because it insists on the consolidation of the ego, and one—which lies at the heart of feminine subjectivity, of feminine masochism—where the ego surrenders itself to the other. Silverman privileges the masochistic form of identification over that leading to "the consolidated ego." One may ask what the necessary benefits, political and other, are for the ego to be in a constant state of dissolution. One may also ask how these two forms come to be somewhat unproblematically gendered. What is the value of sustaining a notion of "feminine subjectivity" as that which surrenders itself? Indeed, in her analysis of T. E. Lawrence's *Seven Pillars of Wisdom*, the problematic nature of such a politics openly returns when Silverman is forced to confront not Lawrence's sexual politics of self-dissolution but the fact that his politics can be performed only within the context of a colonialist discourse. As a consequence, she distinguishes between a feminine masochism, now marked as negative, and a reflexive masochism as a conscious or performative moment of self-undoing, thereby isolating subjectivity from its historical form of existence, a move contrary to the explicit goals of her project.

Following Lacan, Slavoj Žižek, in an essay entitled "Courtly Love, or, Woman as Thing," locates masochism in the phenomenon of courtly love—a move justified, he claims, by the necessity to read history retroactively: the rise of the masochistic couple at the end of the nineteenth century makes it possible to understand the economy of courtly love. Yet this move justifies another shift, for Žižek focuses not on the masochistic man but on what he calls the empty, abstract character of the Lady. She becomes, as she also does in Lacan's formulation of courtly love, a cold, indeed terrifying and inhuman partner, occupying that place of radical Otherness beyond the symbolic order that Lacan calls the Thing or the Real.[10] Since woman occupies the space of the Other onto which man projects his own narcissistic ideal, it is man who thus stages in its most theatrical possibilities his own servitude. From here derives the importance of disavowal that is noted also by Deleuze. The masochist remains at all points the stage director of his own fantasy, but without thereby destroying the illusionary quality of his game. This, the complete externalization of the man's desires through a contractual staging with the Lady, means, according to Žižek, that the masochistic theater is completely nonpsychological: "the surrealistic passionate masochistic game, which suspends social reality, none the less fits easily into that everyday reality."[11]

The idealization of the Lady in the masochistic scenario is not, however, a form of desire created by the presence of obstacles. On the contrary, what masochism points to is the mechanism by which an impossible object, the Real or the Lady, is transformed into a prohibition. Masochism stages this transformation—where the object of desire becomes attainable—paradoxically, only via a detour, via a process of unending postponement. The prohibitive language of violence and pain creates the object of desire and elevates that object into what is unattainable: "The Lady therefore functions as a unique short circuit in which *the Object of desire itself coincides with the force that prevents its attainment.*"[12] Žižek, like Lacan, names this process sublimation: "'sublimation' occurs when an object, part of everyday reality, finds itself at the place of the impossible Thing."[13] Sublimation is here then bound to the process of castration, or rather to the phallic signifier qua signifier of castration. Sublimation means that the very agency that demands renunciation does so only to the extent that it also commands enjoyment. The phallic signifier stands for both the gain and the loss of pleasure. Thus Lacan states in a passage that is also quoted by Silverman: "Something becomes an object of desire when it takes the place of what by its very nature remains concealed from the subject: that self-sacrifice, that pound of flesh which is mortgaged in his relationship to the signifier."[14]

What are the consequences, political and theoretical, of Žižek's use of masochism? A first, and highly dubious one, is his celebration of a kind of logical impasse, or what he calls a "certain deadlock in contemporary feminism."[15] Although he concedes that the Lady's semblance of power conceals male domination, that the beatings the masochist receives are designed to alleviate his guilt for his political and social hegemony, that the Lady's elevation renders her the passively blank screen of man's projections, nevertheless, it also true, he insists, that this same structure provides woman with her own fantasy and hence with a sexual identity whose effects are real. From this, Žižek concludes that woman's opposition to "patriarchal domination" does nothing but undermine the support of her own feminine identity. Opposition to patriarchal domination is what leads to a deadlock. It is worth quoting Žižek in full here:

> The problem is that once the relationship between the two sexes is conceived of as a symmetrical, reciprocal, voluntary partnership or contract, the fantasy matrix which first emerged in courtly love remains in power. Why? In so far as sexual difference is a Real that resists symbolization, the sexual relationship is condemned to remain an asymmetrical non-relationship in which the Other, our partner, prior to being a subject, is a Thing, an "inhuman partner"; as such, the sexual relationship cannot be transposed into a symmetrical relationship between pure

subjects. The bourgeois principle of contract between equal subjects can be applied to sexuality only in the form of the *perverse*—masochistic—contract in which, paradoxically, the very form of balanced contract serves to establish a relationship of domination. It is no accident that in the so-called alternative sexual practices ("sadomasochistic" lesbian and gay couples) the Master-and-Slave relationship re-emerges with a vengeance, including all the ingredients of the masochistic theatre.[16]

What takes place here is a naturalization of masochism to the extent that it is placed at the level of the Real. In other words, by asserting that sexual difference pertains to the order of the Real and therefore resists any form of symbolization, it remains indeed condemned to the structure of asymmetry and thus impervious to any kind of intervention, either political or critical. Even worse, in Žižek's logic such interventions do nothing but reaffirm this structure of violence. What for him is but the fantasy of sexual reciprocity is precisely what defines the masochistic contract. While Žižek may argue at some level that this structure of reciprocal desire or the desire for reciprocity is the product of a historical configuration named courtly love, it is nevertheless the case that in his own words this same configuration can be understood only through the lens of today's masochistic couple. In the name of a formal anti-essentialism, we are left with a kind of masochistic essentialism, a deadlock from which it is logically impossible to escape.

Whereas masochism is a constitutive part of the sexual relationship between man and woman for Žižek, and it is so to the extent that it signifies an encounter with the Real, for Leo Bersani masochism is constitutive of sexuality per se. Bersani wishes to read the "Freudian Body" of work in terms of a necessary theoretical collapse or failure, a failure to be celebrated rather than amended for its more proper (clinical) application. Psychoanalytic truth reveals, he states, the terms of its own failure, and it is this that aestheticizes it and turns it into a literary event. What the Freudian failure reveals, then, is a body inevitably inscribed by failure or self-dissolution, a shattering of the self that defines sexuality. Sexuality is not that which is constitutive of the self or the subject but the moment of its undoing. The mystery of sexuality lies in its inherent violence and cruelty: sexuality "could be thought of as a tautology for masochism."[17] Masochism is thus for Bersani both an ontological and a biological category. The human fact of sexual stimulation (experienced as unpleasure) as it runs headlong into conflict with the binding functions of the ego demands a masochism capable of operating as a psychical strategy in order to defeat "a biological dysfunctional process of maturation."[18] Sexuality is not "an exchange of intensities between individuals, but rather a condition in which others merely set off the self-shattering mechanisms of masochistic *jouissance*."[19] The actualization of this self-shattering effect of *jouissance* in sadomasochistic practice constitutes a "melodramatic version of the constitution of sexuality itself, and the marginality of sadomasochism would consist of nothing less than its isolating, even its making visible, the ontological grounds of the sexual."[20] Since what is at stake is not the representation of sexuality but its very coming-into-being through representation, sexual excitement must always be represented as an alienated commotion before it can be felt at all. It is for this reason that Bersani finds in aesthetic practice a replicative elaboration of masochistic sexual tensions. This is what constitutes sublimation, the repeated representation of self-shattering as the enactment of a traumatic induction into sexuality.[21]

As with Žižek and with Deleuze, such a scene is gendered. Sexual trauma comes from the at once over-present and all-too-distant mother; it is she who commands a form of "cultural symbolization as a continuation rather than repressive substitute for sexual fantasy."[22] Sublimation is a form of aesthetic experience in which renunciation is no longer part of the fantasy, or, more accurately, in which renunciation, now loosened from repression, is not experienced as such since pleasure is located precisely at the point where the self gives all, including itself. The edge or boundary of masochistic fantasies of self-annihilation is marked by the repressive agency of the Oedipal father. The father ends the fantasy as soon as he immobilizes sublimation and at the same time promotes a self-destructing sexuality as repressive renunciation, "a derivative masochism which threatens both the individual and civilization."[23] Bersani is not advocating a return to the mother, however; he is advocating her replacement: the paternal figure needs to be de-Oedipalized, that is, dislodged from his role as the inhibiting law and given the possibility of socializing the "traumatic loving initially experienced at the mother's breast."[24]

Bersani, Deleuze, and Žižek then agree that masochism has an inherently subversive potential vis-à-vis patriarchal gender relations. At the very least, masochism is seen to have demonstrative and performative qualities that illustrate the constructedness of gender relations under capitalism. Feminist criticism has noted, however, that such analyses of masochism do not necessarily benefit women: Kaja Silverman points out, for example, that Deleuze himself disavows patriarchal power, for, though the woman may occupy the father's place, the triangularization of the Oedipal family structure has not been thereby subverted. Carol Siegel, on the other hand, has recently argued that Deleuze's theory might very well lend itself to a feminist interpretation insofar as the male masochist may be interpreted as the site of both the critique *and* the subversion of patriarchal relations. What Deleuze cannot explain, in her view, is how in certain literary texts masochistic men actually come to find true satisfaction in a reciprocal relationship. Siegel demands that one analyze masochism in terms of gender relations precisely in order to dislodge it from standard understandings of femininity and passivity. Such an analysis is possible only if one detaches masochism from its psychoanalytic paradigm: otherwise masochism is nothing but an attempt to rewrite the traditional love story into a tale of man's failure to achieve sufficient masculine mastery over woman in order to make them both happy—a story of love in which psychoanalytic theory participates.[25]

It is undoubtedly the case that Freud, like so many of his contemporaries, was obsessed with the possibility that the father's position had come under serious threat in the late nineteenth century. Freud and other contemporary critics read masochism as one of the most obvious symptoms of a modern European civilization that had produced and was continuing to produce men who were incapable of living up to the demands of acculturation and that had created an increasingly large proportion of women who were demanding an equal part in the social contract. Masochism thus pointed to a crisis in gender relations. However—and this will be the essence of my argument and where I depart from much of current theory—masochism also became the site by and through which masculinity was not only redefined but again made hegemonic. Furthermore, what masochism achieved was the reorganization of the relationship between culture, pleasure, and masculinity. In other words, the disintegration of the paternal function became the new cultural matrix, the new means by which men were socialized and turned into cultural subjects. Late nineteenth century writers on the collapse of the paternal function saw themselves as involved in an unceasing struggle to channel sexual energy in such a way that it could at the height of its passion express itself as culture. Paradoxically, sexual passion found itself not in opposition to culture but the most efficient vehicle by which the frail male body could be tyrannized into submitting to cultural demands. Freud, and psychoanalytic theory after him, named this process sublimation. Here, woman came to occupy the place of "the sublime object": she functioned both as moral agent and as demonic figure (indeed, as Freud was to show, the two were becoming difficult to distinguish) who punished man in the name of civilization. This reordering of the relationship between subjectivity and culture did not create a new position for woman, however, nor did it point to the existence of masculine self-dissolution; *for masochism signified*—and this was the fundamental paradox at the very heart of the phenomenon—*a novel form of self-control.*

It is in this latter fact where I most strongly disagree with the analyses of Deleuze, Bersani, Žižek, and Silverman: I believe neither that the masochistic position has involved self-dissolution nor that such undoing of self or subjectivity is in some self-evident manner even politically desirable. If masochism comes into being as a result of a widening gap between the phallic signifier and concrete forms of male subjectivity—if, that is, it is a symptom of a general crisis of masculinity that has its origins in specific historical configurations—then this gap is and must remain historically concrete and be analyzed as such. The problem with so many postmodern theories of the subject is the elevation of the failure of subjectivity into a general condition of all subjectivity, a failure that is then celebrated as necessarily subversive. The result is an equation of a whole series of terms: masochism, trauma, the sublime, and the demonic all become names for an enigmatic site that holds the place of self-dissolution in the name of a critique of all normativity. History is reduced to the traumatic return of the same; all subjectivity is inevitably doomed to undo itself in a generalized crisis of the possibility of making any normative claims for anything at all.

The dissolution of the self or the decentered subject has, as Carolyn Dean points out, a history of its own.[26] In significant ways this book poses questions similar to Dean's, for it explores the historical configurations necessary for the construction of such a new form of subjectivity. Whereas her focus is on France, mine is on the German-speaking world. Whereas Dean locates the origin of this decentered self in the interwar years, in the fractured male body produced by the Great War, I claim it originated earlier, in the mid-nineteenth century. Dean posits the origins of this new subjectivity in the writing of psychiatrists, psychoanalysts, and avant-garde writers, in particular Lacan and Bataille. I argue that the discussions around masochistic men in the German world precede French arguments about a self that finds its mode of existence only in the Other.

As Dean herself also notes, any such analysis raises the extremely difficult question of the relationship between theory and history. Her expressed goal is to trace how theory and history implicate one another, how meaning is constructed as meaning in the theoretical efforts to account for historical versions of the subject. The question is, if one wants to avoid a simplified reduction of theory to history, how does one account for one's own theoretical assumptions? This book raises this problem most clearly in relation to Freud. Freudian theory is asked here to play a double role, for on the one hand I subject Freud to the same scrutiny as Sacher-Masoch and Wagner; on the other, my own theoretical framework depends on psychoanalytic categories as a tool of cultural critique. Nowhere is the problem more acute than with the concept of the phallic or Master signifier, the place where all injunctions or authoritative statements originate and against which all historical forms of subjectivity seem to measure themselves. But is it in fact a transhistorical category? The phallic signifier stands for the fact that the subject is constitutively split, has in other words an unconscious that is structured in its very being as and to a relation of power. The gap between the phallic signifier and subjects, I believe, is transhistorical, while the nature of this gap is always historically determined and thus demanding of analysis.

Ultimately, I would claim, the force of this demand is of an ethical nature. In an analysis of the demonic, Ned Lukacher has remarked that ethics paradoxically obliges the subject to assume the responsibility or causality of its own self, even as it forces the subject to realize that he or she is not the cause of him/herself. It is this paradox that causes a fundamental displacement in the act of willing. Lukacher names this split the demonic, another name for the phallic signifier, "the signifier that brings loss and absence to presence, makes them *felt*, brings them into the realm of experience precisely as loss and absence.... It is from this enigmatic topology that law derives its force." [27] The enigmatic place, the gap that is opened up by the divided act of willing, is the place, according to Lukacher, from whence the ethical injunction originates; it does not derive from any given context or determination. While it is true that the act of willing is divided within itself, I disagree with Lukacher that ethics therefore arises where all determination breaks down. On the contrary, ethics originates precisely as a determination, as the demand made from and by a context. The phallic signifier is not that which can be reduced to the demonic; it protects the subject from the demonic. The ethical moment, conceived indeed as a paradoxical moment in the act of willing, is much closer to what Žižek has termed a "forced choice." The prototypical example of such a forced choice is the Protestant theory of predestination, where it is precisely the knowledge that one's fate is sealed that impels the subject to frantic activity. Thus, "every belonging to a society involves a paradoxical point at which the subject is ordered to embrace freely, as a result of his choice, what is anyway imposed on him." Žižek's point is that this paradox takes place only at the level of symbolization: "The gap that exists in the demand to embrace freely the inevitable can only be the gap that forever separates an event in the immediacy of its raw reality from its inscription into the symbolic network—to embrace freely an imposed state of things means to integrate this state of things into one's symbolic universe."[28] Thus, the gap opened up between the phallic signifier and historically concrete subjects, the gap created within the act of willing, is not a space devoid of determinations; it is historically "loaded," formed by concrete politico-historical configurations that produce a specific form of subjectivity capable of finding a way to enter the symbolic order. As Žižek points out, this is always a forced choice, to the extent that such choice cannot exist outside of some form of symbolic articulation. In other words, normative structures are always at play in the act of willing, and these structures either sustain dominant power relations or undermine and change them.

If the gap between phallic signifier and concrete subjects is then historically concrete, and if the ethical moment resides in an act of choice made from within that historically determined place, two problems arise: how to avoid a kind of situational ethics or pragmatism, and how to articulate one's own position vis-à-vis the phallic signifier? How, in other words, to place oneself within the tension between the dangers of a diluted ethical relativism and an absolutism produced by the submission to a Master signifier, between history on the one hand and theory on the other? In the end, I do not believe that the tension can or should be resolved: it is this tension that remains the site where a self can most productively be created and where power relations can be critically engaged. It is productive because it is the only place from which it is possible to allow for one's own positioning within the gap between subject-position and phallic signifier. My own understanding of such a gap is close to D. W. Winnicott's notion of the transitional object, of which it can be said that "it is a matter of agreement . . . that we will never ask the question: 'Did you conceive of this or was it presented to you from without?' The important point is that no decision on this point is expected. The question is not to be formulated."[29] Winnicott points to a fundamental paradox involved in the use of the transitional object (its givenness *and* its imaginary construction) and demands that this paradox "be accepted and tolerated and respected, and . . . not . . . be resolved."[30]

Winnicott is referring here to the infant's position vis-à-vis the transitional object, to the process, that is, of the construction of a mature self. Nevertheless, Winnicott's paradox has broader applications: it can also be applied to a broader philosophical formulation of the relationship between subject and object, in which objects are conceived as pre-given and created. An acknowledgment of this paradox is, then, the only place from which the phallic signifier itself can be questioned—in other words, where the historical nature of the most transhistorical of objects can come into full view.

I have chosen to write this book on masochism because the masochistic phenomenon produces so clearly the ethical and political problems raised by a subject-position that claims its own undoing as the precondition of its very existence. Against this tendency, I argue that masochism establishes a new normativity in the name of anti-normativity, and that this new normativity has questionable political effects. The masochistic claims of male renunciation as staged, as rhetorical, must be taken at their word, even though this rhetoric has had real social and political effects: masochism, as it was formulated both as a medical diagnosis of the age and as an aesthetic concept that ordered a new relationship to the culture at large, contributed significantly to the rearticulation of male subjectivity. In the name of marginalization, a new norm was constituted: men were viewed and viewed themselves as always already wounded or fragmented, subjected and enslaved to modern civilization by their own desires, which, of necessity, remained unfulfilled. Masochism expressed both a crisis of male subjectivity and the positive valorization of that crisis whereby crisis itself became a constitutive feature of that same masculinity.

The relationship between the male masochist and modern culture was gendered, for in the masochistic universe modernity came to be feminized: the adoration of and submission to the products of culture were also sexual; the male masochist perceived himself as subjected to a dominatrix, to a topos called the Cruel Woman. The masochist himself created this Cruel Woman as aesthetic object and in that move attempted to reassert control, both over the means of cultural production and over the woman's body. Since the Cruel Woman was always this aesthetically created object, a close link was established between masochism and the Freudian concept of sublimation. Indeed, Freud himself drew on discursive practices that had already created such a connection through the notion of the sublime. Masochistic scenarios, whether in literature, music, the visual arts, or medicalized diagnoses of the fin-de-siècle *malaise*, staged the male shriveled body as a body that submits to an aestheticized and eroticized gaze and voice, thus conceiving of man as deeply penetrated by relations of political and sexual power.

Such are the claims of my first, introductory chapter. In Chapter 2 I analyze the role of the gaze in the constitution of the male masochistic subject through a reading of Leopold von Sacher-Masoch's 1870 novella *Venus in Furs*. Sacher-Masoch—the first official or paradigmatic case of masochism—wrote here a story about how to see and be seen by paintings. The possibility of making and seeing paintings is articulated as a scopophilic hunger predicated on the simultaneous visibility of the Cruel Woman and the blindness of a new, Samsonian man. In Chapter 3, I argue that Richard Wagner's 1882 opera *Parsifal* turns on the problem of possessing the female operatic voice, a possession made possible through the simultaneous acceptance and disavowal of castration. It is this double relationship to castration that enables Parsifal's role as new redeemer and political leader. Chapter 4 continues this interrogation of a sexually ambiguous leadership through an analysis of Freud's cultural writings, specifically *Group Psychology and the Analysis of the Ego* (1921) and *Civilization and Its Discontents* (1930). I argue that the sexual ambiguity of the Freudian leader—is the leader a man or a woman?—must be understood in the context of his theory of narcissism, and that it is at the intersection of narcissism and the hegemony of the cultural and political superego that Freud's new man—the masochist—is constituted.

Male masochism, as I state in the final chapter, is one way by which fin-de-siècle culture reflected and sought to come to terms with a serious crisis of liberalism and of the bourgeois subject. Masochism explicitly took up and staged the most salient constitutive features of that bourgeois liberalism: the contract, which assumes a preconstituted, coherent subject equal to and capable of entering into relations with other subjects, the clear demarcation of the private and the public domain, the distinction between natural constraints and political freedoms, the "obviousness" of male and female sexuality. Through such stagings, masochism subverted the contract (in its economic, civic, and political meanings), as well as the hitherto more easily maintained distinctions between male and female, public and private, consent and compulsion. And yet, such subversions remained politically ambiguous at best, for they were predicated on the silencing of women whose position as victims of a sexual hierarchy had been triumphantly usurped by a male claim to the margin that, once so claimed, became the new center. Male masochism's staged renunciation of power to the Cruel Woman created what Tania Modleski recently has described as a feminism without women.[31] In this sense, though the prostration to cultural objects of beauty might appear as a reversal of traditional gender roles, this reversal was inevitably rhetorical, for it was predicated on the fact that Our Lady of Milo could have no arms.

1

"A FAMILIAR SMILE OF FASCINATION": MASOCHISM, SUBLIMATION, AND THE CRUELTY OF LOVE

The Man . . .

In the second half of the nineteenth century the Western World came to understand itself as increasingly traversed by and enclosed within an ever-tightening network. Yet, as contemporary witnesses observed, this network was of a peculiar if not paradoxical nature, denoted by two of its descriptive terms: traversal and enclosure. For while the lineaments of such a network certainly made the world smaller—one's body, voice, language could move across greater distances at ever greater speed— they also opened up the possibility of striving for ever greater, even un- reachable, destinies. Indeed, enclosure and expansion, restriction and generalization, were so firmly linked together that language itself was infused with the network's peculiar energy. Language was to submit to the network, to become part of its functioning, to reproduce it and be reproduced by it (via Bell's telephone, say, or Edison's phonograph), to copy both it and itself; at the same time, it had to be original, to break out of the network, or drag it along behind itself, to conquer new terri- tories in the same act of exposing itself as condemned to its imitative or mimetic functions. The materiality of language, its nervous energy, rested in its dual function as symptom and diagnosis.

This network was, then, fundamentally energetic, endowed with the capacity for infinite expansion and ultimate mastery, manifestly capable of making more out of less. Crisis and loss were generative of order and gain, not simply because the modern age dispensed with outdated modes of economic production or traditional bases of authority but because in such a network productivity and generation had their origin in the moments of their own collapse or degeneration. The very notion of subjectivity came to model closely this strange economy, where loss of control could double itself into positions of power, where the patient turned inevitably into his own clinician, compelled as he was both by his submission to the network that mercilessly traversed and invaded his body and by a language that equally mercilessly commanded his own diagnosis.

Judge Daniel Paul Schreber, from behind the bars of the newly organized German asylums, was one of the no doubt grandest of these patient-clinicians, and he experienced the network in the form of rays that spoke to him in an ur-language, commanding him to write their diagnostic account so that they might be heard and tried before the Saxon courts of law.[1] His patience and diagnosis were so thoroughly soldered together into a coherent discourse that Schreber was released by the judges, having thus won for himself the official right to his own diagnosis. Freud understood this matter very well, and in his only case history treating psychosis, he concurred with the judges' verdict:

> The psychoanalytic investigation of paranoia would altogether be impossible if the patients themselves did not possess the peculiarity of betraying (in a distorted form, it is true) precisely those things which other neurotics keep hidden as a secret. Since paranoiacs cannot be compelled to overcome their resistances, and since in any case they only say what they choose to say, it follows that this is precisely a disorder in which a written report or a printed case history can take the place of personal acquaintance with the patient.[2]

Although the language of paranoia justified Freud's distance from the whole matter, thus obviating the need for personal contact, it could do so only to the extent that this language was in fact virtually identical with that of psychoanalytic investigation. Since Schreber's network of rays were "in reality nothing else than a concrete representation and external projection of libidinal cathexes," [3] Freud himself had to call on a "friend and fellow-specialist" to bear witness to the fact that, though Schreber's system was remarkably similar to his own, Freud had conceived of it first.

In 1923, only two decades after Schreber's *Freispruch*, the art historian Aby Warburg was to give a repeat performance of this effort at simultaneous submission and control. This time the stage set was Binswanger's clinic itself, the audience fittingly both patients and doctors. Warburg was able to demonstrate his own victimization to the network of serpents, lightning flashes, and electric currents, and in that move make himself master of the serpent ritual.[4] That his audience was so quickly convinced, that he veritably mesmerized, hypnotized, and locked it within the structure of its own transferential desire, thus dispensing with the need for higher courts of appeal, may have been because Warburg, unlike Schreber, had a slide show to back up his facts.

To gain mastery of submission, Schreber had to reach for the heavens of Ahriman and Ormuzd; Warburg for the distant Hopi tribe of the American West. Leopold von Sacher-Masoch had the advantage over both of them: he was born in the right place (Lemberg, Galicia) at the right time (1836), this being in the East, right around the corner from his Transylvanian cousin Dracula, who was continuing his experiments in network-playing with the aid of blood transfusions. Sacher-Masoch's nerve endings were in neither the skies nor the American West but at home in his "native" Galicia, as he would so fondly repeat. For him, the place to begin is not just close to home but home itself:

> I was born on January 27, 1836 in Lemberg, the capital city of Galicia. A Siberian cold ruled that day, and this perhaps may explain my preference for furs, a preference that has been the cause of headaches for many a German critic, though this still would not solve the riddle as to why I only love sable and ermine on beautiful women.[5]

Sacher-Masoch eagerly took on the role of both patient and clinician, adopting the discourse, if not of psychoanalysis, then of a language Freud would later use himself, a language based on the assumption that personality structures were to be explained as originating in and at birth. There remained, of course, the issue of furs on beautiful women, though this too he could explain by recourse to a "primal scene" that occurred when the writer was only nine years old. Sacher-Masoch's life was to have no secrets; like Schreber, he wished freely to exhibit his childhood fixations, and in that act provide a diagnostic self-analysis in the form of laws that had the quality of a ruling, Siberian cold. Sacher-Masoch was one more of those late-nineteenth-century patient-clinicians who led his shadowy yet highly visible existence in a space that straddled the public domain of political power and the private domain of intimate sexual desire.

. . . And His Place

When in 1931 Benedetto Croce looked back at the nineteenth century's particular *mal du siècle*, he was moved to locate this malady in the borderland between a now collapsed ancient and hereditary faith and the new but not yet digested faith of liberal and philosophical ideals. This new faith could not be found "by going in search of it with restless combinations of desire and imagination" but required instead "courage and manliness, and the renunciation of certain outworn motives now grown impossible, flattering and comfortable though they may be."[6] It furthermore demanded "experience and culture and a trained mind." The new age required then, in his opinion, two kinds of subjects, subjects who would be strong enough to live up to these new demands: on the one hand, it needed "robust intellects and characters, who followed [the new faith's] genetic process without allowing themselves to be entangled in it and, passing through their inner storms, reached the haven"; on the other hand, it needed "clear and simple minds and straightforward hearts who at once learned and adopted its conclusions, and put them into practice, conquered and held by the light of their goodness and good." Unfortunately, there were few of these individuals about: the age appeared dominated instead by new idolaters who "identified the infinite with this or that finite, the ideal with this or that phenomenon," ruled as they were by "feminine souls"—"impressionable, sentimental, incoherent and voluble"—and stimulated by excessive and excited doubts within themselves that they were unable to master. These "moral romantics," as Croce called them, were both "nerve-sick" and "fancy-sick"; they had transformed political ideals into political fantasy, the value of poetry for life into poetry-life or life-poetry, liberty into "egoarchy" or anarchy. It was because of these "feminine souls" that so much of the age was simply perverse: they had put lust and voluptuousness in the place of ideals, had flavored cruelty and horror with sensual pleasure, and were altogether guided by a "taste for incest, sadism, Satanism and other like delights."[7]

Croce was certainly not first or alone in his worries about nerve- and fancy-sick feminine souls caught in the bodies of males—or, more accurately, hordes of male bodies unfairly stuck with feminine souls.

Indeed, this Crocean no-man's-land appeared to be becoming rather overcrowded, since, though it belonged "to all times,"[8] it nevertheless seemed to have gained a particular consistency in the course of the second part of the nineteenth century and was still thriving well into the twentieth. Richard von Krafft-Ebing, in his obsessive compilation of the sexual aberrations of his male contemporaries, was disturbed to find that perversions were on the increase during the decades in which he conducted his research (the last quarter of the nineteenth century), and furthermore that it appeared the contagion hit the traditional paterfamilias most strongly. Indeed, it seemed that not only was the public employee, the *Beamte*, failing to remain at his post, but he had the audacity to advertise such failure in the newspapers. No longer content with the satisfaction of his sexually perverse desires in the privacy of his bedroom, the deviant appeared to gain pleasure from the exhibition of his afflictions in the public sphere.[9] Whereas the cultural domain had earlier been the place where one sought the sublime (in either its religious or aesthetic manifestations), it had now become the place where sexual pleasure showed itself in its most pathological forms, in particular as the collapse of the most basic distinctions—for instance, those between male and female, between public and private, and between culture and nature. Indeed, its time and place coordinates remained frighteningly uncertain, for undecidability was one of its main characteristics: although many contemporary observers sought to historicize it by viewing it as a particular feature of modern life, it seemed to flourish most not only in the highly visible public domain of city streets but also in the secret, almost invisible substratum of the mind. It was the place of imagination, fantasy, reverie, and dreams, of uncontrolled and uncontrollable passions, a place that Freud, at the end of the century, was to call "eine andere Lokalität" or "ein anderer Schauplatz," a place that one unwittingly, uncannily, walked into if one were strolling about in the streets. It was the place where pathology and perversion came to be inextricably linked to what appeared as an inevitably wandering imagination; in fact, pathology and perversion became, as Carolyn Dean has noted, the very sign that such a thing as human imagination existed.[10]

There was no question in the minds of most contemporary observers that the wanderings of fantasy were the first signs of a possibly catastrophic change. Eduard Fuchs, in his massive study of the role of the erotic in caricature, not only noted the increase among his contemporaries in erotic popular literature and iconography but also proclaimed: "For, with any such epochal overturn [*Umwälzung*] of state and society there has always been a general erotic expansion connected to this over-turn. . . . This expansion of the erotic . . . usually precedes political and economic change, that is, it begins at the very moment when the new forces work underground and increase to such an extent that conflicts come to a head in a revolutionary manner, enduring until the ferment-ing political and historical tasks find their solution."[11] Not all critics were as confident as Fuchs that there would be an eventual solution to the brewing crisis, since a fundamental component of this crisis was woman, and in particular the New Woman, for it was she who had made special contributions to the blurring of distinctions: the New Woman stood for the impossibility of distinguishing between virtuous woman and prostitute, and by extension, between woman and man. The eman-cipation of women, so it was feared, would lead to one of two possibili-ties: either it would turn women into men, or it would bring about the complete victory of a rampant female sexuality. However, as Michael Salewski has pointed out, male anxiety of being castrated by a domineer-ing woman was not a new phenomenon, nor was the fascination with such figures as Salome, Delilah, and Judith. What *was* new was the grow-ing suspicion that such women were not the exception to the norm of the domestic and domesticated women but in fact prototypes of femi-ninity in general.[12] If the struggle was no longer against a selection of wayward women, then the battle lines had to be redrawn, and the result was an all-out war between the sexes, a battle of cosmic proportions that would have to finally answer the question whether women would suc-ceed in pulling down men's trousers.

This war was held to be of cosmic proportions since at stake was the very possibility of culture itself, for the victory over women signified the victory also over nature. Armed with Darwin's theory of evolution, the American Joseph Le Conte announced in the late 1880s, "There can be no doubt that we are now on the eve of a great revolution," a revolu-tion that would find its fulfillment in man's complete liberation from na-ture. Man was at present still bound by the forces of nature, like an em-bryo that has not yet severed his connection with the earth-mother. "The whole mission and life-work of man is the progressive and finally the complete dominance, both in the individual and in the race, of the higher over the lower. The whole meaning of sin is the humiliating bond-age of the higher to the lower."[13] Nonetheless, while the battle lines seemed clear, while sin appeared so obviously located in the humiliating bondage to Mother Nature, it was equally true that the evil mother was also the source of all culture. Had it not been Eve, after all, who put man in his post-lapsarian state of dependence on all the evils of civilization? As Owen Meredith reminded his male readers in 1887, "A penal law controls Man's fallen state. / It's name is Progress: and, to stimulate / That progress to its destin'd goal, Decay, / Woman, with growing power, shall all the way / Its course accompany—from happiness / And ignorance to knowledge and distress."[14]

Sigmund Freud shared the same confusion about woman's role in the civilization process: on the one hand, it had been man's efforts at overcoming woman's "retarding and restraining influence" on civilization—given her sole interest in family and sexuality—that had granted him the possibility of making culture; on the other hand, a rule of mothers had apparently preceded that of fathers, and it had been "women who, in the beginning, laid the foundations of civilization by the claims [Forderungen] of their love."[15] The claims of love are what most perplexed fin-de-siècle men, for they seemed to guarantee stable attachments to men, while making those same attachments into the very force that prevented men from becoming fully civilized subjects. As Bram Dijkstra has shown, one of the favorite metaphors for this dilemma was woman as a clinging vine. While woman was encouraged to remain loyal to and dependent on her man, the problem with this obedience was that as a clinging vine she had the capacity to smother the very trunk on which she grew. Since woman had no understanding of man's aspiration toward cultural ideals, since, as Freud was to point out, she had no capacity for sublimation, she acted not like a garland or flower but more like a chain. As one critic pointed out, too many women were taking the claims of love too literally: "Accepting as they do, the oak-and-vine theory as regards man and woman, they make no attempt to stand erect without support, but swing wide their graceful tendrils in every breeze, if haply they may find some oak to cling to."[16] Love understood too literally meant that men would be incapable of withstanding the seductions of women, and it was this that led to the feminization of men as they were sucked dry by the voracious desire of consuming and consumerist women.

Man then found himself in a bewildering place where nature and culture were less easily distinguished than demanded and called for by his explicit tasks and strivings. Quite strangely, the more control he sought to gain over nature and women, the more power he seemed to be handing them. The closer he came to his ideal, the further he seemed from it. The constantly shifting horizons of his world challenged wholeness, his own wholeness, and it became ever more difficult to maintain the hitherto obvious connection between gender and sex. Thus, Havelock Ellis was moved to write, "we may not know exactly what sex is, . . . we do know that it is mutable, with the possibility of one sex being changed into the other sex, that its frontiers are often mutable, and that there are many stages between a complete male and a complete female."[17]

If the privileged pathological source for the crisis of masculinity was woman, then the privileged pathological institution of it was the family: first, because it had been the traditional domain of women, and second, because the family occupied an increasingly uncertain position between the private compulsions of man's soul and his public obligations toward the state. Eduard von Hartmann envisioned the typical bourgeois husband of the second half of the nineteenth century as under constant attack by his wife, who, it appeared, was no longer willing to fulfill her domestic duties: "It never enters her mind that her husband's occupation, which is undertaken for the support of the family, entails a far severer martyrdom on him than she suffers by fulfilling all her natural duties, and that it shortens his life in a far greater degree."[18] In the early part of the twentieth century, one French critic was to observe that the typical bourgeois family now consisted of a weak father, a tyrannical mother, a passive son, and a frigid or lesbian daughter. The mother's (and daughter's) contempt for men was seen as the cause of her desire to become a lawyer, a doctor, or an engineer, while the embattled male in the wake of the collapse of his authority inevitably became a passive intellectual. But even if woman refrained from becoming a lawyer or an engineer, even if she remained at home in her own boudoir, the axis of power nevertheless seemed to have shifted, for the power of feminine sexuality was such that it could trick man into making political decisions against his own will.[19]

In 1908, Freud was to reaffirm the close connection between sexual morality gone awry, the excessive demands of civilization, and a particular form of modern nervousness. He too gathered a veritable symphony of voices in support of the idea that the majority of modern men were incapable of getting a hold of themselves because of their excessive and overstimulating doubts, and because they labored with a basic confusion between sexuality and civilizing ideals. There was a direct connection between the physiognomy of this nervousness (whose effects, according to the diagnostician of the age, Richard von Krafft-Ebing, are immediately visible in the structure of the brain) and the organization of modern civilization, though it was not immediately clear whether modern civilization was the result of degenerate brain cells or whether the demands of civilization had created handicapped subjects. There appeared, in any case, a specular, homologous relation between the frenzied and restless activity of man's drives and the nervousness of the modern social order:

> The demands made on the efficiency of the individual in the struggle for existence have greatly increased and it is only by putting out all his mental powers that he can meet them. At the same time the individual's needs and the demands for the enjoyment of life have increased in all classes; . . . The immense extension of communications which has been brought about by the network of telegraphs and telephones that encircle the world has completely altered the conditions of trade and commerce. All is hurry and agitation; night is used for travel, day for business, . . . political life is engaged in quite generally: political, religious, and social struggles, party-politics, electioneering, and the enormous spread of trade-unionism inflame tempers, place an ever greater strain on the mind, and encroach upon the hours for sleep, recreation and rest. City life is constantly becoming more sophisticated and more restless. The exhausted nerves seek recuperation in increased stimulation and in highly-spiced pleasures, only to become more exhausted than before. Modern literature is predominantly concerned with the most questionable problems which stir up all the passions, and which encourage sensuality and a craving for pleasure, and contempt for every fundamental ethical principle and every ideal.[20]

Too much of civilized sexual morality led to bad health and eventually affected the aims of civilization, was Freud's conclusion, a conclusion that for him took on the status of a natural supposition. And by the time he came to write *Civilization and Its Discontents* in 1930, this relationship between bad sexual health and civilization was not only a natural supposition but so widespread that it had become common knowledge: "Our inquiry concerning happiness has not so far taught us much that is not already common knowledge [was nicht allgemein bekannt ist]," he worried at the beginning of chapter 3, and in concluding the same chapter, he wrote, "so far we have discovered nothing that is not universally known." Freud's problem, shared by so many other contemporary observers, was partly an anxiety about waste: "In none of my previous writings have I had so strong a feeling as now that what I am describing is common knowledge and that I am using up ink and paper and, in due course, the compositor's and printer's work and material in order to expound things which are, in fact, self-evident." Such waste of ink, paper, and the work of others was evidently giving him a guilty conscience: "All that has been said above about conscience and guilt is, moreover, common knowledge and almost undisputed."[21] Freud worried whether there was not some unknown or uncanny connection between sexuality and civilization that led to commonness and waste, and did so in the very process of his writing it down and making others work for it.

Phonographic accuracy, according to Friedrich Kittler, means doing away with the constitutive repressions of discourse.[22] Or so it was at least believed. And this was of course true not only for the phonograph but for any type of writing machine, be it Remington's typewriter, Schreber's psychotic *Aufschreibesystem*, or an army of female secretaries. Writing machines had the peculiar quality of doing away with sexual differences: "Machines everywhere, wherever one looks! There is a replacement for the countless tasks that man performed with an able hand, a replacement and one with such power and speed. . . . It was only to be expected that after the engineer had taken the very symbol of feminine skill out of woman's hands a colleague would come up with the idea of replacing the pen as well, the symbol of masculine production, with a machine."[23] If women had the peculiar ability to be reduced to the level of writing machines, if they could simply take dictation, then this depended on the special connection between writing and sexual fantasy: "On the one hand, a desexualization permits the most intimate diaries and most perverse sexualities to be textualized; on the other hand, there is the truth. Indeed, precisely the truth corresponds to Freud's original insight and was simultaneously being publicized by an extended juristic-journalistic dragnet: the fact that hysteria consists in having been seduced by a despot."[24] Now, the problem was that the gender of this despot had become unclear, if not outright questionable. What if, Nietzsche wondered, truth turned out to be a woman? What if this were the most fundamental fantasy of all? Fantasy, Freud was to repeat, was always implanted or inscribed; but when reproduced accurately, that is as text or story, fantasy had the potential for being redirected toward nonsexual activities and therefore freed from the structures of repression. Freud was to call this sublimation, and the concept was to bear the weight not only of his own "writing-down system" but also of that same borderland or "anderer Schauplatz" that was both the object of psychoanalysis and its simultaneous Other: the waste and commonness of the all-too familiar sexual drives.

Masochism: Perverse and Moral

In 1870 the prolific Galician writer Leopold von Sacher-Masoch published his perhaps most famous novella, *Venus im Pelz*. Like so many of his other stories, *Venus* traced the history of love as a battle between the sexes whose outcome would have to remain forever uncertain. Above all, what Sacher-Masoch sought to lay bare was the desire by men to succumb to a dominating, cruel woman. The German sexologist Richard von Krafft-Ebing, in his monumental 1886 taxonomy of sexual perversions, adopted the Galician author's tendencies as the purest expression of what Krafft-Ebing then named "masochism." As may be gleaned from Krafft-Ebing's *Psychopatia Sexualis*, it was clear that Sacher-Masoch was not the only late-nineteenth-century male suffering from this affliction: a veritable plague of masculine submission to dominating women seemed to be spreading through Europe, striking at its worst in the domain of the bourgeois family. Such geographic infectiousness was subsequently repeated in the term's theoretical impact: Sigmund Freud adopted the term in 1905, making it into one of the component instincts of infantile polymorphous sexuality.[25] Masochism in this Freudian conceptualization thereby became a constitutive part of human sexuality, though one that would ideally be overcome once sexuality submitted to the dictates of its genital telos.

And yet the term continued to spread. We know that Freud returned repeatedly to the phenomenon and that he did so because it challenged his theory of the libido. Indeed, the last essay Freud dedicated explicitly to masochism—"The Economic Problem of Masochism" (1924)—forced him to leave the phenomenon just there: as an *economic* problem. And yet the nature of this problem of masochism had shifted for Freud. According to his first theoretical articulations, masochism challenged the opposition between what Freud described as the principle of pleasure, on the one hand, and the self's drive toward preservation, on the other. In this context, the psychic investment of pain with pleasure was conceived as and referred back to an intrapsychic disorder that made its appearance first in the context of infantile polymorphous sexuality and later in adult sexuality as a regressive fixation or reevocation of that same earlier phase.[26] Only in this latter instance was masochism to be understood as a *perversion* in its proper sense, for it constituted a disruption of the sexual instinct in its telic movement toward heterosexual genital organization. Freud's early formulation of masochism as perversion, then, saved Freud's dual theory of the drives: masochism was perverse not just because it stood for sexual practices working against a genital logic that required male aggression and feminine passivity—a complementarity turned on its head by masochism—but more urgently because it wreaked havoc with Freud's drive theory.

Yet the problem persisted. In part, Freud was able to answer the continuing doubts over this phenomenon that gained pleasure from its opposite by formulating a new dualism of the drives in 1920, positing a death drive, a "beyond the pleasure principle," a force of absolute disintegration in opposition to the binding force of Eros, where the two drives nevertheless always appeared together in some amalgamated form. "The Economic Problem of Masochism" in fact rewrote the masochistic story along just those lines. Like the repetition compulsion, like negative therapeutic reactions, or like anxiety dreams, masochism was exemplary of this peculiar though also normal amalgamation.

Nevertheless, and as the title of Freud's essay announced, masochism was still a problem, and more specifically an *economic* problem, and like all economic problems, masochism appeared incapable of fulfilling an essential need: "If pain and unpleasure [*Unlust*] can be not simply warnings but actually aims, the pleasure principle is paralyzed." It was to this seeming paralysis of pleasure that Freud addressed himself. Right away, what masochism created was a kind of political crisis in the relations between the "two great principles," the pleasure principle and the death drive: which of the two ruled the psychic apparatus? Since pain appeared to involve a heightening, and pleasure a lowering of stimulus-tension in the mind, it would seem that the pleasure principle was completely in the service of the death drive, and the pleasure principle could not act as the "watchman over our mental life." And yet Freud finds this proposition not correct. The mind may also perceive a heightening of stimulus as pleasure (in sexual foreplay, for example) and a lowering of the same stimulus as painful. Pain and pleasure cannot be understood in purely quantitative terms; a qualitative factor must enter into their description, though Freud is unable to say what this factor might be. What is clear, however, is that both instincts exist separately but equally and that they thus democratically represent conflictual impulses in the mental apparatus: the "*Nirvana* principle expresses the trend of the death instinct; the *pleasure* principle represents the demands of the libido; and the modification of the latter principle, the *reality* principle, represents the influence of the external world." These three principles cannot cancel each other out, they must always have a working relationship with each other, even when conflict arises: "As a rule they are able to tolerate one another, although conflicts are bound to arise occasionally from the fact of differing aims that are set for each—in one case a quantitative reduction of the load of the stimulus, in another a qualitative characteristic of the stimulus, and, lastly [in the third case], a postponement of the discharge of the stimulus and a temporary acquiescence in the unpleasure due to tension."[27] The pleasure principle as watchman thus "cannot be rejected," even if the consideration of masochism has forced it into a power-sharing situation.[28]

Freud now moves on to a classification of masochism: he distinguishes between three types—the erotogenic or primary form (which grounds all subsequent developments of the libidinal drive and thus cannot be overcome), feminine masochism (considered a perversion when exhibited by men but a natural tendency of feminine passivity when manifested by women), and moral masochism (which catapults Freud into the cultural domain, for here masochism becomes the mechanism by which cultural allegiance if not obedience is instilled as guilt). What is striking is that Freud shows relatively little interest in the first two types: both are discussed rather quickly and then put aside. In fact, primary masochism adds little that is new to Freud's *Three Essays on the Theory of Sexuality* or "Instincts and Their Vicissitudes," and feminine masochism appears as simply another formulation of an adult perversion; indeed, he calls it the "least mysterious form" of masochism. It is clearly *moral masochism* that constitutes the focus of Freud's concern, though he never relinquishes the perverse meaning of masochism in general.[29] Freud continues to straddle this dual understanding of the concept, and in that sense participates in a wider discourse of cultural malaise and degeneration and at the same time provides a place from which to criticize this same discourse.

It is clearly moral masochism that is the economic problem. What is remarkable about moral masochism is that it has loosened its ties to sexuality, whereas in the other forms of masochism, pain must always be administered by a loving person, here "the turning of the other cheek" is administered by an impersonal force. Moral masochism always involves therefore an elision of the gender of the punishing force. Pleasurable punishment comes here from the superego, though this agency may find substitutions in the outside world. But why does the superego terrorize the ego so much and why does the ego eagerly accept this punishment?

The superego, Freud answers, is the representative of both the id and the outer world; it is constituted as the introjection of the parents who both forbid and are cathected with desire. The superego comes into being after the passing of the Oedipus complex; it is its rightful heir and thus necessarily requires a desexualized relationship with the parents, a desexualization that has taken place precisely through their introjection. At the same time, these figures of authority belong to the outside world; their power is "one of the most strongly-felt manifestations of reality."[30]

Ever since Freud's initial formulations of the superego and the ego ideal, he had placed the birth of morality and conscience in that same agency. The obvious question is, what is the difference between morality and moral masochism? How can the two be kept apart? In the case of morality, Freud answers, the accent falls on the sadism of the superego, in moral masochism it falls on the ego itself. Freud immediately realizes that this hardly solves the problem, that more must be involved than simply a matter of perspective. The crucial difference is that the sadistic superego is perceived consciously by the ego, whereas its masochism must remain hidden to it. Moral masochism must remain unconscious because it hides a desire: "Conscience and morality have arisen through the overcoming, the desexualization, of the Oedipus-complex; but through moral masochism morality becomes sexualized once more, the Oedipus-complex is revived and the way is opened for a regression from morality to the Oedipus complex."[31] The problem with moral masochism is that it resexualizes what had previously been desexualized: whereas morality remains desexualized—that is, not cathected as an object of desire—moral masochism disturbs morality because it requires a transgression of the law in order to generate the desired punishment. Yet Freud had introduced moral masochism as a form of masochism that had loosened its ties with sexuality, for if it had not done so, it would be merely another form—probably the feminine version—of masochism.

Moral masochism thus appears to be a desexualized form of resexualization, a difficult compromise formation chosen by the ego in response to the civilizing demands made by morality. And in fact, moral masochism turns out to be not only a response to but also an effect of the civilized suppression of the instincts, that is, of the work of the sadistic, moralizing superego: "The sadism of the super-ego and the masochism of the ego supplement each other and unite to produce the same effects. It is only in this way, I think, that we can understand how the suppression of an instinct can result in a sense of guilt and how a person's conscience becomes more severe and more sensitive the more he refrains from aggression against others."[32] In other words, *if the ego were not masochistic, the superego's hold over it would simply cease*; once the ego had fulfilled the superego's commands, guilt would disappear and morality would collapse. What moral masochism in effect provides is a guarantee that social relations will be permanent, and it provides this guarantee precisely because it can harness or fuse libidinal instincts to the agency of repression. Moral masochism, then, represents a "classical piece of evidence" for fusion at several levels: an instinctual fusion of libido and death drive; a topographical fusion of ego and superego who together produce the same effects of political stability; a fusion of libido with that which is to stem it—the agency of repression—a fusion, that is, of the id and the superego; and lastly, a fusion of libido and the outer world, the forces of civilization, which Freud articulates as the forces of morality. It follows, then, that *all* egos are moral masochists to the extent that they are moral, civilized human subjects. With one notable exception: since women have a weaker superego and since women are therefore for Freud less moral, they can never be true masochists. Subjectivity in modern civilization, so Freud seems to conclude, is male and masochistic.

After 1920—that is, after the formulation of the death drive and the construction of the new topographical model of the psychic apparatus— Freud thus relegated to second place an understanding of masochism as individual perversion. This shift reflects a more general one in the concept's use. Freud, after 1920, comes to increasingly think of masochism in social or societal terms: masochism, insofar as it was an economic problem, was also a political problem; qua moral masochism, masochism became for Freud the central point at which the real entered into the constitution not only of the ego but of the psychic system as a whole. Providing the basis from which Freud was able to think of the social as a specifically modern category, masochism became in a fundamental sense constitutive of the social itself. Thus, the concept of masochism articulated for Freud a meeting place for his egology and his sociology.[33]

If Freud situated masochism at the very center of civilized culture, it was because he located it in that place where trauma entered both the Freudian psychic apparatus and the body of psychoanalysis. At stake was nothing less than the demarcation of the historical and political context in which Freud was writing. In his later work, this context was provided first and foremost by that of post–World War I Europe, and Freud, like most of his contemporaries, was conscious that a new man had emerged out of the trenches of World War I and that this new man was trauma-tized. World War I had produced a generalization of trauma. On a first level, such generalization was linked for Freud to the sheer massiveness of the war neuroses visible on the streets of Europe and endlessly repro-duced in the period's iconography: war neuroses derived not simply from the bloodiness and cruelty of the war but from the fact that it was fought with civilian, conscript armies whose members had been unable, as they marched off to the battle-fields, to leave behind their peacetime egos and to adopt the psychic protections previously afforded to merce-nary soldiers. The soldiers had lacked a preparedness for trauma, lacked what Freud in reformulating his anxiety theory in 1926 was to call an *Angstbereitschaft*. Traumatized at the front, the soldiers had returned home to find that neither side of the warring nations could claim true victory, which would command some sense of closure or end to the con-flict and the political crisis. Instead, war was brought home; it was gen-eralized and continued by other means. War became part of peace, and everyday life became a new form of trench warfare.[34]

The war, according to Freud, had brought in its wake the disillusion-ment of our belief that violence and aggression could ever be overcome through the civilizing process; it had also altered our relationship to death.[35] This return to violence as the return of the repressed and as the new relationship to death was given theoretical elaboration in Freud's *Beyond the Pleasure Principle* (1920). Nevertheless, what is striking in this text is the everyday quality of the sources of danger: Freud speaks of rail-way accidents not aerial bombardments of civilians. Yet this is indeed Freud's point: not only is the specifically modern inhabitation of Eros death, but in and because of this inhabitation, it had become increas-ingly difficult to know with certainty the boundaries that divided the so-cial from the psychic. Of note here are important continuities in Freud's thought. For while the difficult demarcation between the psychic and the social had become particularly acute with the crisis generated by the World War, the need to articulate clearly the domain that was properly individual or psychic had haunted Freud from the very beginning of his career: how, he had wondered ever since his earliest essays on sexual trauma and anxiety neurosis in the 1890s, did the extrapsychic impinge on the psychic apparatus? The question of how the world, how culture and civilization, not simply affected but beleaguered the individual was probably one of the most pressing problems in fin-de-siècle culture. Freud's answer—and one that distinguished psychoanalytic discourse from so many of the other answers—was already in his early writings characteristically complex: the psychic apparatus produces anxiety when it "feels itself incapable of fulfilling . . . a task (danger) *emanating from without*"; it produces anxiety neuroses, on the other hand, when it cannot alleviate the sexual excitation that has arisen from within the psyche. In this latter instance, the psychic apparatus "*acts, therefore, as though it had projected this excitation outwards.*" [36]

From the point of view of the psychic apparatus, therefore, it was impossible to distinguish between real anxiety and neurotic anxiety, since sexual excitation arising from within is registered as coming from without. It was precisely this *uncertainty*, however, this lack of differentiation, that Freud made constitutive of psychic reality itself.[37] The mechanism of anxiety is homologous to that of seduction: when Freud abandoned his seduction theory, this was not because he denied the reality of parental seduction of the child but because he realized that from the viewpoint of the psychic apparatus, from, that is, the viewpoint of fantasy, it made no difference whether there really had been a seduction or not: the effects were the same if this seduction had been imagined. Yet, as Laplanche and Pontalis have shown in their seminal essay on Freudian fantasy, it was precisely this fantasy of seduction that makes fantasy or psychic reality a possibility.[38] As Freud was to reiterate throughout his life, the constitution of the subject was predicated on a certain anxiety, the loss of an object that had never been owned, a feeling of unpleasure that nevertheless made pleasure possible. Or, even more dramatically, the subject was born from excitations that were registered as the unpleasure of pleasure and the pleasure of unpleasure.

In his insistence on the intimacy of Eros and violence, Freud's war texts shared compelling similarities with Ernst Jünger's essay "On Danger" (1931).[39] The human heart, wrote Jünger, is made up not only of security or stability and order but also of danger; danger is always the other side of order, and society is simultaneously utterly constant and utterly mobile. We are at the same time completely civilized and completely barbaric. What gives modernity its specificity is that it for the first time in history enabled men to *register* this barbaric danger. Freud would certainly agree with Jünger's diagnostic analysis that the increased intrusion of danger in daily life, its constant presence rather than its exceptionality, had brought with it radical changes in the inner and outer world. But Freud's normative assessment was, of course, radically different. Jünger settled for an aestheticized celebration of rupture and decisionism as a protest against bourgeois values: "after an era that sought to subordinate fate to reason, another followed which saw reason as the servant of fate. From that moment on, danger was no longer the goal of a romantic opposition; it was rather reality, and the task of the bourgeois was once again to withdraw from this reality and escape into the utopia of security. From this moment on, the words *peace and order* became a slogan to which a weaker morale resorted."[40]

Freud neither escaped into the utopia of security nor did he cling to a simple notion of education and enlightenment in order to ward off the dangers to bourgeois security. He shared Jünger's sense that the greatest victim of the war had been the bourgeois autonomous subject who as a result had become feminized and weak. He too dreamed of a re-masculinization of European society, but contrary to Jünger, he laid this task at democracy's door. He was able to do this precisely to the extent that he believed the threat to democracy to be inherent to democracy itself, a threat that had been present ever since the birth of democratic subjectivity. In that sense, Freud was perhaps less traumatized by the war than Jünger, since he never believed, despite his later pessimism, that democracy was simply a lie. In order to save the autonomous, liberal subject, Freud felt compelled to think the "outside," the "other," both as that which was the source of the greatest threat to the contours of the ego and to psychoanalytic theory, and as that which was most fragile and vulnerable to the incursions of the (narcissistic) ego. Like the ego, Freud's later texts circled here and enclosed, while they also opened up the problem of repression, a concept that would take on increasing political meanings. Repression, Freud would finally claim, was not exterior to desire; it was always already deeply implicated in the libido, and vice versa, the libido was always already deeply implicated in repression or power. Was not masochism just that, the fantasmatic staging of repression as desire and of desire as another form of repression? Masochism forced Freud to think about the relationship between love and authority, and more specifically about the love of authority. This love of authority constituted a threat not only to the classical autonomous subject but also to the subject of psychoanalysis, since it posited a love that was exorbitant and thus absolute, a love that placed the subject there, outside itself, staged and spectral; and Freud would attempt to save this subject, both political and psychoanalytic, through an authority that would have the power to create new boundaries around the subject. As I argue in Chapter 4, Freud would think of this authority as the authority of love.

The *Jouissance* of the Law

In *The Sublime Object of Ideology*, Slavoj Žižek insists that people today are no longer ideologically blind subjects but have become instead the products of cynical reason, perfectly aware of the lie of power:

> Confronted with such cynical reason, the traditional critique of ideology no longer works. We can no longer subject the ideological text to "symptomatic reading," confronting it with its blind spots, with what it must repress to organize itself, to preserve its consistency—cynical reason takes this distance into account in advance. . . . ideology is, strictly speaking, only a system which makes a claim to the truth—that is, which is not simply a lie experienced as truth, a lie which pretends to be taken seriously. Totalitarian ideology no longer has this pretension. It is no longer meant, even by its authors, to be taken seriously . . . its rule is secured not by its truth-value but by simple extra-ideological violence and promise of gain.[41]

Cynical reason does not, however, imply that we are living in a post-ideological society: although people no longer take ideological truths seriously, and ideology no longer functions simply as an illusion that masks the real state of things, it nevertheless operates as a fantasy that structures social reality itself: "Cynical distance is just one way—one of the many ways—to blind ourselves to the structuring power of ideological fantasy: even if we do not take things seriously, even if we keep an ironical distance, *we are still doing them*." For Žižek, the relationship to reality constructed as "I know, but nevertheless . . . " constitutes a reversal of the usual sense that belief is something interior and knowledge something exterior. Belief here turns into a radical exteriority. Since belief is not some intimate state but is always materialized in effective, social behavior, "I can think about whatever I want, I can yield to the most dirty and obscene fantasies, and it does not matter because . . . whatever I am thinking, *objectively* I am praying."[42]

Law in what Žižek calls the "post-liberal" environment begins increasingly to take on the features of the Freudian superego: its effectiveness is predicated on the ego's loss of relative autonomy vis-à-vis both the id and the superego, whereby the ego loses its mediating function between unconscious drives and the agency of social repression; this law furthermore relies solely on its enunciation, on its performative aspect—act as if you believe, and belief will come: "The externality of the symbolic machine ('automaton') is therefore not simply external: it is at the same time the place where the fate of our internal, most 'sincere' and 'intimate' beliefs is in advance staged and decided. . . . our belief is already materialized in the external ritual; in other words, we already believe *unconsciously*. . . . Belief is an affair of obedience to the dead, uncomprehended letter."[43]

Žižek insists that this process of internalization never fully succeeds, and indeed it is precisely this failure that constitutes the very condition of the subject's full submission to the ideological command. In other words, the superego does not act in the form of an internalized law but "assumes the form of a hypnotic agency that imposes the attitude of 'yielding to temptation'—that is to say, its injunction amounts to a command: 'Enjoy yourself!'" It is the failure of the ideological command, of the symbolic mandate and its leftover in the form of blind, compulsive behavior, that gives this new law its full authority. It is also, for Žižek, the *jouissance* proper to ideology: "The function of ideology is not to offer us a point of escape from our reality but to offer us the social reality itself as an escape from some traumatic, real kernel."[44] Therefore the work of post-liberal ideology is always the work of a certain renunciation, of the subject's aphanisis, his self-obliteration, but one that nevertheless produces its own surplus enjoyment.

What Žižek describes as the surplus enjoyment generated by the act of renunciation is what structures masochistic pleasure insofar as the masochist reorders his relationship to the law as a relationship of pleasure. Indeed, Žižek raises several issues that seem particularly pertinent to the masochistic phenomenon. First, masochism, like ideology, asks the important question of how and why people consent to domination. In the case of theoretical speculations on the role of ideology, the answer usually given is that ideology has the function of disguising or masking relations of power so that obedience is rendered unknowingly or unconsciously. In the case of masochism, power relations remain overt and obedience is voluntary. It is in the latter case not a question of a lack of knowledge but of pleasure gained in submission. Second, and relatedly, since repression does not appear as a factor in the masochistic scenario, the role of repression in the constitution of subjectivity is radically altered. Žižek, and in this he follows Lacan—posits the emergence of a new type of subjectivity, a subjectivity that is non-psychological. Modern subjectivity lacks interiority because the Law or the Lacanian symbolic order now has direct access to regressive forces (the id, the Real) with the result that the ego loses its capacity or function as mediator between internal psychic drives and external, social constraints.[45] Third, given the complicated relationship between compulsion and consent within the masochistic universe, the term has fluctuated in its emphasis on either *compulsive behavior* (i.e., a sexual perversion driven by unconscious forces that the afflicted individual has little or no power over) or *consensual practices* (i.e., performative acts that are perceived as parodies of concrete historical relations of power). These two meanings—the first medical, the second politico-aesthetic—come together in the contract. The contract (written or verbal) made between the masochist and some authority figure is a fundamental characteristic of all masochistic scenes and is always initiated by the masochist himself. The politics of masochism thus inserts itself within a liberal discourse that assumes from the very beginning two individuals who are equally free to enter into a binding contract; it differs from liberal discourse in that it makes explicit that such a contract will and must lead to the pleasurable self-dissolution of that same previously assumed subjectivity.

The Son's Aesthetic of Suspense

As a political gesture, masochism sustains a critical relationship to representation, both in its immediate political sense and in its epistemological and aesthetic inflections. What characterizes the masochistic aesthetic are its predominantly fantasmatic qualities, its theatrical suspense, its structure of disavowal, and its consequent dependence on fetishization. Masochistic fantasies are frequently expressed as archaic national customs, folklore, and ritual. The masochistic story is thus often told in the form of a mytho-historical narrative and indeed as a rewriting or reworking of the mythic tradition.[46] This fantasmatic structure is supported by its quality of suspense: masochism takes place as a staging, as a series of *tableaux vivants* where gestures and bodies are frozen in time and space, creating an atmosphere of suffocation and waiting. These moments of suspense as the expectation of punishment are what provide pleasure; suspended or postponed pleasure constitutes, paradoxically, the climactic moments of the masochistic universe. Given this suspense element in the narrative of masochism—that is, the feeling that nothing ever happens—such pleasurable suspense is in fact displaced from the dramatic to the aesthetic itself. Violence and pain remain "muted, sexuality diffused, suffering aestheticized into spectacles, of disappointment."[47]

The masochist creates an ideal reality through the mechanism of disavowal, that is, through a radical contestation of the validity of that which is. The masochist suspends belief and thereby neutralizes it; he does not negate or destroy it. The primary mechanism for such a disavowal is the fetish (the mother's phallus), a frozen image capable of abolishing movement and time, discovery and exploration. Formally, the masochistic scene is most typically initiated by the man through a contract of pain with the cruel woman, the dominatrix, a contract that is to ensure the rules of the game and to fix the players into prescribed roles.[48] According to Gilles Deleuze, what is disavowed in this game is the power of the father, and this disavowal has two important consequences: first, it calls for the suspension of orgasmic gratification, for it is this suspension that symbolically expels the father; second, the actual occurrence of gratification is linked to its basis in pain as the price paid for this expulsion. Deleuze conceives of masochistic guilt as part of this game: "When guilt is experienced *masochistically*, it is already distorted, artificial and ostentatious."[49] Or as Gaylin Studlar phrased it, "the narcissistic ego seeks to mystify the superego's repressive demands for pain, which becomes an empty signifier, the masquerade for guilt."[50]

Since the power of the father is disavowed, it is the woman/mother who is ultimately both love object and controlling agent within the masochistic fantasy. Masochism denotes simultaneously the wish for complete union with this oral mother and the fear of such a symbiosis:

[The mother] is the figure of the cold oral mother who represents the good mother from the infantile stage of imagined dual unity or symbiosis between mother and child. Bad mother traits are projected on this imago and are then idealized. In a process that eliminates the father from the symbolic order, the good oral mother assumes and transforms the bad mother functions of other maternal imagos, such as the Oedipal mother who is associated with sadistic elements, and the seductive uterine mother who is connected in fantasy with prostitution. The father's punishing superego and phallic sexuality are then symbolically punished in the child-subject, who must expiate likeness to the father and reject his law.[51]

The masochistic universe is that of the humiliated father, of the father who is forever banished from the symbolic order; it is a mythic universe where everything has always already happened and where all takes place between mother and son. The contractual relation between son and mother accounts for the specifically masochistic relation to the law as well as the peculiar "Catholic" quality of masochistic culturalism (from nature to contract; from "free" sensuality to playing "as if"; from drives to their aestheticization). Here one may locate a double displacement: from father to mother with the consequent reformulation of masculine subjectivity; and from religion to culture with the rearticulation of self-renunciatory or self-sacrificial practices expressed as highly controlled, ritualistic, and sublimated artistic objects.

Masochism elevates the abject to the constitutive principle of subjectivity. As Julia Kristeva has argued, the abject is that which cannot be assimilated; it is both a jettisoned object, an object which is thrown out and up, and also a subject that is always already displaced, destitute, or exilic. The abject is the in-between, the ambiguous, the composite, and bears a primary, undifferentiated relationship to the maternal. It is constituted in a pre-symbolic maternal anguish and hence is diachronically the most archaic form of the object. The destitute or abject subject includes within himself his own exclusion; he casts "within himself the scalpel that carries out his separations"; he inevitably strays. And yet the more he strays, the more he is saved, for this eternal wandering provides him with his *jouissance*: "jouissance alone causes the abject to exist as such. One does not know it, one does not desire it, one joys in it. Violently and painfully. A passion . . . a jouissance in which the subject is swallowed up but in which the Other, in return, keeps the subject from foundering by making it repugnant. One thus understands why so many victims of the abject are its fascinated victims—if not its submissive and willing ones."[52]

The masochistic art of suspense places us, as Deleuze has insisted, on the side of the victim and forces us to identify with him, even if both the victim and the viewer's identification with him are always determined by the moment of consent. Thus, says Kristeva, this identification is perhaps more a possession, a composite of judgment and affect, of condemnation and yearning, of signs and drives. The nature of this consent—and here I differ from Deleuze's analysis, which reads masochistic stagings of the political contract as a subversion of the law—remains undetermined; that is, it remains undecidable, whether it functions as a critique of "real" power relations (demonstrating that even the most freely chosen political relations are inherently relations of power) or whether it imbues those same power relations with erotic fascination. Masochism enacts the specifically modernist claim that one is always already guilty before the law, that modern law as contractual consent implies a reversal between conscience and renunciation.[53] It parodies law, it demonstrates its absurdity and its pleasure by showing how it does not prevent erections but actually guarantees them. According to Deleuze, when the threat of the law originates from the father, the effect is the prevention of incest; but when it originates with the mother, it guarantees incest, that is, it guarantees the castration of the son: in the masochistic scene, love is always staged as interrupted, suspended love while at the same time it constitutes the very condition of possibility for incest.

The severe or cruel law generated from the contract between mother and son always leads straight into ritual, a ritual designed to lead to the son's rebirth. The cruel mother ensures the parthenogenetic rebirth of the son; she makes a man of the masochist, a New Man, a Christ-like figure who, like Jesus, is born of woman alone. Founded on the elimination of the father, in castration and interrupted love, the masochist practices, as Deleuze states, three disavowals at once: he magnifies the mother by attributing to her the phallus necessary for his own rebirth; he excludes the father from this rebirth, thus disavowing the paternal symbolic order; and he disavows genitality so that sexual pleasure is reconfigured as the pleasure of being reborn. The masochist is, in the words of its first "case," Leopold von Sacher-Masoch, the man "on the Cross, who knows no sexual love, no property, no fatherland, no cause, no work."[54]

Masochistic ritualistic parthenogenesis depends on the participation of the mother in the creation of a cruel law. Nevertheless, she can only participate in this process through her own sacrifice: the cruel woman guarantees incestuous love by her formal dominance within the masochistic fantasy, but this position depends on her submission to the law's dictates through her self-obliteration. Love as interrupted love is here always a male fantasy whereby Woman is constructed as sublime object of desire, never as its subject. In other words, the displacement from father to mother involves not a transfer of power but the rearticulation of male subjectivity, posited in this universe as a rhetorical self-renunciation, as a subjectivity of the son or the brother in a context where the father as Law is formally dead.[55]

From its very inception, the term "masochism" represented both a fundamental developmental aspect of human sexuality and a diagnosis of a concrete historical configuration. More specifically, and in the combination of this double function, it made possible a medical or scientific assessment of what was described as the cultural malaise or degeneration of European bourgeois culture. Masochism thus operated as a theoretical concept (and in that sense, one believed, it could be validly used for the diagnosis of any historical period and thus had universal, transhistorical applicability) and at the same time as a symptom of a particular historical juncture. The concept's application thus made visible a historical crisis—the fact that there were a growing number of bourgeois men who desired to be beaten and humiliated—and simultaneously naturalized that same crisis by its generalization. The paradoxical result—and here we find the very essence of masochism—was precisely the generalization of crisis: crisis became the constitutive mechanism by which male subjectivity could function within a new political-social order no longer able to take for granted an independent, coherent individual who was capable of simply renouncing his origins in some state of nature as he entered a civil society of contractual relations. Within the masochistic universe, male subjectivity was articulated as always already wounded; man was by definition, if not by constitution, at the margins, and it was this marginality, paradoxically, that was to guarantee his continuing hegemonic position.

Sublimation

How does woman come to occupy the position of the Cruel Lady? How does she come to speak from the position of the dead father, now interiorized as superego? The theoretical concept that articulates this position and this voice is that of *sublimation*; it is through the process of sublimation that it becomes possible to think of the peculiar structural position assigned to woman as the cruel agent of the Law and at the same time as the sublime object of man's desire. In Lacan's analysis, the sublimatory function is explicitly linked to the structure of courtly love, that is, to the poetic function that raises an object to the dignity of the Thing (*das Ding*), where this Thing is understood as the emptiness that lies at the center of the real.[56] The question here—which must center precisely on this claim to emptiness, this deprivation that man demands in courtly and in masochistic love—is as follows: is this space indeed an empty space, or is it not "filled out" by a marker, a marker that is named Woman as void or vacuole?

The concept of sublimation questions the relationship between psychoanalytic interpretation and the interpretation or critique of cultural products. For if sublimation produces a nonrepressed object—that is, a cultural object that cannot be traced back to unconsciously structured desire—then it follows that sublimation can only with difficulty be theorized as a psychoanalytic concept and that furthermore the product of sublimation cannot be submitted to the methods of a psychoanalytic or symptomatic reading. Many critics have noted Freud's difficulties in formulating a theory of sublimation. Mary Ann Doane has remarked that the concept represents Freud's attempt to deny the historical assault on the sublime by designating a realm of sublime cultural objects safe even from his own psychoanalytic techniques. She sees his difficulty in maintaining this space as arising not only from the pressures that modernity puts on auratic art but also from Freud's resistance to accepting limits to his own theory.[57] Leo Bersani, on the other hand, views this failure of a theoretical formulation as strategic: a theory of sublimation would only be necessary if one wanted to account for culture as an ultimately reductive process of repression and substitution. A failure to theorize, on the other hand, allows for an engagement with cultural products that he visualizes in terms of "the play of a consciousness resolutely attached to the always ambiguous pleasures of its own vibrations."[58]

At stake, then, in the concept of sublimation is the issue of reading and the localization of the critical voice. On the one hand, we encounter a critical voice that must be disloyal to its object of criticism insofar as it seeks out the desire that is hidden in the text, and thereby destroys the sublime character of aesthetic production as it drags it through the mud of secret and hidden desires. On the other hand, we are requested to be loyal to the cultural object created by "the most resolutely superficial reading of texts"[59] that, however, necessitates the self-abnegation or self-sacrifice of the critic's own voice. It is in both cases a matter of substitution; or, as Freud saw it, it is always already a matter of desire or transference, to which someone or something must succumb. On the one hand, Freud was forced to wrestle with the problem in terms of the difficulties, if not the temptations, of writing "merely" psychoanalytic novels. The problem was not simply that his case histories, under the pressure of the material treated, were in constant danger of turning into "romans à clef," as he was to worry repeatedly; pressures also came from within Freud himself.[60] In his most extended meditation on sublimation, *Leonardo da Vinci and a Memory of His Childhood*, he was forced to wonder whether there had not been some mismanagement on his own part, caught as he was by the mysteries of the powers of sublimation: "Like others I have succumbed to the attraction of this great and mysterious man, in whose nature one seems to detect powerful instinctual passions which can nevertheless only express themselves in so remarkably subdued [i.e. sublimated] a manner." Leonardo had to remain a mystery: "Since artistic talent and capacity are intimately connected with sublimation we must admit that the nature of the artistic function is also inaccessible to us along psycho-analytic lines."[61]

On the other hand, if it was not Freud himself who succumbed, then it had to be the material at hand that gave way. Psychoanalysis usually dealt with "frailer men [schwächlichem Menschenmaterial]," he states at the beginning of *Leonardo da Vinci*, but when psychoanalysis attempted to treat the "great," then it was not in order to "blacken the radiant and drag the sublime into the dust." Freud assures his readers that there was not and should not be any satisfaction in "narrowing the gulf which separates the perfection of the great from the inadequacy of the objects" that are the usual concern of psychoanalysis. After giving these assurances, he moves to the attack: those who oppose the writing of pathographies because such investigations merely seek to denigrate the achievements of great men are simply transferentially bound to their subjects of analysis. No one, Freud insisted, is so great as to be "disgraced by being subject to the laws which govern both normal and pathological activity with equal cogency." The sublime object that is Leonardo was then not "so great"; though he embodied to the highest degree the capacity for sublimation, both this capacity and its products were inevitably tinged with the pathological or the symptomatic: sublimation and the sublime could, indeed had to, subject themselves to the laws of psychoanalytic investigation. The great Leonardo himself would not have objected— and this was at least partly why he was so great. Due to his "love of truth and his thirst for knowledge," he would have encouraged Freud to study the trivial peculiarities and riddles of his own character, to make them a starting point for "discovering what determined his mental and intellectual development."[62]

The concept of sublimation occupies a strange, liminal position in Freud's work, straddling the sexual and the nonsexual and marking the moment when the sexualized individual enters the cultural domain. In this sense, it is Freud's conceptual tool for building a bridge between psychoanalysis as clinical practice and as cultural analysis—indeed, as he was so often to repeat, between his need to establish a science of the mind and his equally great need to indulge in metaphysical speculations. As such, the concept of sublimation both denotes a medical diagnosis of what happens to drives once they are civilized and acts as the site of broader cultural speculations that silence his drive theory in the name of higher, aesthetic goals. Freud remarked once that sexuality, as it is conceived by psychoanalysis, is to be understood as being located both below and above the question of the reproduction of the human species. Sublimation, one might say, is in turn located both above and below psychoanalysis in that realm that no longer allows for its simple reduction to all-too-human bodily drives.

Sublimation is one of the vicissitudes the sexual instinct may undergo where the resultant activity is no longer directly connected to its sexual origins. An instinct is sublimated when its aim has been redirected and when its object has been replaced by a socially valued (nonsexual) one: "A certain kind of modification of the aim and change of the object, in which our social valuation is taken into account, is described by us as 'sublimation.'"[63] Therefore, since Freud insists that the object is not originally connected to the instinct, and since objects are therefore easily substitutable, sexual instincts are capable of activities that are widely removed from their original modes of attaining their aims. One such new mode of satisfaction is achieved by the process of sublimation. Sublimation is thus linked to the question of the sexual object but in a "widely removed" sense. It addresses not only the transformation of the sexual instincts but also the genesis of cultural objects. Indeed, since sexual instincts can only be known in a state of transformation—that is, as products of culture—Lacan argues that it is not sexual instincts that generate sublimation but sublimation that retroactively creates sexual instincts. For Lacan, sublimation results precisely from a crisis concerning the object: it is motivated by the void that signals the relationship between the Real and the Symbolic, whereby an object is raised to the status of a Thing. The quintessential or first sublime object is the vase as the embodiment of that void and as the instantiation of (artistic) creation ex nihilo, and the paradigmatic form of sublimation is courtly love, which relies on and guarantees the unattainability of that same object.[64] As I will discuss, Lacan's choice of vase and courtly love are not coincidental ones for an understanding of sublimation.

Since it generates socially valued objects, sublimation must be distinguished from repression. Yet sublimation has its source in sexual drives, and it remains difficult to know whether any given object is the result of repression or sublimation, whether the object must be subjected to a symptomatic or an aesthetic reading. If read at the level of the symptom, as Freud does in his *Leonardo da Vinci and a Memory of His Childhood*, then sublimation is homologous and indeed simultaneous with seduction. If seduction describes the moment when sexuality is implanted and propped onto nonsexual, self-preservative drives, then sublimation is in some sense its inverse: the path established by sexual instincts toward nonsexual activities. However, this redirection of sexual aims and the substitution of objects characteristic of sublimation has, Freud continuously warns, its limits; there must always be an element of non-sublimation for sublimation to take place without damage:

> To extend this process of displacement indefinitely is, however, certainly not possible, any more than is the case with the transformation of heat into mechanical energy in our machines. A certain amount of direct sexual satisfaction seems to be indispensable for most organizations, and a deficiency in this amount, which varies from individual to individual, is visited by phenomena which, on account of their detrimental effects on functioning and their subjective quality of unpleasure, must be regarded as an illness.[65]

Although sublimation is the rarest and most perfect of the vicissitudes of the sexual instinct, Freud warns that no substitute is harmless. Ultimately, sublimation must be correlative to repression. In the words of Jean Laplanche,

> Investigation, research, becomes to a certain extent *compulsion* (Zwang) and substitution (Ersatz) for the sex act, but because of the radical difference in basic psychic processes (sublimation rather than emergence from the depth of the unconscious) [sublimation thus forestalls the formation of a symptom arising from the unconscious] the characteristics of a neurosis being absent, the subjection to complexes arising out of childhood sexual investigations does not occur and the drive can freely work actively in support of intellectual interests. However, sexual repression—which, through the sublimated libido, has been strengthened—continues to mark the drive by forcing it to eschew sexual subjects.[66]

Yet sublimation can also have restorative functions. In *The Ego and the Id*, Freud describes displaceable, desexualized libido as sublimated energy because it retains "the main purpose of Eros—that of uniting and binding—insofar as it helps towards establishing the unity, or tendency to unity, which is particularly characteristic of the ego."[67] Here sublimation is identified as the creation of a whole or "beautiful" object, viewed simultaneously as the *restoration* of the narcissistic wound of incompleteness (castration) and the *disavowal* of genitality: "In the course of cultural development so much of the divine and sacred was ultimately extracted from sexuality that the exhausted remnant fell into contempt," which explains, according to Freud, why in aesthetics the genitals come to be consistently marked as ugly.[68]

The effects of sublimation, both seductive and restorative, return in Freud's distinction between scientific investigation and artistic or pictorial creation as two separate sublimatory processes. In *Leonardo da Vinci*, these two forms are anaclitically but also hierarchically related: "Leonardo's researches had perhaps first begun . . . in the service of his art," and it is the growing prominence of Leonardo's scientific inclinations at the expense of his artistic side that constitutes Leonardo's neurosis.[69] This shift, according to Freud, in Leonardo's sublimatory energies clearly constitutes a loss. It is the loss of Leonardo's energy that drives Freud to his own scientific investigation into Leonardo's childhood trauma. The drive to investigate is always already active in childhood in the form of infantile sexual researches (as in the question "where do babies come from?"), and this drive has, according to Freud, three possible vicissitudes. First, research may share the fate of sexuality; like sexuality it may be repressed and thus result in neurotic inhibition. Second, thinking may recall its connection to sexuality and assist in evading sexual repression: thinking becomes here sexualized, resulting in compulsive brooding and colored by the pleasures and anxieties proper to the sexual processes. Third, research may escape both the inhibition of thought and compulsive thinking, in which case thought may reach its most perfect form:

Sexual repression comes about, but it does not succeed in relegating a component instinct of sexual desire to the unconscious. Instead, the libido evades the fate of repression by being sublimated from the very beginning into curiosity and by becoming attached to the powerful instinct for research as a reinforcement. . . . the quality of neurosis is absent; there is no attachment to the original complexes of infantile sexual research, and the instinct can operate freely in the service of intellectual interest. Sexual repression, which has made the instinct so strong through the addition to it of sublimated libido, is still taken into account by the instinct, in that it avoids any concern with sexual themes.[70]

This most perfect form is what describes sublimation. Since it is founded in infantile sexual researches, it constitutes a form of mastery over the trauma not only of sexualization but also of the failure to gain an answer from the parent to the question of (sexual) origins: "The impression caused by this failure in the first attempt at intellectual independence appears to be of a lasting and deeply depressing kind."[71] Investigation is always based in fantasy since it must remain a search for something that is both hidden and representable: "With investigation we go from a potentially complex research . . . to the search for something hidden, something necessarily capable of representation, beyond appearances. It is not surprising that the 'hidden' and 'representable' should be linked to the emergence of the sexual. To it we should . . . add that it is a matter of something interiorized, a kind of representative schema that is already no more than fantasy."[72] The interiorization described by Laplanche is what sexualizes vision: the nonsexual activity of seeing becomes *Schaulust*, or scopophilia, "as soon as it becomes *representative*, that is, the interiorization of the scene," and it is thus difficult to keep apart Freud's distinction between sublimation as pictorial creation or representation and sublimation as scientific investigation.[73]

Sublimation names the work that goes into the transformation of the sexual into the nonsexual, and it is this work that makes sublimation not only a requirement for civilization but indeed the mechanism that *is* civilization. This work also constitutes its enigmatic nature: "Sublimation of instinct is an especially conspicuous feature of cultural development. . . . If one were to yield to a first impression, one would say that sublimation is a vicissitude which has been forced upon the instincts by civilization. But it would be wiser to reflect upon this a little longer." Freud speaks of sublimation as a kind of energy or labor-power that is subject to laws similar to those of the economy, laws to which individuals have different access, depending on their place in that economy. These economic laws are troublesome, indeed uncanny: they clearly describe some kind of loss or renunciation, and at the same time they point to a gain within the cultural arena. For Freud, too, the demands on his scientific work are severe, and much requires explanation: "it is not easy to understand how it can be possible to deprive an instinct of satisfaction. Nor is doing so without danger. If the loss is not compensated for economically, one can be certain that serious disorders will ensue."[74]

The problem is first and foremost to locate this loss or waste that, paradoxically, is translated or to be registered as gain. Freud's concept of sublimation, the discovery of its laws, might be compared here to Marx's analysis of value under capitalist relations of production. How, Marx asks, is it possible for money (which for Marx is the ultimate embodiment of commodity fetishism) to be transformed, seemingly magically, into more money? How does M turn into M'? How can value increase—seemingly of itself? Marx's critique of political economy—which takes this equation as given—will of course entail the discovery, below the surface of an apparent, mysterious identity, of the laws of exploitation, conceptualized as a transfer of work and named the theory of surplus value. I would argue that Freud's concept of sublimation performs a similar kind of work—that is, it seeks to provide an answer to a mysterious transformation of bodily needs into cultural products. And yet Freud creates such a tightly intermeshing network between sublimation, civilization, and work that his own writing on the subject turns into a serious economic problem. A series of equivalencies and differences is established between terms that are hard to follow but that provide the basis for Freud's elaboration of a phylogenetic or collective fantasy based on the flow or current of psychic energy. Work is a form of sublimation; it allows for the displacement of libido and thus not only provides satisfaction but contributes to the process of civilization: "Professional activity is a source of special satisfaction if it is a freely chosen one—if, that is to say, by means of sublimation it makes possible the use of existing inclinations, of persisting or constitutionally reinforced instinctual impulses."[75] Yet it is precisely the coexistence of free choice and constitutionally reinforced impulses that is a problem. First, people do not like to work: they work only "under the stress of necessity, and this natural human aversion to work raises most difficult social problems." If work is one form of sublimation, then the opposite is also true: for sublimation designates both the work needed to convert libido into nonsexual activity and the fact that pleasure in this work is itself hard work.

Second, like labor, sublimation is subject to laws of division. Individuals are not endowed with equal capacities for sublimation, and different forms of labor do not provide equal sublimating outlets:

The relationship between the amount of sublimation possible and the amount of sexual activity necessary naturally varies very much from person to person and even from one calling to another. An abstinent artist is hardly conceivable, but an abstinent young *savant* is certainly no rarity. The latter can, by his self-restraint, liberate forces for his studies; while the former probably finds his artistic achievements powerfully stimulated by his sexual experience. In general I have not gained the impression that sexual abstinence helps to bring about energetic and self-reliant men of action or original thinkers or bold emancipators and reformers. Far more often it goes to produce well-behaved weaklings who later become lost in the great mass of people that tends to follow, unwillingly, the leads given by strong individuals.[76]

In civilization the instincts are enslaved; it is the "weaklings" that inevitably succumb in this process, while the "stronger" characters are able to get some form of compensation for their (self-)sacrifice.[77] It is because only a minority can attain mastery through sublimation that the majority must come to grief by becoming neurotic, he tells us in *"Civilized" Sexual Morality and Modern Nervousness*; the greater the disposition to neurosis, the less abstinence can be tolerated. Neurosis is thus a form of abstinence, a form of sublimation, while in turn abstinence or sublimation is a form of neurosis.

Differential capacities for sublimation are grounded in gender. Since women are "the actual vehicle of the sexual interests of mankind," they have only very limited capacities of sublimation: "they are scared away from *any* form of thinking, and knowledge loses its value for them."[78] This inability to sublimate is linked to those types of women evoked by Freud in relation to the mechanism of transference: "These are women of an elemental passionateness; they tolerate no surrogates; they are children of nature who refuse to accept the spiritual instead of the material; . . . they are amenable only to the 'logic of gruel and the argument of dumplings.' With such people one has the choice: either to return their love or else to bring down upon oneself the full force of the mortified woman's fury."[79] It is the woman's role to function as *object* of the sublimatory process, and it is therefore quite natural that she will be incapable of engaging in the act of substitution of objects that is so necessary for sublimation. And yet, if the act of substitution is not harmless, or if the act of substitution is never quite manageable, it is because of women. This is either because they are simply unable to do it, and thus demand, as the guardians of sex, an equal return on their investment; or because they *do* engage in substitution or sublimation with disastrous consequences for the male: a woman "may find a sufficient substitute for the sexual object in an infant at the breast," but by being overly tender to the child, she "awakens it to sexual precocity."[80] In other words, when women sublimate or substitute, they seduce, thereby creating false objects. Nevertheless, if women in this scheme are incapable of being producers of culture and hence incapable of being subjects, they can, however, be themselves sublimated; that is, *women stand in for the sexual instinct* and thus represent the latter in sublimated form. Women can and indeed must, if cultural objects are to be made, be converted into Lacan's "vase," his quintessential object of desire.

The level of civilization and the level of sublimation are, according to Freud, intimately connected. And yet the demands of modernity, when sublimation has reached its height, either lead to the collapse of sublimation or demand a higher price for it than its actual worth. And it is this "too much" or "too little" that engages the specificity, the novelty or modernity, of psychoanalysis. The new economy has its basis in the peculiar nature of modern power, located in the superego and experienced as an ever-increasing spiral of conscience and guilt. While conscience may have been the first cause for instinctual renunciation, this relationship is reversed under the dominance of the superego; renunciation now feeds conscience and guilt so that every new act of renunciation must increase the severity and intolerance of conscience insofar as the superego is now the principal cathected object. It is no longer possible to pay off one's debt to the law, the always guilty individual is roped into a strange economy that must continually remain open, giving the simultaneous appearance both of a libidinal drain toward the outside and of an ever-growing, self-generated growth in the form of libidinal cathexes. This is an economy where less appears to turn into more, and it is in this strange place that we are finally brought "to something that is foreign to people's ordinary way of thinking," to an idea that "belongs entirely to psychoanalysis." Here, what really happens or happened is not the point: "Whether one has killed one's father or has abstained from doing so is not really the decisive thing. One is bound to feel guilty in either case."[81] This, then, is the true site of civilization's *Unbehagen*, as well as of the psychoanalytic project itself: the economy of drives, psychoanalytically expressed as the principle of pleasure, is intruded upon from the *inside*—an inside that is external to itself. Freud points to a traumatic foreign body inside the pleasure principle itself, the death drive, which disrupts the economy of pleasure but in the form of a pleasure in displeasure: a repeated, pleasurable striving for an always missed or unattainable object. Freud calls this pleasure in displeasure, this strange economy embodied in the superego, "masochism" when speaking of the ego and "sublimation" when pointing toward its object. Masochism and sublimation name a form of cruelty, a certain *jouissance*, a laughing and persecuting agency of conscience and guilt.

Teste che ridono

Leonardo was apparently obsessed with laughing heads. The laughing heads of women and children at the beginning of his career and the "mysterious smile" that characterizes the artist's last work provide, according to Freud, the key to the secret of Leonardo's sublime economy: "The familiar smile of fascination leads one to guess that it is a secret of love. It is possible that in these figures Leonardo has denied the unhappiness of his erotic life and has triumphed over it in his art, by representing the wishes of the boy, as fulfilled in this blissful union of the male and female natures."[82] It is not clear whether this "familiar smile of fascination" reveals or conceals the secret of love. But this, too, remains part of its fascination, for the smile functions as a condensation of all the conflicting and contradictory powers of sublimation. The woman's smile has "produced the most powerful and confusing effect on whoever looks at it" (107), because it has combined "two distinct elements." Freud elicits the words of an international army of critics to describe these contradictory elements: "this woman . . . now appears to smile on us so seductively, and now to stare coldly and without soul into space," says one such critic. Another writes, "Jamais artiste . . . a-t-il traduit ainsi l'essence même de la femininité: tendresse et coquetterie, pudeur et sourde volupté, tout le mystère d'un coeur qui se réserve, d'un cerveau qui réfléchit, d'une personnalité qui se garde et ne livre d'elle-même que son rayonnement. [Never before has an artist . . . so translated the very essence of femininity: tenderness and flirtatiousness, modesty and secret sensuality, all the mystery of a guarded heart, a reflective mind, and a reserved personality that reveals itself only through an aura]." And still another says, "Buona e malvagia, crudele e compassionevole, graziosa e felina, ella rideva. [Good and malevolent, cruel and compassionate, graceful and feline, she laughed]" (108–9).

Freud returns with this smile to Leonardo's childhood memory— the memory, that is, of the vulture. Everything hinges on this vulture, though the vulture, of course, is not a vulture.[83] Leonardo recalls this scene from childhood in connection with an explanation of his desire to fly, that is, of the foundation of his investigatory drive: "It seems that I was always destined to be so deeply concerned with vultures [Questo scriver si distantamente del nibio par che sia mio destino (*writing* so extensively about the *kite* seems to be my destiny)]; for I recall as one of my earliest memories that while I was in the cradle a vulture [kite] came down to me, and opened my mouth with its tail, and struck me many times with its tail against the lips" (82). Freud reads the memory as a scene of seduction by Leonardo's mother that results in Leonardo's confusing gender identifications, first, because it enacts a series of reversals between activity and passivity, and second, because it assigns to woman attributes that remain ultimately undecidable: "The mother who suckles her child—or to put it better, at whose breast the child sucks—has been turned into a vulture that puts its tail into the child's mouth" (93). In Freud's analysis, the mother begins as the agent and immediately becomes a passive object that takes the form of a vulture. Freud himself is unclear how this happens: "But we do not understand how imaginative activity can have succeeded in endowing precisely this bird which is a mother with the distinguishing mark of masculinity" (93); it is a "puzzling psychological fact that the human imagination does not boggle at endowing a figure which is intended to embody the essence of the mother with the mark of male potency [the 'coda' or tail] which is the opposite of everything maternal" (94). Freud finds his answer to this puzzle in infantile sexual researches and in the early infantile denial that women lack the phallus. He can therefore "translate" Leonardo's memory back to his early sexual researches, which "had a decisive effect on the whole of his later life": " 'That was a time when my fond curiosity was directed to my mother, and when I still believed she had a genital organ like my own' " (98). This may explain the phallic mother, but it does not shed light on the second reversal, namely, that from activity back to passivity: whereas Freud himself had previously made sure that all imaginative action is with Leonardo, he now concedes that the memory's "most striking feature, after all, was that it changed sucking at the mother's breast into being suckled, that is, into passivity, and thus into a situation whose nature is undoubtedly homosexual. . . . the question is forced upon us [this is Freud's own passivity] whether this phantasy does not indicate the existence of a causal connection between Leonardo's relation with his mother in childhood and his later manifest, if ideal (sublimated), homosexuality" (98).

Freud needs further proof of this connection, and he finds it by referring back to the curious because erratic and apparently meaningless accounting techniques Leonardo employs for his domestic economy. Leonardo's diaries contain a series of entries pertaining to two categories of expenses: the first belong to trifling amounts of money spent on clothing for his young, male pupils ("he had chosen them for their beauty and not for their talent, none of them . . . became a painter of importance" [102]); the second belong to extravagant and wasteful sums spent, Freud concludes, on the mother's funeral. The point is that these figures are supposed to add up and provide Freud with yet another translation: "'It was through this erotic relation with my mother that I became a homosexual'" (106), since Leonardo's reckonings provide "scanty remnants" of his libidinal economy, which had found expression in a sublimated but obsessive manner.

When not keeping his books or wanting to fly, however, Leonardo painted: "Kindly nature has given the artist the ability to express his most secret mental impulses, which are hidden even from himself, by means of the works that he creates" (107), which brings us back to the laughing heads. Whereas Leonardo's researches and domestic, economic problems are wasteful at best, "these works have a powerful effect on others who are strangers to the artist, and who are themselves unaware of the source of their emotions" (107). Indeed, Freud resolves to "leave unsolved the riddle of the expression on Mona Lisa's face" (109). "We should be most glad to give an account of the way in which artistic activity derives from the primal instincts of the mind if it were not just here that our capacities fail us. We must be content to emphasize the fact . . . that what an artist creates provides at the same time an outlet for his sexual desire; and in Leonardo's case we can point to the information which comes from Vasari, that heads of laughing women and beautiful boys . . . were notable among his first artistic endeavors" (132–33). They were also among his last.

Freud thus provides us with two models of sublimation. In the first, artistic one of laughing heads, sublimation is based on "work without inhibition," without reserve, where creativity is active because modeled on the father; it is "masculine creative power." This "work without inhibition" is furthermore unexplainable. In Leonardo's case, however, this productivity cannot last because "the almost total repression of a real sexual life does not provide the most favourable conditions for the exercise of sublimated sexual trends" (133). Therefore he succumbs to a second—and, I would argue, masochistic—form of sublimation, which is founded in a regressive return to infantile sexual researches: here Leonardo assumes the passive, feminine position of the investigator, dictated by a rather different kind of relationship to the symbolic order: under the influence of maternal seduction and uninhibited by the presence of his father, Leonardo attained "an equally sublime achievement in the field of scientific research" (122) because the father's absence allowed for the critique of authority: "in teaching that authority should be looked down on and that imitation of the 'ancients' should be repudiated, and in constantly urging that the study of nature was the source of all truth, he was merely repeating—in the highest sublimation attainable by man—the one-sided point of view which had already forced itself on the little boy as he gazed in wonder on the world" (122).

Everything seems to hinge on how sexuality and work are combined. When sexuality and work are combined in a masculine manner, the result will be good, artistic, and ultimately unanalyzable sublimation. When, however, sexuality and work are combined in a feminine manner, the result will be cultural products that can be traced back to scenes of maternal seduction. Yet these two forms, masculine and feminine sublimation, ultimately cannot be held apart, for what the true, unanalyzable sublime object produces is the "blissful union of male and female natures." Leo Bersani has argued that Freud wavers between a paternally and a maternally centered account of sublimation, that in fact Freud "is continuously shifting positions on the question of shifting positions."[84] Freud's first model of sublimation commits Freud to "an art of secure statement." Here, aesthetic expression depends on a post-Oedipal inhibition of sexual indeterminacy, the manifestation of castration anxieties resulting from the overcoming of the Oedipus complex and a critical reading of texts dedicated to a demystifying interpretation in the form of a nonrepressed metadiscourse. In the maternally centered account, on the other hand, Bersani views sublimation as nonrepressed sexual energy that depends on

> the "absence" of the father, or more exactly, on a certain failure on the part of the father during the Oedipal period to crystallize into the prohibitive Law, that is, on the defeat or at least subordination of the so-called dominant Oedipal configuration. Thus the play in Leonardo's work of indeterminate relations between the indeterminate identities of mother and child, and of male and female. . . . Freud can't help but suggest that a certain kind of unsuccessful repetition, or of mistaken replication—the repeated attempts to identify an erotically traumatizing and erotically traumatized human subject—is in fact the source of Leonardo's aesthetic power, and that his artistic achievement therefore depends on (rather than is inhibited by) a certain *failure to represent.*[85]

Bersani is correct in locating the origin of sublimation in the erotically traumatizing and traumatized human subject. Yet representation does take place, that is, a certain work does go on and objects do get made. Sublimation, particularly within the context of masochism—and this is what interests Bersani above all—requires the absence or killing of the father in the form of a disavowal, and this act of disavowal, in turn, hinges on the creation of the mother or woman generally as sublime object. It is precisely a certain gender indeterminacy operating within the relation between work and sexuality that attempts a *reinscription* of sexual identity insofar as the object of sublimation is not indeterminate at all; its structure is never empty. It is, in fact, historically quite concrete, for it is occupied by Woman. Bersani in fact repeats the same Freudian gesture: whereas he insists that the Oedipal father inhibits or immobilizes a sublimation modeled on masochistic, maternal seduction, his desire is for a paternal form of sublimation that would "provide the opportunity for a socializing of the traumatic loving initially experienced at the mother's breast."[86] It is noteworthy that so much of the theorizing of sublimation returns to Woman, though not in the form of theory (which appears impossible) but as "example." This is certainly the case with Freud himself: insofar as woman in the form of the powerful and seductive mother stands at the origin of the need for man to sublimate in order to free himself from her grip, she thereby constitutes the very limit of sublimation, for she embodies a form of human subjectivity incapable of this transformation of desire into civilization. For Lacan, sublimation is captured by the "empty vase" in the form of courtly love and the figure of the Cruel Lady; for Bersani, sublimation stems from the seductive and seducing mother, who is to be replaced by the "de-Oedipalized" father; for Laplanche and Pontalis, who view sublimation as first and foremost a fantasy of seduction, the "exemplary" mode of fantasy is "prostitution, street-walking."[87] In all these cases, Woman marks the limit of sublimation while remaining mysteriously placed at its very center; Woman as sublime object marks the site where sublimation takes place, yet also the site where sublimation is in constant danger of collapsing.

If sublimation names the work that produces a movement from libidinal energy to culture or civilization, then it simultaneously names the place where sexuality and work come together, where the two cannot in fact be held apart. As Mary Ann Doane has argued, the quintessential place of such a place of collapse is prostitution. During the later part of the nineteenth century and well into the twentieth, there was in fact much interest in the problem of managing expenditure and waste. From within this perspective, prostitution was viewed as the site of a triple waste: of the woman herself, of the client, and of money.[88] Many critics have observed that the prostitute was the late nineteenth century's object par excellence, that she became a kind of metacharacter of modernity.[89] The prostitute was the female embodiment of Benjamin's flaneur; her sexuality was out of bounds not only because she indulged in wasteful activities but because she refigured woman's relation to public space, ultimately making the distinction between the prostitute and the consuming bourgeoise difficult if not impossible to maintain.[90] Above all, the prostitute became the very mark of the commodification of the human body; she "demonstrates the new status of the body as exchangeable and profitable image."[91]

It is this profitability of an image that is ultimately at work both in the Freudian theory of sublimation and in the work of theory as itself a sublimatory act. Sublimation allowed for a strange process of substitution and reversal: by making woman into a sublime object in order to convert sexual desire into cultural objects, her place on a pedestal was guaranteed to be lubricated, as Bram Dijkstra has remarked, with nitroglycerin. Hatred of woman could be transformed into a fear of woman, into the submission that was so necessary for culture to be made. This sublime image marked the site where waste originated, but also where much work could be done and immense profits could be reaped; the site where exchangeability or substitution was overcome (*aufgehoben*) as Value but where this exchangeability nevertheless became the law; the site of renunciation and self-abnegation because it always demanded to be avoided, but also the site to which one erringly returned (as Freud noticed with discomfort in "The Uncanny"); the site of a laughing power because, as hard as one might have tried, the account could never be closed in this system of revolving credit and interminable debt and interminable analysis; and finally, the site of representation, of *Schaulust* either as pictorial representation or scientific investigation that produced a fantasy of culture and a culture of fantasy.

The notion of the sublime plays a crucial role within the masochistic scenario, both because it undermines all representation and because it marks the point toward which aesthetic and religious practices strive, while it nevertheless undoes them. Within the masochistic scenario, the sublime becomes connected to that strange Freudian boundary concept of sublimation—that is, the transformation of the sexual drives and desire into cultural products that through this process of desexualization can find a path of expression without the need to succumb to repression. This transformation of libidinal drives into cultural or aesthetic objects is achieved by making woman occupy the place of sublime object, an object that the masochistic male creates and seeks to control but which he himself posits as an infinitely powerful entity to which he must submit. More specifically, masochism follows the rules of the sublimatory process—thus eluding the demands for repression—by elevating the *gaze* and the *voice* (perceived as occupied by woman) to sublime objects of desire and therefore to constitutive principles of subject-formation.[92] Although masochism may not be placed under repression, its unconscious content remains excluded insofar as it remains disavowed. This exclusion is always strange or uncanny: ultimately, what is disavowed (the function or the name of the father) returns to reassert itself and it forces the masochistic fantasy to narrate its own death.

The two chapters that follow will trace the specific vicissitudes of these two drives—that of the gaze and that of the voice—in Leopold von Sacher-Masoch's *Venus in Furs* and Richard Wagner's *Parsifal*. Whereas Sacher-Masoch attempts to articulate the crisis of masculinity as a problem of possessing the gaze, that is, as a problem of holding a privileged point of view, Wagner articulates this same crisis in terms of the problem of the voice—that is, in terms of a vocational crisis. In both cases, masculinity is articulated as masochistic self-loss, as a renunciation of the self, in order to circumvent the cultural demands of the repression of bodily drives, and this is achieved, paradoxically, by an attempt directly to occupy the position of the gaze and the voice in the name of their own marginalization.

In *Language and Symbolic Power*, Pierre Bourdieu quotes Charles Schulz's Snoopy on top of his doghouse as saying, "How can one be modest when one is the best?" Bourdieu's answer is, quite simply, by acting according to the common knowledge that one is indeed the best— that is, by simply being who one is. Bourdieu's principal claim is that power operates precisely as a symbolic function, or what he calls the performative magic that is the essence of all acts of institution.[93] Such performativity is always an act of investiture, a calling to which the subject must respond: "All social destinies, positive or negative, by consecration or stigma, are equally *fatal*—by which I mean mortal—because they enclose those whom they characterize within the limits that are assigned to them and that they are made to recognize." At stake here is always an act of naming and of inheritance or transmission, an act that, in Bourdieu's terms, can go wrong:

There are exceptions: the unworthy heir, the priest who abandons his calling, the nobleman who demeans himself and the bourgeois who turns common. . . . That is . . . the function of all magical boundaries (whether the boundary between masculine and feminine, or between those selected and those rejected by the educational system): to stop those who are inside, on the right side of the line, from leaving, demeaning or down-grading themselves. Pareto used to say that elites are destined to "waste away" when they cease to believe in themselves, when they lose their morale and their morality, and begin to cross the line in the wrong direction. This is also one of the functions of the act of institution: to discourage permanently any attempt to cross the line, to transgress, desert, to *quit*.[94]

My own reflections begin with the rather puzzling fact that both Sacher-Masoch and Wagner, along with many other nervous men of the fin-de-siècle, seemed to be crossing this line in hordes, that the late nineteenth century appeared to be overrun by whole regiments of quitters. In the name not just of modesty but indeed of outright abjection, in the name of marginalization, Sacher-Masoch and Wagner posit the crisis that Bourdieu marks as the exception and turn it into the rule. They perform this crossing and thus capture for themselves that power which for them emanates from the gaze and the voice.

WHEN MEN CAN NO LONGER PAINT: ACTS OF SEEING IN LEOPOLD VON SACHER-MASOCH'S VENUS IN FURS

What approaches is the law of frigidity, of minimum fellowship.
—Gottfried Benn, *Pallas*

In one of his most pained exclamations regarding his condition, Daniel Paul Schreber despairs that what his persecuting rays fail to understand is that "a human being who actually exists *must be somewhere.*" Even while he was separated from them in space, these rays were making direct contact with him and forcing him to compulsive thinking. Continual thinking means continual enjoyment, which is impossible for a human being: one is both constantly invaded and always abandoned, a condition Schreber likens to the "phenomenon like telephoning; the filaments of rays spun out towards my head act like telephone wires; the weak sound of cries of help coming from an apparently vast distance is received *only by me* in the same way as telephonic communication can only be heard by a person who is on the telephone." This constitutes the essence of Schreber's "soul murder." The mechanism, indeed the real cause, of Schreber's compulsive thinking is what he calls "picturing": "To picture . . . is the conscious use of the human imagination for the purposes of producing pictures (predominantly pictures of recollection) in one's head, which can then be looked at by the rays."[1] He footnotes his remark:

Picturing in the *human* sense is the representation of objects on a surface ... *without colour* ... and especially *either* mere *copying* ... that is reproducing objects actually seen in the outer world, in which human *imagination* plays no part, *or* the creation of pictures representing objects not yet existing in the outer world, for either purely artistic purposes ... or for practical purposes ... the latter implying *imagination* (fantasy ...). The German word [Einbildungskraft] indicates clearly the notion of "something being *put into* the head or into human awareness," which is not present outside.[2]

Pictures are implanted into the head and into human awareness during sleep, or as Schreber has it, during half-sleep, and the results are "highly peculiar": "it really must be rather pleasant to be a woman succumbing to intercourse."[3]

Picturing is Aby Warburg's primary concern as well. The process of sublimation, which is the essence of civilization, brings with it the creation of distance. This distance Warburg understands as the transformation of pictures into words, of *Bildsprache* into *Wortsprache*, of the magical cosmos of the *Greifmensch* to the rational cosmos of the *Denkmensch*, where the world can no longer be physically grasped by man, nor can he be grasped by the world. At the center of this transformation, both synchronically and diachronically, stands human symbolic activity, whose embodiment or constitutive symbol is the serpent. The serpent occupies a crucial because paradoxical role in cultural sublimation: in one sense it is the picture of anxiety (that is, the way anxiety can come to be represented); at the same time it is by virtue of its pictorial form thus tamed. The serpent brings anxiety closer while distancing us from it. It is the symbol of lightning, since only captured momentarily in a snapshot (*Augenblicksaufnahme*) or as a Benjaminian "dialectical image." The serpent as symbol and the symbol as serpent can only ever be momentarily registered as a flash of recognition occurring in the twinkling of an eye (*Augenblick*). Thus the serpent's contradictory, paradoxical status in culture: it is not only culture's agon and disruptive sickness but also its healing agent and cure, and it is this dual nature of the serpent that makes it into the dominatrix (*die Herrscherin*) of the house of culture. But when tamed in the modern age, the serpent is destroyed, bringing with it the destruction of culture as a whole: modernity's suppression of the serpent ritual leads to what Warburg describes as simultaneity, a fact that in itself can only be captured in a snapshot:

The conqueror of the serpent cult and of the fear of lightning, the in-
heritor of the indigenous peoples and of the gold seeker who ousted
them, is captured in a photograph I took on a street in San Francisco.
He is Uncle Sam in a stovepipe hat, strolling in his pride past a neo-
classical rotunda. Above his hat runs an electric wire. In this copper serpent of Edison's, he has wrested lightning from nature. . . . The lightning imprisoned in wire—captured electricity has produced a culture
with no use for paganism. What has replaced it? Natural forces are no
longer seen in anthropomorphic or biomorphic guise, but rather as infinite waves obedient to the human touch.[4]

Destroyed in this process is a certain kind of distance, a distance that
Warburg terms a space for devotion and a space for thinking. Modern
technology is a soul murderer because it destroys a feeling for distance
(*Ferngefühl-Zerstörer*): "Mythical or symbolic thinking strive to form
spiritual bonds between humanity and the surrounding world, shaping
distance into the space required for devotion and reflection: the distance
undone by the instantaneous electric connection [*Augenblicksverknüp-
fung*]."[5]

Sacher-Masoch's literary output is extensive, though with the exception of his novella *Venus in Furs* (1870), it is virtually unknown today. Yet
he was widely read during the second half of the nineteenth century,
indeed was hailed as the literary successor of Turgenev both in Vienna
and in Paris. Nevertheless, his immortality was to be assured by another
path: in 1886 Richard von Krafft-Ebing published his *Psychopathia Sexualis*, in which he outlined a particular sexual perversion whose victims were

> dominated in the realm of their sexual feelings and ideas by the idea of
> being completely and unconditionally subjected to a person of the op-
> posite sex, of being treated by this person in a domineering manner, of
> being humiliated and even abused. This idea affords them pleasure; the
> person thus seized revels in fantasies in which he *paints to himself such
> pictures*; he often attempts to realize them and is often, due to this per-
> version of his sexual drive, increasingly unable to respond to the nor-
> mal attractions of the other sex; he becomes incapable of a normal vita
> sexualis—that is, he becomes psychically impotent.[6]

Krafft-Ebing called this particular perversion masochism, a term that he
had derived from Sacher-Masoch's name, following here, he asserted, the

standard scientific practice of word formation: "'Daltonism' (after Dalton, the discoverer of color blindness)."[7] The parallel between Dalton, the discoverer of color blindness, and Sacher-Masoch does not hold, of course, for strictly speaking it is Krafft-Ebing who should have lent his own name to his newly discovered perversion. And that Krafft-Ebing should have chosen Masoch and not Sacher in his taxonomy of abnormality was perhaps also not a coincidence, for Masoch designated not only the Eastern side of the latter's family but also the maternal one.

Indeed, Krafft-Ebing clearly felt that he had to explain: such a choice was occasioned and legitimated, he claimed, because "not only had Sacher-Masoch been the poet of masochism, but himself had been afflicted with said anomaly."[8] Because he painted pictures of his fantasies, the issue, if not the real source of Sacher-Masoch's perversion, lay in the latter's transferential relationship to his work—that is, in the way in which he transformed sexuality into literature:

> As a human being, S.-Masoch certainly does not lose anything in the eyes of intellectuals simply because he was innocently afflicted by anomalous sexual feelings. As an author, however, this anomaly has been seriously damaging to his work and creation because he was, as long as he did not move on the grounds of his perversion, a very gifted writer, and would certainly have achieved great things, if he had been a person of normal sexual feelings. He is in this respect a noteworthy example of the powerful influence, both positive and negative, that the vita sexualis may gain over a person's spiritual sensibility and character.[9]

Krafft-Ebing set the tone and the parameters for all later debates on the concept of masochism insofar as the latter became the name for a psychological perversion designating a pleasurable investment in physical pain and psychic humiliation. Thus the term was quickly taken up by psychoanalysis, and by 1905 Freud had made it into one of the basic component instincts of polymorphous infantile sexuality. Masochism came to be identified with passivity, the inverse, that is, of the active or aggressive instinct of sadism.

Sacher-Masoch's work itself has been read, if at all, in two forms, and both these approaches reproduce to an astounding degree the masochistic structures that Sacher-Masoch himself enacts. First, starting with Krafft-Ebing, the work has been read diagnostically, usually taking the form of a psychobiography or pathography. Such readings are, even at their best, inevitably reductive, in terms of the relationship both between author and text and between text and context. Sacher-Masoch and his fictive characters are collapsed, all transformed into patients who must in some form respond to the critic who functions here as the text's and the author's physician. Since Sacher-Masoch is here the patient, it is a foregone conclusion that he has somehow failed, as person or as writer. In the first case he is marked as perverse; in the second, as banal. This form of reductionism leads paradoxically both to an overcontextualization of Sacher-Masoch's work (that is, it reduces his texts either to the intentionality of their author or to the historical context in rather simplistic terms) and to an undercontextualization insofar as such diagnostic reading requires a theory of masochism that depends on the assumption of the latter's universal, transhistorical existence.

The second reading of Sacher-Masoch is celebratory. Here the writer is credited with not only having outlined a new aesthetic practice but also having diagnosed the historical malaise of late-nineteenth-century relations of power. In other words, where in the first reading Sacher-Masoch was the patient, here he turns clinician; where in the first he was perverse, here he is subversive; and where he was banal, he now becomes parodic. While the first reading had depended on the centrality of character analysis, the second depends on the primacy of fantasy and the consequent laws of desire. In positive terms, this has of course meant that Sacher-Masoch's texts have been submitted to much closer readings; yet these readings suffer from a paradox similar to the one suffered by the first, diagnostic readings: these celebratory interpretations remain either overtextualized because they do not refer to the historical context at all, or undertextualized because they simply exaggerate Sacher-Masoch's subversiveness by ignoring the fact that, however else one wants to describe Sacher-Masoch's texts, they certainly were a constituent part of a collective and *dominant* cultural fantasy.

Sacher-Masoch's *Venus in Furs* is a story about the *Augenblick*—that is, in its double German meaning, both about the gaze and about the moment. Like Krafft-Ebing or like Schreber and Warburg after him, he posits this *Augenblick* as an activity of painting. In terms of both its form and its content, *Venus in Furs* is a snapshot or *Augenblicksbild* designed to carve out a cultural space that captures the moment as picture. Whereas Freud in *The Interpretation of Dreams* writes pictures down, that is, (re)-presents pictures by converting these pictures back to words, Sacher-Masoch moves in the opposite direction: he wants to convert the act of seeing into a picture, to make the gaze into a substance in order to fix it there in space and time, and he does this by what Freud calls sublimation as pictorial activity. Sacher-Masoch's gaze is always the gaze of desire, which in the sublimatory process turns into a substance, a Thing—rays—that in turn are able to produce an immensely productive or working image.

The plot of *Venus in Furs* is a rather typical one for Sacher-Masoch: like so many of his novellas, the story is embedded in a narrative frame taking the form of a conversation between two male friends, the unnamed narrative "I" and the hero of the story, Severin von Kusiemski. The narrative frame itself is divided into two parts. The novella begins, unannounced, with the narrator's dream of a conversation with Venus; the dream's narration to Severin inspires the latter to tell his "ridiculous story [eine dumme Geschichte]," a dream of Venus he had with his eyes open. As Severin sits staring into the fire, the narrator reads Severin's "Confessions of a Supersensualist." These confessions make up the story proper, and the narrative frame is returned to only briefly at the end to provide the "moral" of the story, which is that men and women are, given the historical conditions, absolute enemies, that one must be the anvil, the other the hammer, and that it is preferable to be the hammer. Hence the banal but puzzling moral of the tale: "whoever allows himself to be whipped deserves to be whipped."[10] The "Confessions" then trace the stages of Severin's coming to this recognition, ending in a final whipping that cures him once and for all: since he has had the poetry whipped out of him, from now on he will do the whipping.

The "Confessions" themselves bear a tripartite structure, again typical of Sacher-Masoch's work. Each part announces a new stage in Severin's relationship to Wanda, the dominatrix of the story, and each is signaled by new places of action, new backdrops, new wardrobes, new "scenes." When Severin first encounters Wanda in an isolated villa in the Carpathian mountains, she is a beautiful and young widow. Indeed, most of Sacher-Masoch's cruel women are either widowed or divorced; they are women of experience and thus not capable of further character development, for they have already put behind them the tragedies of life and the mourning over loss.[11] Wanda is here the goddess of love of antiquity; she is both loving and demonic insofar as she embodies Southern passion and a disregard for Northern morals. Although this initial meeting takes place in the North, Wanda's wardrobe is predominantly made up of white, diaphanous gowns. During this first stage of Severin and Wanda's relationship, Severin announces that he prefers his women in a dominating position: "If I were faced with the choice of dominating or being dominated, I would choose the latter. It would be far more satisfying to be the slave of a beautiful woman. But I should hate her to be a petty, nagging tyrant—where would I find a woman to dominate me in a serene and fully conscious manner?" (163).

It is immediately clear that Wanda is to fit Severin's model of woman. Yet she does protest, for to her this means abandoning the ways of the South and giving in to "modern ways": "It would seem that for you love and particularly women are hostile forces; you try to defend yourself against them. However, you are quite overcome by pleasurable torments and exquisite pain which they afford you. A very modern view" (159). Whereas the South or antiquity represents for her a situation where "desire would follow upon look, enjoyment on desire" (159), it is Christianity and through it the modern age that has introduced a hostile element into innocent pleasures: "The struggle of the spirit against the senses is the gospel of modern man. I do not wish to have any part in it" (159). However, have a part in it she must, and Severin embarks on a campaign for Wanda's education into the ways of the North. He challenges her with reasoned arguments: "do you believe that your theories could be put into practice in our present century? Do you think that Venus could display with impunity her joyous, naked charms amongst trains and telegraphs?" (162; translation modified). If nothing else, she would catch cold; and Wanda, under the weight of this logic, concedes that women must now wear furs.

The relationship gets underway. Wanda is to take on the role of the dominatrix; this is signaled most clearly by the furs she wears and the whip she carries. Both Wanda and Severin are compelled at this stage to theorize their relationship: he as her educator and she as his at times reluctant pupil. The force of this theorizing is the question of will and consent. A typical conversation between them runs like this (Wanda speaks first):

> "I shall grant you all the rights of a husband, a lover and a friend. Are you satisfied?"
> "I have no choice."
> "You are not forced to accept it."
> "So be it."
> "Splendid! Now you are talking like a man. Here is my hand."
> (168–69)

While Wanda continues to insist that Severin has a choice, he just as eagerly tries to force that choice back onto her ("So be it!"), so that Wanda's statement that his forced choice is what makes him into a man must remain highly ambiguous. Severin is ultimately able to place Wanda into an impossible situation. While both agree that one can love only that which stands above one, Severin demands that she forfeit this love object, a fact that must remain for her slightly "repulsive," for she replies:

> "Then you are attracted by what others find repulsive?"
> "That is right. It is my peculiar nature."
> "Come now, there is nothing really so peculiar nor remarkable about your passion. Who does not find beautiful furs irresistible? We all know, we all sense how closely related are sensual pleasure and cruelty."
> "But in my case these things are taken to extremes."
> "You mean that reason has little power over you and that you are weak and sensuous by nature?
> "Were the martyrs also weak and sensuous? . . . the martyrs were *supersensual beings* who found positive pleasure in pain and who sought horrible tortures, even death, as others seek enjoyment. I too am *supersensual*, madam, just as they were."
> "Take care that you do not also become a martyr to love, the *martyr of a woman*." (172)[12]

Wanda and Severin draw up the famous masochistic contract wherein Severin relinquishes all rights as a citizen and Wanda has the sole obligation to wear furs, particularly when she is inclined to treat Severin in a cruel manner. The previous rights of a husband and lover are relinquished in favor of whippings, a fact that understandably gives Wanda only limited pleasure.

The second stage of the relationship between the lovers requires a change of scenery. Interestingly, the contract can only be signed in the South, and Wanda and Severin move to a hotel in Florence where Severin is renamed Gregor (a typical name for Russian servants) and put into servant's clothes.[13] Wanda's wardrobe also changes: her clothes turn darker, increasingly black, reflecting ever more the colors of her boots and whips. She also becomes colder, indeed icy, and Severin/Gregor dreams that she has turned into a polar bear with claws that rip him to shreds. Under these favorable conditions, the contract is finally signed, though Wanda has added a second contract to the first in the form of Severin's suicide note: she now has absolute power of life and death over him.

This second stage constitutes the most perfect form of their relationship, alternating between moments of cruelty and tenderness, between fantasy and reality. Yet a fundamental instability is produced by the question of how seriously to take the act of role playing. Before their departure for Italy, it is already clear that Severin's identity relies on the authenticity of role playing. As long as Wanda is resistant, Severin may play his role without any problems:

> "Severin, . . . I am a young and frivolous woman. It is dangerous for you to surrender so totally to me, you will end up becoming my plaything. Who will protect you then? I might take unfair advantage of your folly."
> "You are too noble to dream of that."
> "Power makes one presumptuous."
> "Then be presumptuous! . . . trample on me!"
> "I am afraid of not being capable of it, but for you I am willing to try, for I love you, Severin, as I have loved no other man." (182–83)

Presumptuousness, however, is only applicable to moments of cruelty, and that only within certain limitations.[14] Presumptuous love is the first and immediate threat to Severin's identity. Although Severin insists that Wanda do with him as she will, such limitless behavior is ultimately disastrous:

> Wanda . . . drew me back onto the ottoman and began to kiss me again. This silent language was so easy to understand and so persuasive. . . . It told me more than I dared to interpret. A languid abandon came over her whole being. What voluptuous softness in her half-closed eyes, in her red hair shimmering under the white powder! The red and white satin rustled with each of her movements, and the ermine caressed her shoulders with a snakelike movement. . . . I kissed her; no, she kissed me—wildly, passionately, as though she wanted to devour me. I was almost delirious, and had long since lost my reason; panting, I tried to free myself from her arms. (188–89)

Severin ultimately loses consciousness as his only way of escape, and when he comes to, he finds blood running down his arm: Wanda has bitten him. This is clearly not the form of domination that Severin had in mind, and he continually insists on punishment and humiliation instead of passionate lovemaking.[15] Here too, however, Wanda seems unable to get it right. Obviously her capacities for imaginative activity are limited; she takes things too literally. In response to a moment of great cruelty on her part, Severin has this to say to her:

"You take my fantasies too seriously."

"Too seriously? When I undertake something, there can be no question of jesting. You know that I detest all playacting and melodrama. Was it my idea or yours? . . . At any rate we are now in earnest."

"Wanda, . . . be reasonable and listen to me. We have such enormous love for each other, we are so happy, would you sacrifice all our future to a whim?"

> . . . .

"Leave me alone. You are not a man."

"And you!"

"I am selfish . . . I am not like you, strong in imagination and weak in action."

> . . . .

[Severin:] "You are mistaken . . . you are making yourself out to be more evil than you really are; you are far too good, far too noble by nature. . . ."

"What do you know of my nature? . . . You will get to know me as I really am."

> . . . .

"Wanda!"

"You wretch [Mensch]!"

> . . . .

"Yes, you must be a slave and taste the lash, for you are not a man." (200–202)

The question of sexual identity and its close connection to fantasy reaches its limits during the third and last stage of the masochistic relationship. Wanda and Severin/Gregor have moved to a villa outside Florence. The atmosphere in the villa is heavy; the color scheme turns into a dominating blood red. Wanda herself is now increasingly likened to a "red lioness." Her education is now complete, and it is here that Severin loses control over his pupil. She has taken on her role of cruel woman. Severin now indeed suffers, both beneath her whip and from her boredom with him. It is at this stage that the other man enters the picture in the form of the "Greek," the "red lion" whose own sexual identity is however ambiguous. Although he is described as rich, educated in Paris, cruel, brave, an atheist, a racist—"a real man," as Wanda concludes—Severin has this to say about him:

> What a beautiful man, by God! I have never seen his like in the flesh, only his marble replica in the *Belvedere*: he has the same slender, steely musculature, the delicate features, the wavy locks and the feature that makes him so distinctive: he has no beard. If his hips were less slender, he could be taken for a woman in disguise. . . . I cannot remain indifferent to his erotic power and my heart is filled with admiration for Socrates, who had the strength to resist the seductive Alcibiades. . . . Like a woman, he knows he is beautiful and behaves accordingly. Always elegant, he changes his costume four or even five times a day like a courtesan. He has been seen in Paris dressed as a woman and men showered him with love letters. An Italian singer, famous for his talents and for his passionate temperament forced his way into his house and threatened to kill himself if our hero did not yield to him.
>
> "I regret," the Greek replied with a smile, "I should have granted you my favors with pleasure, but alas, I can only sign your death warrant, for I am a man." (246–50)

The arrival of the Greek, and Wanda's incipient relationship with him, provoke Severin to draw the important distinction between cruelty and meanness (*Gemeinheit*, implying both a form of spitefulness and commonness or vulgarity): "So long as you were only pitiless and cruel I was able still to love you, but you are now becoming vulgar [*gemein*]" (255). The capacity for cruelty is to be understood here as the ability to sublimate, whereas vulgarity is merely a literal understanding and performance of bodiliness. Women, as Severin will eventually prove, are incapable of sublimation, a fact Freud will later also affirm. And yet it is the Greek—and here lies the true source of his androgyny—who finally ends the masochistic fantasy by taking the whip into his own hands and whipping the poetry out of Severin. Severin is left behind, as Wanda and the Greek leave together, and he finds himself cured for good. He is now able to return to his "father's house," where he learns the art of husbandry and administration, and where he learns to enjoy work and the fulfillment of duties. Once his father dies, he "quite naturally and without altering [his] way of life . . . became the master of the house" (269).

Venus in Furs presents the reader with two kinds of pictures: dream or fantasy pictures and art works that, when gazed at and when they gaze back, construct and articulate a specific form of male subjectivity. It is Severin's relationship to these pictures that constitutes his particular form of masochism, a relationship that Sacher-Masoch places into the history of human picture-making activity in Western civilization from antiquity to the present. The story that emerges is quite literally a *Heilungsgeschichte*: the word is made flesh, is incarnated, made real and tangible; poetry is converted into aching flesh, and thus Severin is cured. The course taken by Sacher-Masoch is thus the converse of Freud's: whereas Freud makes analysis and all interpretative activity dependent on the transformation of dreams and fantasies into words—that is, into a diachronic narrative—Sacher-Masoch's goal is to fix these images in time, to freeze them into an immobile, albeit always unstable construct, and thereby render unto them their redemptive power. His novella constitutes an explicit engagement with the development from paganism through Christianity to new secular forms of transcendence, a development that in Sacher-Masoch remains firmly anchored in the Catholic tradition of the redemptive power of images. The tensions in his work come from two sources: the level of content, because these images themselves (and they are invariably of cruel women, of "Venuses in furs") must move in order for the story to be a story in the first place, and because he must submit these pictures to his own interpretative and diagnostic analysis; and the level of form, because in writing these images down, he compels them to a certain diachronic existence.

Sacher-Masoch's Venus in furs is first and foremost a male creation, a *Kopfgeburt*, but nevertheless "the real thing." She first appears at the very beginning of the novella, in the narrator's dream: "I was in delightful company: the lady who sat facing me across the massive Renaissance fireplace was none other than Venus; she was no *demi-mondaine* who had taken a pseudonym to wage war upon the masculine sex, but the goddess of Love in person" (143). We quickly learn that the narrator's dream had been excited by a memory trace, or by what Freud was to call a remnant from the previous day's experience: the narrator's dream had been occasioned by his having seen a painting in Severin's study, a painting that turns out to be an image or representation of Severin's own imaginings:

It was a large oil painting done in the powerful colors of the Flemish School, and its subject was quite unusual. A beautiful woman, naked beneath her dark furs, was resting on an ottoman, supported on her left arm. A playful smile hovered on her lips and her thick hair was tied in a Grecian knot and dusted with snow-white powder. Her right hand played with a whip while her bare foot rested nonchalantly on a man who lay on the ground before her like a slave, like a dog. The pronounced but well-shaped features of the man showed quiet melancholy and helpless passion; he gazed up at her with the fanatical, burning eyes of a martyr. This man, this footstool for her feet, was Severin, beardless and ten years younger by the look of him. (148)

The narrator instantly recognizes the painting of Severin's gaze, in particular his burning eyes, as the cause of his own dream: "That is how I saw her in my dream!" (148). Severin responds that he too had dreamed of this Venus in furs but, as is demonstrated in the painting, with his eyes open. Severin is moved to allow the narrator and reader to see his "Confessions," a written document compiled from his personal diary of the period in question—"since . . . it is impossible to describe the past objectively"—thus giving the story "a flavor of the present" (151). First, however, we are invited to view yet another painting, a painting directly facing the representation of Severin's open-eyed dream. It is a "remarkably good copy" of Titian's *Venus with the Mirror*, another Venus in furs, that is, which represents "a biting satire on modern love: Venus must hide herself in a vast fur lest she catch cold in our abstract northern climate, in the icy realm of Christianity" (149). Interestingly, this Venus is less the real thing, more the demimondaine than in the other painting, though art historical discourse had seemingly covered this up with furs:

[Titian] simply painted the portrait of some distinguished Messalina coldly inspecting her majestic charms, and he was tactful enough to paint Cupid holding the mirror. . . . The picture is merely a piece of flattery. Later some connoisseur of the baroque dubbed the lady "Venus," and the despot's furs in which Titian's model wrapped herself (more out of fear of catching cold than from modesty) became the symbol of the tyranny and cruelty that are common to beautiful women. (149)

Severin's story, both in its unfolding and in its reception (it has, after all, the flavor of the present), takes place between these two images, which are, to a certain extent, structurally similar, for they both represent the cruel woman in furs. The paintings face, indeed are mirror images of, each other and can only be understood or interpreted with reference to each other. The reading of the "Confessions" is to be understood as a mediation between these two paintings. On the one hand, there

Leopold von Sacher-Masoch and Baroness von Pistor

is the "superbly good copy" of Titian, a fake but "biting satire" on modern love, a flattery represented by the fact that the Messalina dressed up as Venus sees no one but herself. Titian's painting can only be viewed in terms of the history of its reception and of receptivity in general. It describes the history of love, how love transforms its object into a sublime object. The painting thus functions as an allegory of art historical vision.[16] On the other hand, the real Venus, who looks at the real Severin with his eyes wide open, is a representation of Severin's dream and fantasy life. Readers will come to understand this history as the history of the masochistic subject, founded as it is in a "personal history." A double chronology therefore traverses Sacher-Masoch's text: on the one hand, the history of love as the movement from South to North, and on the other hand, Severin's personal history as the history of male subjectivity. The first explains how pleasure and power come to stand one for the other; the second, how Severin is allowed to participate in that history. Whereas the second painting guarantees an authenticity that the first, "fake," painting lacks, the first painting in turn guarantees the second's authenticity as a form of aesthetic or sublimated representation.[17] Mas-

Titian, *Venus with a Mirror*, Andrew W. Mellon Collection, © 1997 Board of
Trustees, National Gallery of Art, Washington

ochistic reading or readability takes place between these two central images of Sacher-Masoch's text, a space of vision where the two gazes of
the paintings meet, where the two histories are merged as a history of
the representation of the Cruel Woman (represented in the three stages
of Severin and Wanda's relationship), which in turn produces the reader's
gaze at the text insofar as he himself in turn has gazed—with his eyes
wide open—at those same images.[18]

Eine dumme Geschichte, Part I: The History of Love,
or How Venus Got Her Furs

The history of love is marked by the repeated appearances of Venus.
When we encounter her the first time in the narrator's dream, she is described as having a pale face, a body of marble, and a magnificent head,
despite the fact that her eyes are stony and lifeless. These eyes are Venus's determining characteristic. Although here a speaking subject, she
is in fact only a statue of the ancient goddess of love, Aphrodite/Venus,
who is looked at but cannot or will not look back. As a statue, Venus appears in the garden of the Carpathian villa and is the woman Severin is
in love with before meeting Wanda. In a photographic copy of Titian's
painting, Venus is the verso of Severin's first poetic outpouring to Wanda;
then the goddess reappears as the Medici Venus, whom Severin visits in
Florence. Furthermore, both Wanda and Severin seem to have imbibed
her image with their mother's milk. Wanda was taught to be a Greek by
her father, who had surrounded her with replicas of classical statues from
an early age; Severin, after rejecting "the healthy breast of his nurse,"
had become shy with women but had fallen in love with a plaster cast of
the goddess of love that stood in his father's library. Indeed, the library
seems to be Venus's preferred abode, since it is here that men can take
refuge from the advances made by real and therefore vulgar or common
women. Thus, Severin narrates how as a young boy he used a copy of
Tacitus against a chambermaid who had made sexual overtures to him.
The novella's narrator, who awakes from a dream of Venus, had fallen
asleep while reading Hegel. And Sacher-Masoch himself, in his first
masochistic contract with Anna von Kottowitz, included a clause that allowed him six hours a day in the library in order to write. This escape
clause gave him not only a respite from common women but also a space
from which to report on his own life: the result is *Venus in Furs*.

These Venuses, who for centuries had been able to draw the desiring
gaze of male viewers, do not return it in kind: either they have eyes
of stone or are too busy looking into mirrors. Due to an inherent self-
sufficiency and a primary narcissistic pleasure (the mirror is the goddess's emblem and a reminder that Aphrodite was the ancient goddess of
prostitutes), their gaze remains directed inward. In Sacher-Masoch's
novella, this blank look turns, as Monika Treut has noted, into an empty
screen onto which the "learning experience" regarding the Cruel Woman
can be projected as a mastered because past event.[19] Two initial moves

are necessary for such a projection: first, Venus must come alive; and second, she must get her furs. Within the structure of the "Confessions," these two necessities occur simultaneously. Severin sends the as yet unknown widow some reading material while "remembering too late that the photograph of my Venus" (156) is in one of the books. The photograph of Titian's Venus bears Severin's inscription: "*Venus in Furs.* You are cold and yet you fire the hearts of men. Wrap yourself in your despot's furs, for they become no one so well as you, cruel goddess of Beauty and Love" (154). Severin hears the widow laugh, forcing him to wonder whether he is an amateur or a fool. Wanda answers by dressing the statue in the garden with a fur: "The goddess is draped in fur: a dark sable cloak flows from her marble shoulders down to her feet. I stand bewildered, transfixed; again I am gripped by an indescribable panic. I take flight. In my hurry I take the wrong path and just as I am about to turn off into one of the leafy avenues, there before me, seated on a bench—is Venus" (156). This time, however, it is the "real" Venus: not a marble statue, but "the goddess of Love in person." This is truly miraculous, though Severin instantly perceives that the miracle is not yet complete: "her hair still seems made of marble and her white dress gleams like moonlight" (157); however, she is wearing furs, and "suddenly her eyes shine with a wicked green glitter—she is laughing!" (157).

Here begins Severin's personal history, in which he is eventually transformed from a dilettante, one who is "an amateur in life"—"I have never progressed far beyond the first brush stroke, the outline of the plot, the first stanza" (152)—to a gentleman and landowner, described by the narrator as "surprisingly lucid and serious almost to the point of pedantry." He becomes a man capable of following a "rigorous philosophical and practical system" under "the dictates of the thermometer, the barometer, the aerometer, the hydrometer, Hippocrates, Hufeland, Plato, Knigge and Lord Chesterfield" (148), his story describing a curative transformation that is interrupted only by occasional attacks of violence. Within this transformative process Wanda is simply the bearer of furs and the blank screen of masculine self-mastery. She herself does not even get near such mastery. As Albrecht Koschorke points out, the descriptive adjectives of mastery focus increasingly in Sacher-Masoch's narratives on these furs and less and less on their wearers: it is the furs that eventually become Severin's quintessential fetishistic object and thus come to embody the symbol of power and mastery.[20]

Yet, as Treut has remarked, these furs, though they increasingly take on the symbolic meaning of power, mastery, and cruelty, have themselves to undergo a historical process of transformation. The history of furs is the history of power and cruelty as it intersects with the history of sexuality, a joint history that arises out of necessity. As we learn both from the history behind Titian's painting and from the narrator's dream, Venus is forced to don furs because of the cold. With the development of civilization, passions must be controlled and sublimated as they are forced to take up habitation in the North. The South/North vector of civilization is, of course, a common trope of Romanticism which describes the process whereby energy and passion must submit to the laws and dictates of reason.[21] Sacher-Masoch is well aware, as Freud later would also insist, that passion does not disappear in this move northward. What takes place is not an obliteration of passions but their substitution or sublimation in mitigated form. According to Treut, the strength and form of passion is displaced in Sacher-Masoch's work into anger, unrest, storming, and domination, a fact that shows up symptomatically in the cured Severin's sudden outbursts of rage. Such displaced passion takes the form of furs, which become the symbolic attributes of beauty and power, since they allow men to participate in that electrified passion that is viewed as characteristic of the South:

> It is a natural law that fur has a stimulating effect on highly strung people. It exerts a strong and mysterious physical attraction to which no one is immune. Science has recently established that there is a relation between electricity and heat and that their effect on the human body is similar. Torrid climates make for passionate natures and warm atmospheres produce exaltation; the same is true of electricity. This is why cats have always had such a beneficial and magical effect on spiritual and impressionable people: the movement of their long, graceful tails, their magnetism, their fur crackling with electricity. (177–78)

Wanda understands Severin's message and rightly concludes that a woman in furs is simply a large cat, "a sort of highly charged electric battery" (178). Which is why, according to Severin, furs come to take on the attributes of beauty and power, for "in ancient times monarchs and noblemen claimed furs as their exclusive right" (178). Those who were excluded from this right, by virtue of their birth or because passion has become cold, may partake of passion and power at one remove once furs become accessible to all men. Severin's access to furs is, as Treut notes, always indirect; or rather, his access to passion can only take place through his engagement with furs. This is a secondhand passion; it is fundamentally foreign to Severin and can only be experienced passively, in a slavish manner, because it requires the continuous denial or disavowal of the lack of power that is characteristic of the Northern cold. Furs are not simply symbols of passion and power; they are the site where the two come together as a substitute participation in sexual and political relations. Masochistic coldness, as it comes to be embodied in furs, is not a negation of feeling but a disavowal of sensuality. Sentimentality, according to Deleuze, becomes the dominating element of this universe; it constitutes a freezing point that corresponds to the catastrophe of the Ice Age, of the movement from South to North, and of the onset of modern relations. Yet the ice and furs bury and protect a hidden supersensuality: "The coldness is both protective milieu and medium, cocoon and vehicle: it protects supersensual sentimentality as inner life, and expresses it as external order, as wrath and severity." [22]

But Severin has not yet told everything: "Does not fur have a special significance for you personally?" Wanda asks Severin. Indeed it does, for Severin cannot imagine a woman without furs: "she is a strange ideal born of the aesthetics of ugliness, with the soul of a Nero in the body of Phryne" (178). His love for women in furs has its source in the circumstances of his birth and in the structure of his family: he was born into a ruling Siberian cold and therefore must have furs, and he explains his love for cruel women in furs by reference to a primal scene. Severin's narration of this primal scene coincides with an autobiographical event that was supposed to have taken place when the author was nine years old. A beautiful aunt who was given to wearing furs and who was supposedly much feared by Severin/Sacher-Masoch because of her great cruelty one day whipped the child while his parents were out and then forced him to kneel down and kiss her hand. His fear was instantly transformed into adoration, or rather, the two became inextricably combined and geared toward an ideal, sublimated object of desire. From then on he swore to himself that this was what he had to save himself for in the future: "My cato-like austerity and my shyness in the presence of women were nothing more than an excessively developed aestheticism. Sensuality became my own personal cult, and I swore never to squander its sacred treasures on any ordinary being, but to reserve them for the ideal woman, if possible for the goddess of Love herself" (175). In Severin's fantasy the two images of his first loves—Venus and the fur-clad aunt—come to merge: "sometimes she loomed in Olympian garb, with the severe white face of the plaster Venus, and at other times I saw her with the thick tresses of brown hair, the laughing blue eyes and kazabaika trimmed with ermine that were my pretty aunt's" (175–76). What emerges from this fantasy is the image of the Cruel Woman with furs, founded in a chain of female historical figures, in a long catalog of literary and mythological references, and in personal, traumatic memories that are anaclitically attached to this history:

> By making man so vulnerable to passion, nature has placed him at woman's mercy, and she who has not the sense to treat him like a humble subject, a slave, a plaything, and finally to betray him with a laugh— well, she is a woman of little wisdom. . . . the more cruel and faithless she is . . . the more she quickens his desire and secures his love and admiration. It has always been so, from the time of Helen and Delilah all the way to Catherine the Great and Lola Montez. (146)

Treut has traced six structural prerequisites for the resultant masochistic fantasy: Such a fantasy homogenizes the plurality of its historical and cultural references into one semantic picture, that of the cruel woman; the cruel woman structures the masochistic fantasy as a mythic system; masochistic mystification, though formally a cultural enterprise, empties and impoverishes that same enterprise; the myth of the cruel woman leads to the frozen quality of the fantasy (the "icy woman"); this frozen quality evokes suspense as its primary stylistic form; and masochistic suspense indefinitely displaces pleasure into the future.[23] The contradictory impulse—desire to transgress as well as fear of that transgression—is expressed in the distinction between the vulgar or common woman, on the one hand, and the cruel or cold woman, on the other. By creating a sublime object, the masochist maintains control over his transgression, and, as is proper to sublimation, he does so on aesthetic grounds. The cruel woman plays a double role: she is the object of desire, and she prohibits its genital fulfillment (it is unclear whether Severin and Wanda ever consummate their relationship); she constitutes the aim but also the limit of pleasure, that is, both its promise and its prohibition. Her double role takes the form of a double requirement: as the statue of Venus she must come to life, she must look back at the man's desiring gaze; and at the same time, she must prohibit limitless pleasure, the pleasures of the South, where the gaze produces desire, and desire produces enjoyment. The second requirement she can only fulfill by wearing Northern furs, by embodying the icy cold they represent, and thereby turning herself into a picture. It is in this sense that the cruel woman must embody aesthetic sublimation. She provides the site where what

Freud termed "considerations of representability" can be taken into account: insofar as she takes place as picture and also makes it possible to put fantasy into pictorial form in the first place. This picture-making activity, which is one of the four fundamental mechanisms of fantasy and of dreaming (the other three being condensation, displacement, and secondary revision), is also the primary impulse behind Freud's theory of sublimation, the scopophilic drive to create cultural objects that may evade the process of repression in the form of an ever-seducing woman who laughs at man's self-renunciatory efforts at keeping the woman in the picture.

Eine dumme Geschichte, Part II: The Story of the Eye

In a discussion of Freud's essay "Instincts and Their Vicissitudes," John Noyes argues that Freud uses a linguistic model to explain the psychic mechanisms behind the two pairs of component instincts, scopophilia/exhibitionism and sadism/masochism.[24] Freud thus differentiates in his analysis of the couplet sadism/masochism between three separate stages that this instinctual drive undergoes in its development:

(1) Sadism consists in the direction of this drive toward an outside object. Freud describes this in terms of the active voice of "I torture him/her."
(2) The object is abandoned and replaced by the subject's self. This turning around of the drive is expressed in the reflexive voice of "I torture myself." In this stage the turning around of the aim has come about, and thus the passive voice is achieved.
(3) Only in this stage can one speak of masochism proper. Here another person is sought as object of the drive, though due to the change in instinctual aim, the object now plays the role of the subject: "I am tortured by him/her."

Freud claims that the couplet scopophilia and exhibitionism, while undergoing the same three stages as sadism and masochism, in fact diverges from them. This is because in the case of scopophilia/exhibitionism, the first or primary stage is in fact the second, self-reflexive stage. In other words, Freud equates "the subject looking at his sexual organ" with "the sexual organ being looked at by the subject." The autoerotic origin of the sexual drive justifies this claim and is a condition absent in sadism because sadism is initially nonsexual in nature and represents a first attempt by the subject to gain control or mastery over the outside world. Yet Freud hesitates: "it might not be altogether unreasonable to construct such a stage out of the child's efforts to gain control over his own limbs."[25] Freud's hesitation points in fact to a more general problem: not only is it possible that mastery may be self-reflexive from the beginning, but this effort at self-control might in fact also point to the moment when mastery is sexualized. Laplanche has distinguished in Freud's text two forms of sadism: a first, nonsexual form that agrees with Freud's first stage; and a second form that is properly sexual, stemming, like masochism, from the self-reflexive or second stage.[26] Thus, Laplanche reads the self-reflexive move of both sadism/masochism and scopophilia/exhibitionism as describing the moment when sexuality is anaclitically created from nonsexual drives, and the subsequent direction of this moment toward activity or passivity as the vicissitudes of the newly created drive. Freud will, of course, confirm this reading in his 1924 essay "The Economic Problem of Masochism," where he posits an originary form of masochism that he identifies as the constitutive moment of human sexuality.

Laplanche has established the fundamental connection between this second, self-reflexive stage and the genesis of sexuality as the moment of fantasy. In other words, self-reflexivity denotes an internalization in regard not only to autoerogenous zones but also to fantasmatization. Created here is sexuality as an interior space of fantasy. Thus, in the transition to the reflexive voice, sexuality and fantasy emerge in the form of a masochistic excitation:

> We have situated, in the position of what we called reflexive masochism, or the middle voice, a fantasy which, however, has a properly masochistic content in the "passive" sense. . . . But that is because . . . the process of turning round is not to be thought of only at the level of content of the fantasy, but *in the very movement of fantasmatization*. To shift to the reflexive is not only or even necessarily to give a reflexive content to the "sentence" of the fantasy; it is also and above all to reflect the action, internalize it, make it enter into oneself as fantasy.[27]

The genesis of sexuality thus coincides with interiorization conceived as a fantasmatic space; and fantasy in turn is the site where sexuality comes into being. Freud posits this movement in linguistic terms or, as Lacan would have it, as the proposition that the unconscious is structured as language. Fantasy as the place where sexuality comes into being is thus never the object of desire but its setting, and as Laplanche and Pontalis have argued in their seminal essay on fantasy, the subject participates in this fantasy at no predetermined point: "In fantasy the subject does not pursue the object or its sign: he appears caught up himself in the sequence of images. He forms no representation of the desired object, but is himself represented as participating in the scene although, in the earliest forms of fantasy, he cannot be assigned a fixed place in it."[28] Thus, for example, in the "ur-fantasy" of "a father seduces a daughter," the subject may occupy the position of subject, object, and indeed, verb.

Sacher-Masoch's point of entry into his particular fantasy is that of the verb, staged here as the gaze. John Noyes has claimed that what Sacher-Masoch stages is a fantasy where the verb "to see" comes to be nominalized. Seeing, in Sacher-Masoch's text, is made into substance, thus gaining transcendental consistency and the capacity to function virtually autonomously. According to Noyes, the gaze is the privileged site for such transcendence for it is in the act of seeing that the subject both establishes contact with the outside world and realizes his or her own constitutive lack:

> As soon as the subject attempts to confirm his subjectivity in the gaze of the other, that same gaze that floats between them dramatizes a lack that is constitutive of both. . . . The gaze shapes itself in its contact with reality as both active and passive: the gaze received by the subject is for the latter a representation of reality; the subject's gaze calls forth self-consciousness, in that the representation of reality becomes a representation that concerns only the subject. The subject and object of such a gaze are both indeterminate or ambivalent, so that the desire for Being can only be expressed as desire for transcendental mediation.[29]

The specificity of masochism, according to Noyes, is that within the structure of this perversion the grammatically passive voice nominalizes the gaze and constructs the subject's relation to his drive as a relation to the gaze; or, to put it within the vocabulary of Laplanche and Pontalis's analysis, the subject enters the fantasy at the level of the verb. The resultant masochistic gaze is structurally equivalent to a staging of the constituent lack of subjectivity as a putting-into-question of self-consciousness, and therefore the desire to be is the gaze of desire. The gaze of desire functions as a transcendental signifier that posits the subject as split, and the masochistic text, that is, the grammatical form that it takes as passive voicing, serves to pin down this split as writing.

Noyes is correct in positing the nominalization of the verb as the constitutive part of the masochistic scene. Thus, when the statue of Venus comes to life in the garden of the Carpathian villa, she puts on furs and gains eyesight. In the first glimpse Severin gets of these eyes, they are described as "two diabolical, green rays" (157; translation modified), later as green lightning flashes. In other words, this is a gaze that can be seen, it is an object. However, there is also Severin's gaze of desire, the gaze of the dreamer, of the "supersensualist," a gaze that both expresses too much desire and has transcended that desire in sublimatory fashion. Sacher-Masoch describes it as the burning, tearful gaze of the martyr, and it is quite different from Wanda's green rays. Although Wanda gets embodied as green rays, only Severin ever has his eyes wide open. She has no subject-position at all, while his subject-position is constituted by virtue of the fact that he is looked at, or to be more precise, by the fact that he sees himself being looked at. Severin's *Schaulust* takes the form of a certain kind of exhibitionism; his gaze enacts an active passivity that is the very essence of masochistic subjectivity.

Noyes misses this crucial distinction. His theory moves from the specificity of Severin's subjectivity to a general one, where the construction of all subject-positions or all self-consciousness must follow the same pattern. In effect, he collapses the *genesis* of sexuality, fantasy, and subjectivity with one of the drive's possible *vicissitudes*. Seeing and torturing are unproblematically linked, causing Noyes to lose the historical specificity for the connection between the gaze and its passive expression. What remains unanswered by his reading is how Sacher-Masoch is able to move from the self-reflexive moment to an interpretation of it as "naturally" masochistic. Although Noyes concedes that Sacher-Masoch's gaze is shaped as one that vacillates between the public-historical and the private-sexual, he cannot explain why and how this in fact happens. What is the connection between seeing and suffering? Are the subject-positions created by this connection arbitrary or indeterminate, or are they universal?

The thematic and formal center of *Venus in Furs* is constituted by the "mirror scene" and the "painting scene" that follows, as well as by the relationship these two scenes bear to yet another painting: the representation of Samson and Delilah's final encounter before Samson is blinded in punishment for his desire. Wanda desires a bath and demands the ministrations of Severin/Gregor. The bath takes place in a "spacious rotunda" of the Italian villa, lit by a red glass dome in the ceiling, with carpeted stairs leading down to a marble bath. The central decoration adorning the wall is an enormous mirror. Since Severin must "help" in the bathing ritual, he is forced to see Wanda in her full nakedness, that is, without furs. His incipient feelings of arousal are, however, instantly converted into an aestheticization of the scene, most obviously into a reenactment of the birth of Venus (whom he had visited the day before in the Uffizi). Before Wanda throws off her furs, he still feels compelled to gaze at his beloved, as though he were driven by "some magical force. . . . At the sight of her lying on the red velvet cushions, her precious body peeping out between the folds of sable, I realized how powerfully sensuality and lust are aroused by flesh that is only partly revealed" (239). However, as Wanda rises and tosses off her furs, Severin's reaction is instantaneously ("*in diesem Augenblick*") transformed:

> At that moment she seemed saintly and chaste in her unveiled beauty as the statue of the goddess, and I fell on my knees before her and devoutly pressed my lips to her foot. My soul, that had been rocked a while ago by such a storm of emotion, was now suddenly pacified; there was not a trace of cruelty about her. . . . I was able to contemplate her in peaceful joy, untouched by a single atom of suffering or desire. . . . How right is the nihilist aesthete when he says that a real apple is more beautiful than a painted apple, and a living body than a Venus of stone!
>
> A silent rapture overcame my whole being when she rose from the bath, the drops of silvery water and the pink light streaming down her. (239–40)[30]

The transformation from demonic cruelty to saintly nakedness, indeed the birth of this religious icon, signals the transcendence of Severin's passion. This is an inevitably double move: it comprises both the adoration of the transfigured woman/goddess/Virgin Mary and the deification of the female demon with furs. In the first case, as Koschorke has remarked, male asceticism takes the form of the silencing of passions;[31] in the second case, this asceticism is the core of both passion itself and those rituals in which such passion may be expressed. Thus, while Wanda turns into the "real Venus" at a first moment, she must also continue to wear her furs. The moment of birth cannot last forever, for Severin simply has no place in this picture. As Wanda emerges from the bath and dons her furs again, the real apple must be transformed into a painted apple in order to make the moment and the gaze last:

> The supple furs greedily caressed her cold marble body. Her left arm, on which she supported herself, lay like a sleeping swan amid the dark sable, while her right hand toyed with the whip.
> My eyes alighted by chance on the massive mirror that hung opposite and I let out a cry: our reflections in its golden frame were like a picture of extraordinary beauty. It was so strange and fantastic that I felt a pang of regret that its forms and colors would soon vanish like a cloud. . . .
> I pointed to the mirror.
> "Ah, yes, it is beautiful," she said. "What a pity we cannot capture this moment." (240)

Severin, too, shudders at the thought that "this extraordinary beauty, these mysterious green eyes and wild fiery hair, and all the splendor of this body" should die and turn into dust and nothingness. A trace of Wanda's existence must be preserved; her beauty must triumph over death: she must be painted. The moment of mirroring constitutes therefore an epiphanous moment because it is poised between life and death, between movement and immobility, between the Real and the Symbolic. The image in the mirror is uncanny because, as Treut has noted, it also captures both the coming-to-life of the artistic tradition or past and the freezing of the present and future. It marks the point where Wanda, who had before been transformed from the statue of Venus into the "real Venus," must again be captured, fixed in an eternal Now by returning to representation: "The masochist thus experiences his loved one as a moment in time [*Augenblick*] where she appears as the living dead of the past in order to be eternalized aesthetically as a beautiful body."[32]

There will be a transformation: Severin will be part of this new representation, both as observer and as participant. His gaze will now be that of desire in a double sense: as the patient object of the cruel woman, the suffering martyr with burning eyes, but only insofar as he can see himself see and be seen in such a manner. This new painting will have to provide an answer, then, to Severin's question of being: "What would I have to be in order to be looked at in this way? . . . What would I have to be in order to look at something in this way?"[33] Severin must become the simultaneous patient and clinician of his own perverse passions.

The painting of the mirror scene gets on the way. Although no Titian or Raphael lives in Italy today, "our little German" painter, who for a while had been hanging about the villa in silent admiration of Wanda, will do the job, if nothing else because his transference to his object is sufficiently strong: "I shall ensure that love mixes the colors on his palette" (240). Wanda lives up to her promise. The love-struck painter begins his portrait of her, representing her as a Madonna, thus obviously missing the point. His "idealism of a German" obviously needs other influences: "Wait a moment, I want to show you a portrait of me, one that I painted myself; you shall copy it" (241). The mirror scene is reenacted in a veritable orgy of gazes: "Look at me . . . with your deep fanatical look," Wanda orders Severin, while the painter in turn "devours the scene with his beautiful melancholy eyes" (241–42). The German is clearly getting increasingly caught up in both the picture and its story: "'This painting, like many of the Venetian school, is intended to be both a portrait and a story,'" though it is only with difficulty that he can speak:

> "I imagine that the goddess of Love has come down from Olympus to visit a mortal. So as not to die of cold in this modern world of ours, she wraps her sublime body in great heavy furs and warms her feet on the prostrate body of her lover. I imagine the favorite of this beautiful despot, who is whipped when his mistress grows tired of kissing him, and whose love only grows more intense the more he is trampled underfoot. I shall call the picture *Venus in Furs*." (242)

The painting proceeds, but the transferential relationship between the three must grow more extreme and must be played out for the painting to become more "real." This in turn makes the painting process more difficult:

> "I am glad you are in high spirits, madam," says the painter, "but your face has completely lost the expression I need for my painting."
> "The expression you need for your painting," she smiles. "Wait a moment."
> She rises to her feet and deals me a blow with the whip. The painter gapes in childish wonder, half horrified and half admiring.
> As she whips me, Wanda's face gradually recovers the cruel, ironic appearance that fills me with such rapture.
> "Is this the right expression for your portrait?" she asks.

The painter is dumbfounded; he lowers his eyes to evade her piercing stare.

"That is the right expression," he stammers. "But I can no longer paint."

"What is the matter?" asks Wanda mockingly. "Can I be of any assistance?"

"Yes," cries the German, as though taken with madness. "Whip me, too!" (243)

This scene constitutes both the pinnacle or fulfillment of the masochistic fantasy and its simultaneous undoing, captured by the sentence "But I can no longer paint." Although this scene is about the painting of the scene itself—one founded in the masochistic gaze of both Severin and the painter—it also leads to an inevitable doubling and the reintroduction of precisely the mirroring that Sacher-Masoch and Severin had wanted to freeze in time. As long as the painter cannot paint, he can direct his masochistic gaze of desire at Wanda; as soon as he paints and thus stops the mirroring, he must in some fundamental sense relinquish his desire. He must sublimate it.

The doubling is also expressed in the problematic fact that this scene requires a third subject-position, namely that of the witness, expressed here in the doubling between Severin and the painter. The former witnesses the latter's whipping, an event that transforms Severin into the painter of the scene, and the German can in turn only paint the scene by witnessing Severin's whipping. In both cases, the witness cannot be the recipient of Wanda's gaze. Within the completed picture, her gaze is always at some indeterminable point outside the representation, which can only ever represent, then, Wanda's absent gaze. The viewer of the painting or the scene (Severin, the painter, the narrative I, and ultimately the reader) can only receive Wanda's "green rays" by projective identification. Ultimately, this scene can only ever point either backward to historical models (the series of paintings evoked in the novella, the bath scene, the mirroring scene) or forward to a utopian fixing of eternity in the form of a promise of a future painting. Thus, for Sacher-Masoch, art constitutes a momentary flash, a green lightning or instantaneous twinkling of the eye that embodies in the cruel woman both the fantasy of a remembered past and the image of an anticipated future.

In order to put a halt to this mirroring or doubling and thus reverse Severin's undetermined object-position to a passive subject-position, Sacher-Masoch falls back to yet another act of doubling: he constructs a metanarrative or metapainting of the story of the eye. This is the story both of Samson and Delilah and of Severin's relationship to its representation on the ceiling of Wanda's Florentine bedroom. Like the eventually completed picture of Wanda and Severin, this fresco is both portrait and story. Although as biblical narrative it is mentioned early in the novella, as picture Severin sees the painting three times. At first, he hardly glances at the painting but merely remarks that it is a "fine painting." He is all eyes for Wanda, who appears here in a "captivating *déshabillé*" and smothers Severin with kisses. Who can look at paintings when being gazed at with "eyes misty with gentle rapture" (219)? He sees the painting for a second time during the signing of the masochistic contract. On reading the terms of the documents—the signing or not signing of which will determine Severin's question, man or slave?—our hero is gripped with terror, and in this momentary hesitation,

> I gazed up for a moment and only then did I realize the utter lack of historical character in the painting above me (as happens so often with painters of the Italian and Dutch schools;) this gave it an uncanny quality. Delilah, an opulent creature with flaming red hair, reclines half-naked on a red ottoman, a sable cloak about her shoulders. She smiles and leans towards Samson, who has been bound and thrown at her feet by the Philistines. Her teasing, coquettish smile seems the very summit of cruelty; with half-closed eyes she gazes at Samson, while he regards her longingly, crazed with love. Already his enemy has laid a knee on his chest and is about to blind him with the white-hot sword. (221)

Although under the gun himself, in the very instant before signing the contract, Severin is able to read or see the painting in art historical terms. He places it within a school onto which he projects his own lack of historical character. In other words, he fails to see that the representation is in any way connected to his own story of sight and blindness. He sees the painting but is blind to it. Blinded by love himself, he misses, as Treut points out, the allegorical meaning of the painting, and like Samson, who was punished for his seeing/loving with blindness, Severin blindly signs the contract. It is only when he sees the painting for the third time that it becomes an eye-opener. Fittingly, this constitutes the final scene of the "Confessions" and signals Severin's cure. As he stands bound to the pillar of Wanda's bed, with the Greek about to whip all aesthetic pleasure out of him, Severin's eyes drift to the ceiling, where Samson is soon to be blinded by the Philistines: "The painting suddenly appeared as symbol, the timeless image of the love, the passion and the lust of man for woman. 'Each of us ends up like Samson,' I thought. 'We are always betrayed by the woman we love, whether she wears a sable cloak or a linen smock'" (268). The painting thus appears in a progression of awareness that is, however, the inverse of the actual content of the painting itself: while Severin sees, Samson is blinded. Severin begins to see under the sign of blinding love, progresses to the historical interpretation of aesthetic practices under the sign of power (the contract), and ends with the enlightening allegory of the timeless, unhistorical, and nonspecific or general (whether sable cloak or linen smock) relations between the sexes under the lash of punishment. In Treut's view, Severin moves from happy oversight, to the presentiment of horrified fascination, to terrorized awareness.[34]

Ideally, Severin's gaze would have absolutely nothing to do with Wanda—or at least as little as possible. It has everything to do with Severin's identity, however, an identity that he can establish only within what Noyes calls a field of substantive seeing. Wanda's gaze is constructed as substance, and it is within this substance that Severin's identity seeks to take its place. The cruel woman's gaze becomes substance through the act of picturing, through making art and interpreting it, thus putting both Wanda and Severin quite literally into the picture. The most perfect achievement of such an identity always occurs in Sacher-Masoch's work under the sign of the middle stage (not, as one would think, at the final stage of the cure). This moment of achievement takes place under the shadow of horrified fascination, where insight and blindness turn one into the other and where sexual desire can only be inscribed under the sign of power, that is, the contract. It is here, before the signing and the writing,[35] where the question "Am I a man or a slave?" is posed, that Severin finds his identity. Such an identity is neither that of man nor slave but arises as the posing of its question, the very posing of which will always hinge on the act of seeing and being seen. More accurately, it will depend on the possibility or the promise that Severin can see himself being seen, on the condition that the passive phrase "I am tortured by Wanda" means "I can direct my own torture at the hand of Wanda." Thus, the passive or masochistic subject-position must be just that: a subject-position in charge of its own destiny. It must allow for a kind of self-reflexivity that permits a representation or projection that transforms the passive construction of being tortured and being seen into an agent or subject of that same passive sentence. Hence the repeated question posed by Wanda—"Do you still love me?"—which is not, as Noyes as noted, a question belonging to her own affective life but one that should of necessity elicit the question of Severin's being. And yet, the question cannot ultimately be answered, except perhaps with another question and another act of representation that pushes Severin's authenticity farther away. He must, like Sacher-Masoch himself, remain his own reporter: his "writing that registers the constant danger of boredom and the deficit of life reaches for naked and bloody reality, but only to arm itself through a grid of literary barriers and techniques of disavowal against its immediate impact on consciousness."[36] Sacher-Masoch, like all his heroes, remains inevitably caught in a kind of scopophilic hunger.

3

THE THEFT OF THE OPERATIC VOICE: MASOCHISTIC SEDUCTION IN WAGNER'S PARSIFAL

We have, in Galicia, a marvelous legend. Every star that falls becomes, as soon
as it touches the ground, a human being of a strange, hypnotic beauty, whose
angelic face is framed by the fiery golden tresses of a demon. This being, man
or woman, whom no mortal can resist, is a demon who kills those who love it
by sucking out their soul with a kiss.

—Letter of Leopold von Sacher-Masoch to "Anatole"
(assumed to have been Ludwig II of Bavaria)

When Wagner's last and—for many—his most sublime work was staged
for the first time in 1882 in Bayreuth, it instantly created the parameters
of a debate that remain in their essence unchanged to this day: what was
Parsifal, religion or blasphemy? And above all, what constituted the nature of its power to fascinate: an instance of the sublime or a massive
swindle? Wagner himself had viewed his *Parsifal* as a work that could not
be subsumed under his already new category of "music drama" (itself
constituting a displacement of "opera") and had lent it the cumbersome
and virtually untranslatable name "*Bühnenweihfestspiel*" (festival drama of
dedication, or drama of consecration of the stage). In a letter to his pa-
tron Ludwig II of Bavaria, Wagner believed to have "openly staged the
most sublime mysteries of the Christian faith," and if his own descriptions are to be believed, the first performances of *Parsifal* engulfed participants and audience alike in his staged representation of the sublime
rite of the Grail Knights' Love-feast: "Whoever had the mind and eye to

seize the character of all that passed within the walls of that house during those two months, both the productive and the receptive, could not describe it otherwise than as governed by a consecration that shed itself on everything without the smallest prompting." Seemingly everyone was in tune with Wagner's totality, and it was the invisible hand of "Anarchy" that did its bidding. Neither violent outbursts of passion (the domain of common opera), nor etiquette, nor fashion contributed to the "natural grace of sublimity."[1] Apparently the audience was stunned. Franz Liszt commented after the premiere, "During and after yesterday's performance the general feeling was that there is nothing that can be said about this miraculous work. Silence is surely the only possible response to so deeply moving a work; the solemn beat of its pendulum is from the sublime to the most sublime."[2] Such descriptions have endured, ranging from the adulatory remarks by Romain Rolland (also present at the premiere) that *Parsifal* constituted the fifth Gospel, or rather its first and greatest, to more evocative allusions to the cultic, still reflected in current performance practices of the *Bühnenweihfestspiel*. (The Metropolitan Opera of New York continues to stage *Parsifal* at Easter time and retains the practice established at Bayreuth of withholding applause after Act I in order to respect the work's "religious" nature.) That *Parsifal* was performed outside Bayreuth at all, of course, already constituted a heretical act, for Wagner had restricted stagings of the work to his own opera house. It was not until 1903 that *Parsifal* was performed elsewhere, but by then the question of its "authentic version" had become firmly entrenched as a fundamental aspect of any engagement with the work.

Wagner seduces. He himself was quite sure that a good performance — for example, of Act III of *Tristan und Isolde*—would either drive people crazy or be banned by the censors. According to Nietzsche, *Parsifal* would go down in history as the stroke of genius in the art of seduction: Wagner is a swindler, the Klingsor of all Klingsors. Žižek has called Wagner the Charcot of music who dominates a now feminized public with his bag of hypnotic tricks. The peculiarity of *Parsifal* stems foremost from the extreme transferential reaction the work has generated ever since its first performance, a reaction that can only be described as cultic: whether the *Bühnenweihfestspiel* is a religious or secular work has been not so much a question of its thematics (*Parsifal* is clearly *about* religious themes) but rather a question regarding its status as ritual, its performative impact. Standard critiques, such as that of Lucy Beckett, for whom *Parsifal* is unquestionably a religious work, simply avoid the problem of this transference: for Beckett, the opera is religious because it concerns

Parsifal's conversion into a position of responsibility, and this for her is inherently a religious subject. With her insistence on thematic content, however, she misses the work's power of appeal, indeed its *authoritative* impact, and it is, I believe, no coincidence that she never mentions its sexual dimensions, except unproblematically as that which is to be renounced. What she misses, in other words, is the fact that *Parsifal*'s religious appeal is grounded precisely in the mechanisms of sexual desire.

The debates around *Parsifal* have left virtually unchallenged both the music and its precise function in the opera—the music is perceived by all critics as unquestioningly beautiful, indeed sublime—but have tended to focus on its libretto and therefore its historical, philosophical, and religious underpinnings, underpinnings that, nevertheless, remain strangely disconnected from the music. Claude Debussy, otherwise critical of the Wagnerian project, unhesitatingly described the music as "one of the most beautiful monuments of sound ever constructed to the eternal fame of music,"[3] and Nietzsche, Wagner's earliest, most virulent critic, could only wish he himself had composed the music to a work that he nonetheless saw as a product of decadence, a work of meanness, vengeance, a "bad work." Robert Gutman, while seeing in *Parsifal* a work of anti-Semitism, an allegory of Aryan redemption, posits it as an "enigma of genius that Wagner was able to yoke all this bizarre paraphernalia embracing the catalogue of his neuroses to both an allegory of the fallen and redeemed Aryan and a symbolic representation of the developing human soul, to overlay the whole with a rather cheap and cracking veneer of fake Catholicism, and yet achieve a monumental masterpiece."[4] Thus, even if its critics have continued to speak of the opera as pseudo-religion or of a *Parsifal* pseudo-cult, even if on the Christian side there were criticisms that the work was blasphemous because it sought to replace religion with an aesthetic product, the cultic aspect of *Parsifal* has survived. It remains to most viewers and listeners a sublime experience, an overwhelming one, whether one reads its libretto merely as allegory or whether one rejects it altogether and shifts the opera's religious content to the music.

Much criticism of Wagner is engaged simultaneously in continuous efforts at exorcism (this becomes even more prevalent during the postwar period after the association of Wagner with anti-Semitism and Nazism) and in a religious, if not obsessive, pursuit of the composer's intentions. This transferential relation to Wagner has generated a string of strong or mis-readings of Wagner (sacrificial and/or self-sacrificial, disloyal and/or loyal) undertaken in the name of faithfulness to the composer's intentions. But to state that an artist's output has generated a consistent series of misreadings does not yet solve the problem. One may, as Jacques Derrida has remarked with reference to Nietzsche, "wonder how and why what is so naively called a falsification was possible (one can't falsify just anything)."[5] Indeed, close to the investigation into Wagnerian intentions lies the question of whether the tendency to falsification may not be an essential aspect of Wagnerian opera—whether, in other words, Wagner had been *serious*. Nietzsche raised the issue in 1887:

> That poor devil and nature boy Parsifal, whom he finally made into a Catholic by such captious means—what? was this Parsifal meant *seriously*? For one might be tempted to suppose the reverse, even to desire it—that the Wagnerian *Parsifal* was intended as a joke, as a kind of epilogue and satyr play with which the tragedian Wagner wanted to take leave of us, also of himself, above all *of tragedy* in a fitting manner worthy of himself, namely with an extravagance of wanton parody of the tragic itself, of the whole gruesome earthly seriousness and misery of his previous works. . . . Is Wagner's *Parsifal* his secret laughter of superiority at himself, the triumph of his ultimate artist's freedom and artist's transcendence? One could wish that it were, to repeat again; for what would a *seriously-intended Parsifal* be?

It is the seriousness of Wagner's intentions that is most corrupting to the listener because it requires unquestioning faith:

> And yet I was one of the most corrupted Wagnerians.—I was capable of taking Wagner seriously.—Ah, this old magician, how much he imposed upon us! The first thing his art offers us is a magnifying glass: one looks through it, one does not trust one's own eyes—every thing looks big, *even Wagner*.—What a clever rattlesnake! It has filled our whole life with its rattling about "devotion," about "loyalty," about "purity"; and with its praise of chastity it withdrew from the corrupted world.—And we believed it in all these things. . . . Wagner thus represents the Christian concept, "you ought to and must *believe*."[6]

Everything in Wagner is too big, too exaggerated, too theatrical: Wagner, according to Nietzsche, points to the rise of the musician as actor who depends on the hallucinatory power of the stage. Wagner rejects beauty for the sublime, the deep, the overwhelming; he prefers effect, gesture. "Too much music!" Mallarmé exclaimed. And it is this "too much" that takes him beyond music. "As a matter of fact, he repeated a single proposition all his life long: that his music did not mean mere music. But more. But infinitely more.—'Not *mere* music'—no musician would say that."[7] Wagner's seriousness, which in its exaggeration points to a fundamental lack of seriousness, is nevertheless, as Thomas Mann suggested, a deadly serious game, for it is grounded in Wagner's ability to command and to submit:[8]

> Never has obedience been better, never has commanding. Wagnerian conductors in particular are worthy of an age that posterity will call one day, with awed respect, *the classical age of war*. Wagner understood how to command; in this, too, he was the great teacher. He commanded as the inexorable will to himself, as lifelong self-discipline: Wagner who furnishes perhaps the greatest example of self-violation in the history of art.[9]

In the following pages I argue that self-violation stands at the very center of the Wagnerian enterprise, that Wagner's great achievement was to have established the power of impotence and made it into the essence of art. This impotence is quite literally staged and lies behind the composer's seductive appeal. But while Wagner seduces, he also lies, and, paradoxically, we his listeners know this, for Wagner creates a form of reification that does not dupe. The peculiarity of Wagner's performative power, its "as if" quality, is not simply a veneer under which one may still discover some form of individuality or truth. The aestheticization of the political, politics as theater (and this is what is ultimately at stake here), is a thoroughly serious game. It involves, as Slavoj Žižek has claimed, "the 'non-integration of the subject into the register of the signifier,' the 'external imitation' of the signifying game akin to the so-called *as if* phenomenon characteristic of proto-psychotic states."[10] The paradox, indeed the essence of Wagner's work, lies here: the more *Ideologiekritik* we exert on his work, the more we seek to comprehend his work symptomatically, the more we participate in his universe. Wagner invites critique—invites, if you will, a critical beating—in order to generate the required seriousness. The greater the critical distance, the closer lies the seduction. Wagner cannot, therefore, be directly approached at the level of the critique of ideology. This fact constitutes his historical novelty and his power of appeal. Wagner is the first producer of the modern mass medium, the first producer of culture as spectacle, the first producer of totalitarian art.[11] The response he generates is a new form of blindness, a blindness predicated not on a misrepresentation, a false picture, but on the recognition of a picture as a lie, a picture to which obedience is nevertheless given.

Wagner's Invisible Theater and the Law of Music

Parsifal is undoubtedly one of the grandest nineteenth-century examples of the "religion of art," a testament to the fact that the truth-content of religion had shifted to the domain of art. Wagner himself wrote the libretto based on the early-thirteenth-century poem *Parzifal*, by Wolfram von Eschenbach. *Parsifal* describes the knights of the Holy Grail, whose purpose it is to guard and worship the cup or Grail that had caught Christ's blood on the cross, as well as the spear that had wounded him. The first act finds the community in an acute crisis, for its king, Amfortas, is suffering from a bleeding wound that will not heal. Amfortas had received this wound in battle against the evil Klingsor. Klingsor had taken the spear from Amfortas while the latter was being seduced by Kundry, a woman of many guises and in the service of Klingsor. Kundry has been wandering the earth for many years in search of redemption because she, when seeing Christ on the cross, had laughed. The knight Gurnemanz tells how the spear will be returned and Amfortas's wound closed when a young fool made wise by pity is found so that order may be restored to the Grail community.

Parsifal arrives in the first act, and Gurnemanz believes him to be the long-awaited redeemer. The youth is led to the castle but fails to comprehend the ritual of the Grail. Parsifal is banished. In the second act, Parsifal arrives in Klingsor's realm; unlike Amfortas, the youth withstands the seductions of Kundry and captures the spear from Klingsor. The realm of evil turns to dust, and Klingsor is vanquished. The third act takes place many years later: the community, now in despair of ever finding its redeemer, is in complete disarray. Amfortas refuses to perform the ritual of the Grail; his father, Titurel, deprived of the cup's sustenance, has died; and the knights of the order are at war with each other. Parsifal returns to the forests of Montsalvat and there encounters Gurnemanz and Kundry. He reveals himself as the redeemer; Gurnemanz makes him king; and Parsifal blesses Kundry, who can now die in peace. Parsifal enters the castle, heals the wound of Amfortas and performs the ritual. The knights of the order hail their new king as their redeemer while the dove of the Holy Spirit descends over the Grail.

Wagner was quite clear not only that his music drama was to represent the fall of religion and its redemption by a "fool made wise by pity," but that the drama itself was to play this redemptive function. There was, then, in Wagner's mind, no distinction possible between Parsifal, the hero of his opera, and *Parsifal*, the opera as it was to function in its wider social context. Art—and music in particular—was to displace a degenerate and debased religion by its "enrapturing effect [entrückende Wirkung]" on the audience,[12] thus reconnecting it to the older, more authentic Christian virtues of love, faith, and hope, a displacement that would also reconnect the audience with art and consequently with its essence. *Parsifal*'s and Parsifal's roles were to reestablish connections, to "religare," to tie and bind a new community, a new order, through the renewal of ritual. What was needed, Wagner asserted in his 1878 essay "Public and Popularity," was a genuine popularization of the deepest knowledge, an appeal to the Folk and thus an art that was "sublimely popular."[13] Like Parsifal himself, Wagner was aware that such an art would have to be subject to a different law, one that was founded in the disavowal of reality: "we are bound to presuppose a law quite other, concealed from the eyes historical, ordaining the mysterious sequence of a spiritual life whose acts are guided by denial of the world and all its history."[14]

Yet what is the nature of this new law if, as Wagner states, quoting Schiller, the characteristic mark of Christianity is the upheaval of law and therefore the presentation of a "beautiful morality," a humanizing of the Holy? The new law is founded in the "exorbitant" commandment to love, a love "that springs from pity, and carries its compassion to the utmost breaking of self-will."[15] It is Christ, as the embodiment of the refusal of will, who presents the "quintessence of all pitying love, stretched out upon the cross of pain and suffering. A—symbol?—beckoning to the highest pity, to worship of suffering, to imitation of his breaking of all self-seeking Will; nay, a picture, a very effigy!" It is the simplicity, even the rudeness, of such a picture of "the head with wounds all bleeding," not complicated theological dogmas or scientific truths, that fill us with ecstatic throes. The sublimity of Christianity lies in its simplicity, in its direct and unmediated address to the "poor in spirit." Jesus was divine not because he was wise but because he was a fool. He did not offer metaphysical explanations of suffering, since suffering was readily visible and open to feelings: "his own flesh and blood he gave as last and highest expiation for all the sin of outpoured blood and slaughtered flesh, and offered his disciples wine and blood for each day's meal:—'Taste such alone, in memory of me.' This the unique sacrament of the Christian faith; with its observance all the teaching of the Redeemer is fulfilled."[16]

Wagner's entire theological and aesthetic system for *Parsifal* comes together in the Eucharist. Ideally a ritual of participation that leads to real presence, the Eucharist engenders a form of participation that is communal, never representational. It is for this reason that music and music drama in particular must occupy such a privileged space: it is the Wagnerian *Bühnenweihfestspiel* that best captures the ritualistic aspect of participation, its music that may teach a redemption-starved humanity a second speech where "the Infinite can voice itself with clearest definition."[17] Whereas painting, for instance, signifies, music simply makes present; music "ist für sich selbst da." Wagner was fascinated by the indeterminacy of transubstantiation, for the ritual centered on the mystery of the act of transformation of Christ's blood and body into bread and wine as well as the transformation of bread and wine into the presence of Christ among the community of believers. Indeed, Wagner's Grail ritual stages the self-sacrifice of Christ's body both as a source of spiritual and physiological nourishment, as the very fount of pity and love, and as the site of murder and impurity, of cannibalism and devouring. While working on the libretto for *Parsifal* and thus engaged with the legend as told by Wolfram von Eschenbach, Wagner wrote to Mathilde Wesendonck,

All transport, worship, ecstasy, at the wondrous presence of the chalice which reddens into soft entrancing radiance, new life is poured through all [Amfortas's] veins—and death can not draw nigh him! he lives, relives, and more fiercely than ever the fatal wound ravens him, *his* wound! Devotion itself becomes a torture! . . . in the frenzy of despair might he turn entirely from the Grail, shut fast his eyes thereto? Fain would he, for a possibility of death, but—he has been appointed Guardian of the Grail himself. And no blind outer power appointed him,—no! but since he was so worthy, since none had wist the marvel of the Grail so deeply and so inwardly as he; as even now his whole soul ever turns again towards that sight which withers him in adoration, blends heavenly unction with eternal ban!—

And I am to execute a thing like that, to boot? make music for it too?[18]

What is immediately striking here is the proliferation of visual metaphors in the form of an alternation and mutual implication of blindness
and sight leading to uncertainty and indeterminacy. Although Wagner
somewhat coyly suggests at the end that such indeterminacy could never
be put to music, that is of course precisely what he will do some twenty
years later. And not only that, he will ultimately conceive music—invisible and indeterminate—as the very resolution of this dilemma. That is,
music will resolve the question of how to distinguish good blood from
bad blood: Wagner will inscribe this difference musically, and do so,
paradoxically, by (re)presenting this difference in the form of a new relationship between the visible and the invisible. Music or sound will become the vehicle or new vessel for the sacred; it will be made visible as
the Grail/wound, as the ear that receives and contains. At the same time,
music will be the blood that courses through vessel and body, that invis-
ibly penetrates the body.

Michel Poizat has argued that in opera in general, and Wagnerian
opera in particular, the voice gains the status of an object of desire.
Opera, in its quest for the voice, expresses a certain truth: that as humans we suffer from the fact that we are always already inserted into the
symbolic order of language and law and that we therefore gain pleasure
in seeking to forget this necessary subjection to language. Operatic pleasure is always marked by suffering—tears, shivers, sighs—and is closer
to an experience of *jouissance* than to one of pleasure. The *jouissance* that
opera generates is, though Poizat never calls it such, masochistic: opera
produces a "feeling of madness, of captivation, of rapture . . . , an ecstatic gratification in the lost object, the feeling of its recovery, but never
without the pain of remembering its loss, never without the desire for its
pain."[19] In its quest for the voice, then, opera strives to escape the laws
of symbolization; it inevitably seeks to transcend word and meaning and
thus, in its climactic moments, verges on the cry, a moment when the
human voice encounters the Real. According to Poizat, this cry performs a double function: it constitutes an encounter with silence or
death, and it acts as a call, as an invocation. Following Lacan, Poizat describes the quest for the voice as an expression of the invocatory drive
whose impulse it is to identify with or introject the voice-object. There
are several consequences of this identification with the voice: the voice is
eroticized insofar as it is the object of a drive; it is constitutive of subjectivity in that it also performs interpellative functions; and it creates this
subjectivity in terms of self-loss because the object sought, the voice, is

always traversed by death.[20] Wagner's *Parsifal* is, as I will come to argue, an attempt at staging this fundamental operatic desire, this quest for the voice. *Parsifal* is in that sense an allegory of opera's desire; it is opera's embodiment.

The body matters to Wagner. First, it is a body pierced and fragmented by its insertion into a symbolic order that is not merely dysfunctional but indeed functional due precisely to the system's malfunctioning. Exemplary here is Amfortas's suffering, which does not simply disrupt the Grail ceremony but becomes a constitutive part of the ritual itself. Thus, Amfortas's wound is not only a sign of failure or loss but productive of a certain pleasure: "the very symbolic machine which 'mortifies' the living body produces by the same token its opposite, the immortal desire, the Real of 'pure life' which eludes symbolization."[21] Second, the Wagnerian body is a singing, breathing body, a body that produces and receives sound. Wagner brings, according to Friedrich Kittler, the love act in its physiology onto the stage; he generates a "respiratory eroticism" against which the subject is helpless: as subject one must either sing or die, while as audience it is impossible not to hear.[22] Amfortas's wound is both the narcissistically wounded or castrated body and the singing body as always open ear; it joins these two aspects into a subject-position of sexualized passivity.

The one to die on the Wagnerian stage is the classical bourgeois subject, and it is unconscious or regressive elements that become the primary focus of representation. According to Kittler, a conscious subject is able to choose whether to receive input from the outside world as long as that input is verbal or visual. Sound, on the other hand, "pierces the armor called Ego, for among all of the sensory organs, the ears are the hardest to close. . . . The all pervasive power of sound sustains Wagner's imperialism."[23] Unlike the eye, the ear is inherently passive; it can be neither opened nor shut. Wagner deeply distrusts privacy and consciousness and insists on the power of unconscious forces that turn his music dramas into "a permanent invitation to intoxication, as a form of 'oceanic regression.' . . . The basic idea of the music drama is revealed . . . by a sort of mental flight," by the privileging of both acoustic and visual hallucination. It is hallucination created and sustained by music that is to heal the wound in and of the symbolic order; it is music that is to suspend language and signification and return the human being to expressiveness. Wagner's music drama creates what Theodor Adorno calls an intoxicating brew, formulated always in terms of sexual metaphors. And yet the gendering of these metaphors remains highly ambivalent: Wagner's famous claim that words are the male seed of art, while music is the gloriously loving woman, the bearer of art, is continuously subverted by the simultaneous power of music to penetrate, to rape the listener. Music heals the fractured ego and yet is the very source of its fracturing, its undoing. Wagner's musical desire generates a structure, a process whereby the always destitute subject can come to identify with an "oppressive and mutilating power," not only in order to accept it but in order to welcome its disruptive, sublime pleasures.[24]

Wagner conceives subjectivity as a process of specular narcissism and oral or cannibalistic identification.[25] The final result of such a conception is a continuous oscillation between these specular structures and the final elimination of all difference in death. The specular, or what many critics have called the architectonic, structure of *Parsifal* appears in its "three main situations," that is, its three acts, with the third act a repetition of the first (the first scene in both acts takes place in the woods of Montsalvat; the second in the castle itself, where each time a ritual of the Grail is performed; both acts combine these scenes through the transformation music), and the second act functioning as the contrast and turning point, the line of division (the hymen) between these repetitions. This outer form of the opera is reflected in its inner form, that is, in the construction and actions of its characters. And just as the outer form is architectonic or static, the inner form is equally immobile or immobilized insofar as the characters never actually do anything. The defining characteristic of *Parsifal* is in fact this almost complete lack of any positive action. Parsifal himself, as Carl Dahlhaus has claimed, is a passive hero.[26] One of Wagner's longest operas, *Parsifal* has the shortest libretto. The main characters either renounce action or perform actions that tend to be empty, purely symbolic gestures.

The result is the tight specular structure of the opera, a structure whose elements may constantly double themselves and cross over onto the opposite side of the mirror.[27] It is this specular structure that prevents the crisis that haunts the order of the Grail from being reduced either to an external threat (in Gutman's reading of the crisis, the community of the Grail is heading toward erasure due to the external threat of racial degeneration) or to an internal threat (in Žižek's explanation, the community is being assailed from inside because Amfortas can no longer perform his bureaucratic duty because of his inadequate placement in the symbolic order).[28] Whereas an analysis of the crisis as external threat reads this crisis as a sacrificial one—that is, as the need to expel impurity—an analysis of the crisis in terms of an internal threat reduces the problem to one of bureaucratization. While the first analysis sees the problem as a racial one, the second sees it as a crisis pertaining to the Law, that is, as a crisis of sexual differentiation. In fact, the two problems cannot be held apart in the opera: Wagner articulates here the problem of race and sex precisely *as* the question to be posed (or not posed, since the opera is in fact dominated by the absence of the question), and he does this by posing the problem in terms of a subjectivity that is bound either to overidentify with the outside in the form of self-loss or to violently incorporate that outside within its own body.[29] Within the specular structure of the opera, inside and outside cannot be held apart: this undecidability is both the Grail's crisis and its resolution, and the two must be held in a position of perpetual suspense and indeterminacy. Impurity becomes a new form of purity—racial miscegenation is constructed as sexual differentiation, and sexual confusion as racial purity.

The specularity of *Parsifal* invites a very specific act of seeing; it makes visible a crisis and yet also posits that same act as redemptive. Amfortas's gaze at the Grail increases his suffering, whereas the knights depend on the gaze at the vessel for their livelihood. The audience's gaze is continuously directed at Amfortas's wound, the sign of his suffering, which is nevertheless the site where understanding originates (it is Amfortas's wound that gives knowledge through pity to Parsifal). What is rendered visible through this gaze at the gaping, open wound? Does, in fact, this act of rendering visible not provide an effective closure in the Wagnerian universe—quite concretely, of course, in the closure of Amfortas's wound at the end of the opera, even if this is a closure that is displaced onto the possibility of now openly revealing the Grail?

The politics of visibility are extremely complex in *Parsifal* and are intimately bound up with the opera's blind spots. Indeed, *Parsifal* is structured as an open secret. Robert Gutman, in quoting Max Friedlander's analysis of the *Ring*, comes close to the recognition of this structure when he claims that Wagner delighted in setting up stage situations that were at variance with the text, in juxtaposing the seeming and the real. "At these moments the average spectator, satisfied with what appears to be a conventional operatic situation, settles back to drink in the beautiful sea of sound . . . *Parsifal* is . . . a drama characterized not only by the composer's natively obscure and elliptical literary style, but also by the indigenous circumlocutions of allegory, the calculated unrealities of symbolism, and, especially, the sultry corruption of decadence."[30] The result, according to Gutman, of such circumlocutions is that the presentation of religious rituals on stage are really perversions of the Eucharist; they are in reality Black Masses dedicated to sinister gods.

Gutman points here to a fundamental quality of *Parsifal*, to wit, its ability to generate a complete misreading of what is actually taking place on stage. Not only are Black Masses of blood-drinking and cannibalism perceived as Christian rituals, but sexual promiscuity is staged as renunciation, incest as pure and purifying love. Cosima Wagner reports in her diary that her husband told her in reference to the first discussions around the staging of *Parsifal*, "Oh, I have a horror of all costume and make-up creatures! And when I think that figures like Kundry are to be bundled up, I immediately think of those awful artist parties; and after I have created the invisible orchestra, I would also like to invent the invisible theater." He adds that Kundry should really appear onstage prostrate and naked like a Titian Venus. In other words, the more visibly, the more nakedly Kundry is represented, the less visible she will in fact become.

Wagner's understanding of visibility or representation should be understood as a form of "acting-out" in the Freudian sense of the term. Wagner's visibility as acting-out is always performative, gestural, and ritualistic. Most action in *Parsifal* is given to the audience through Gurnemanz's and Kundry's narration of past events, but these narratives tend to be accompanied by visual props or tableaux (the entrance of Amfortas in Act I on his way to the bath serves no other dramatic function except that of backing up Gurnemanz's narrative) or tend to become the occasion for ritual (Amfortas's suffering does not simply disrupt the Grail ritual but becomes itself part of that same ritual). Despite Wagner's desire for an invisible theater, he nevertheless conceived of music drama as finding its fulfillment in stage action, in its "realization." The aim of Wagner's theater is to reveal, to make visible the invisible and, at the same time, to make invisible what is visible. He puts pleasure on display, says Adorno, but only to anathematize it; the dreamlike quality of what the audience sees is always already a waking-up—"inside the illusion dwells disillusionment."[31] *Parsifal* seeks to create an invisible theater in which, however, the unconscious is made visible as presentation, as a form of acting-out. Philippe Lacoue-Labarthe, in his discussion of the relationship between Mallarmé's and Wagner's conception of the theater, calls this the desire for a sublimation of mimesis. What both Wagner and Mallarmé aim for is not a traditional theater of catharsis and mimesis but a "mediation of the group, a 'solemnity,' a frisson and something like a voiceless terror. Unease more than emotion. And the sacred . . . resides in this secret."[32] Wagner seeks nothing less than the presentation, the rendering of the sublime in the form of an open secret. What he renders is the Lacanian Real, for him visually embodied most dramatically in Amfortas's wound.[33] I would argue that he does this in two ways: first, by redirecting the gaze so as to force a certain misrecognition or disavowal; second, by backing up this misrecognition by a new law, expressed in his opera through the music. Kittler is thus not correct in asserting that with Wagner, acoustic hallucination supplants visual hallucination:[34] Wagner generates a sea of sound, what Žižek calls an "aquarium of the real" that surrounds isolated islands or fragments of the symbolic. Wagner's musical wound does not represent; it insists. It renders the Real not only as frozen or suspended immobility but also as "life substance in its mucous palpitation."[35]

This is the very essence of Wagner's masochistic aesthetic, of his masochistic fantasy, for he generates a suspended vision, a disavowal in relation to what is "actually" seen on stage, and he backs up that suspense through a musical law that is itself not unequivocally subject to the pleasure principle. His music is the voice of conscience, that which resides outside the subject and comes from beyond. In that sense it fulfills an interpellative function, constituting a "call to order," a call to the subject to take his place in the symbolic universe, a demand to which the subject must respond if he wants to survive. At the same time the music, the voice, is also the object of desire, a "left-over," a Thing that cannot be integrated into the symbolic order (into visual display, or representation) but that nevertheless resides inside the subject, inside the body (both of the singer and of the listener) *as* desire.[36] Wagner's music is Lacan's *objet petit a*. It is a meaningless object, a hypnotic voice, a leftover of the signifying system that yet "quilts" the symbolic order and holds it together. In this sense, Wagner's new musical law resembles the Freudian superego, in that its paradoxical structure creates a subject who becomes more guilty, the more he or she obeys the law. The more the subject renounces enjoyment, the more enjoyment is accumulated in the superego. The superego thus embodies a law that is exempt from its own authority, and it is here that the essence of Wagner's vocational crisis lies. In Act I of *Parsifal*, Amfortas's father, Titurel, is the purest embodiment of this voice, this call of the superego to perform the law ("Mein Sohn Amfortas, bist du am Amt?"). As a living dead who persecutes the living from an open grave that refuses to shut, he demands the performance of duty by the living so that he may have his pleasure in the form of the Redeemer's blood of pure enjoyment.[37] And insofar as this law is penetrated by enjoyment, it is the very essence of a masochistically conceived law. Wagner's musical telos is paradoxically the production of a kind of speechlessness—indeed this is its promise—for what Wagner promises is self-annihilation as a new form of subjectivity.

Žižek is correct in stating that the obscenity of Titurel transforms the Christian thematics of the opera not only into pagan ritual but also into a law that has lost its formal neutrality. This lack of neutrality has a very specific concreteness for Wagner, for his musical law is always nationally or racially inscribed; it is by necessity German. "Germanness can only be realized," he insists, "if we hear the German voice as Must again."[38] As long as there are only words, there can be no belief; words must be backed up by music. Germany will be condemned to cultural chaos and impotence as long as she does not take note of "a clue that leads to higher outlooks. Perchance that clue would not be visible, but only audible—a sigh of deepest pity, haply, such as once we heard from the Cross on Golgotha, and now goes up from our own soul."[39]

The Wagnerian gaze is anamorphic, that is, it is a gaze of desire that creates the consistency of its object of contemplation only via a detour. Of crucial import here is that the absence of a sexual relationship is founded not in the logic of prohibition but, paradoxically, in the demand for it. Or, alternatively, a sexual relationship is constructed *from within* the logic of prohibition and of the obstacle: "*external hindrances that thwart our access to the object are there precisely to create the illusion that without them, the object would be directly accessible*—what such hindrances thereby conceal is the inherent impossibility of attaining the object."[40] Lacan conceives of the anamorphic gaze as one that can only look from the side, that can only produce the object in its distorted form: a direct look would show the object as a void, or as monstrous: "The detour in the psyche isn't always designed to regulate the commerce between whatever is organized in the domain of the pleasure principle and whatever presents itself as the structure of reality. There are also detours and obstacles which are organized so as to make the domain of the vacuole stand out as such."[41] Anamorphosis makes the object sublime, creating its sacred nature:

The Object, therefore, is literally something that is created—whose place is encircled—through a network of detours, approximations and near-misses. It is here that *sublimation* sets in—sublimation in the Lacanian sense of the elevation of an object into the dignity of the Thing:

"sublimation" occurs when an object, part of everyday reality, finds itself at the place of the impossible Thing. . . . This is how the impossible changes into the prohibited: by way of the short circuit between the Thing and some positive object rendered inaccessible through artificial obstacles.[42]

Conceived thus, the movement of sublimation may be essential to understanding the secular displacement of religion to aesthetic forms of the sublime, for displacement must be conceptualized here not as a movement of putting some essential energy into new forms but instead as the very creation (retroactively) of that energy. Sublimation constructs belatedly (*nachträglich*) its renounced and therefore sublime object of desire. And yet such a gaze is fundamentally unstable, for while it may create the effect of sublimity and sacredness, it can nevertheless turn, at any point, into its opposite, its monstrous double. Its power of attraction—but also its abjectness—lies in this doubling capacity where the sublime joins horror in the form of a fascinated and enraptured gaze. Žižek quite correctly points out that whether it is beauty or disgust that is perceived will depend on the cultural space from within which the gaze originates.

Wagner was most certainly the creator of one such cultural space: not only did he create a cultural space that was specifically German, but he also articulated, as Sam Weber has indicated, another scene (the Freudian *anderer Schauplatz*), a new relationship between *Bühnenraum* (stage space) and *Zuschauerraum* (audience space). According to Weber, Wagner creates a theater of dislocation where the "scene cannot be entirely determined by what it appears to represent since the latter supposes an imaginative effort of the audience as an integral part of its articulation. The audience thus ceases to function as a pure spectator. . . . by reacting to what is *not* shown, it may in a certain sense be said to complete the scene."[43] Weber insists that such completion of the space's borders does not lead to closure but instead to further displacements and dislocations. The picture gets more complicated, however, insofar as what is peculiar to *Parsifal* is less an imaginative addition by the spectator to what is not made visible than a movement of subtraction. Here the audience precisely does not see what is made visible; it disavows through anamorphosis what is made visible; it renounces visibility, indeed participation, in the name of participation and narcissistic identification, though this is an identification that is empowering only insofar as it is always already impotent. As by Isolde in the *Liebestod* the audience is asked: "Seht ihr's nicht?" and like Klingsor, the audience in response takes hold of the spear, of the phallic order and in that move castrates itself.

Masochistic Seduction

> I permit myself to put only one question to my beloved friend in respect to *Parsifal*—why is our hero first converted through Kundry's kiss, why does his divine mission become clear to him through it? Only from this moment on can he transplant himself into Amfortas' soul, can he understand his nameless misery, and feel with him!
> —Letter of Ludwig II to Richard Wagner

> Darling, that is a terrible secret!
> —Letter of Richard Wagner to Ludwig II

Act II is the site of Parsifal's constitution as masochistic subject through an act of renunciation or sacrifice, a subjectivity closely modeled on Ludwig II, the enchanting and seductive *"Weibjünglein"* with political power.[44] The question raised, however—and Ludwig himself understood this very well—is what Parsifal renounces or sacrifices, and this is indeed the terrible open secret of the opera. Unquestionably, the formal and dramatic center of the opera is located in Kundry's kiss in Act II, Scene II. Standard interpretation, even the most sophisticated readings of the scene, hold that Parsifal is drawn into the magical gardens of Klingsor's castle, encounters Kundry, is nearly seduced by her kiss, learns pity through this near miss, identifies with Amfortas's suffering, and may therefore regain the spear. Lucy Beckett, for example, links Kundry to a compelling and compulsive sexuality and, by extension, to knowledge. Kundry's name is of course etymologically derived from *Kunde* (knowledge, message, tidings) and in that sense Kundry as the bearer of news plays an angelic function, though her name is just as powerfully connected homophonically to *Wunde* (wound). The libretto plays on this chain of audial associations. "Ihn dir zu künden, harrt ich deiner hier: was zog dich her, wenn nicht der Kunde Wunsch? [I waited for you here to tell you this: what drew you here, if not the wish to know?]" (Act II, Scene II). When Kundry tells of Parsifal's mother, Herzeleide, and of her fear that Parsifal may come one day to know, she sings, "Nur Sorgen war sie, ach! und Bangen: nie sollte Kunde zu dir hergelangen [She was all concern and foreboding lest you should ever acquire knowledge]." Kundry proposes sexual love as the means for Parsifal's atonement of guilt for his mother's death. But as she kisses him, first to the music of Klingsor, then to that of Amfortas, Parsifal's *Kunde* is transformed into *Wunde*, the wound of Amfortas, an identification that climaxes into "O! Qual der Liebe! [Oh, torture of love]." In the prolonged scene that follows, Parsifal understands that Kundry herself will be redeemed not through desire but despite it, not by Parsifal acceding to her desire but by his victory over her. He leaves her with that promise.

Quite extraordinarily, Beckett refuses the rather virulent misogyny not only of the scene itself but of the opera as a whole. She admits that there is a certain amount of woman-hating to the extent that Kundry is marked as good when old and ugly (in Acts I and III) but as evil when young and beautiful (Act II). "What really counts," according to Beckett, is Kundry's individuality: "Nothing but [Wagner's] own dramatic genius is responsible for her individuality, her fatal *Schadenfreude*, and her pathos as a soul seeking deliverance."[45] She brushes aside even Wagner's worries, for instance, that the seduction scene in *Parsifal* may be a repetition of the Venusberg scene in *Tannhäuser*. She simply proclaims as irrelevant Wagner's comment in reference to a never-completed opera (*Jesus of Nazareth*) that the ideal of chastity is "the most complete and irremediable egoism," which "lies at the bottom of the monk's renunciation." Kundry's kiss is far more complicated, and the tautological reduction of sexual foreplay to "a kiss is just a kiss" shuts down the virtually abysmal meanings of the seduction scene. In fact the failure of seduction must be read here also in terms of the failures and successes that seduction might possibly generate.

The seduction scene proper begins with a classic moment of interpellation: Kundry calls Parsifal by name (this is the first time the audience hears the name). At this stage, both Kundry and Parsifal are in fact "namenlos." Kundry is so because she has many names. In Scene I of Act II, Klingsor calls her several names, beginning, for her too, with "Namenlose": "Herauf! Herauf! Zu mir! Dein Meister ruft dich, Namenlose, Urteuflin! Höllenrose! Herodias warst du, und was noch? Gundryggia dort, und Kundry hier! [Come up! Come up! To me! Your master calls you, nameless one, primeval witch, rose of hell! You were Herodias, and what else? Gundryggia there, and Kundry here!]." Parsifal is "namenlos" because he lacks a name or at least knowledge of one: "Riefest du mich Namenlosen?"

At the beginning of the seduction scene, then, while both characters are initially nameless, it is only Parsifal who will earn his subjective consistency, whereas Kundry will remain unanchored, a floating signifier.

Kundry is the very embodiment of the operatic voice whose privileged site is in the upper registers (the soprano); she is a pure vocal object reduced to its enunciatory function.[46] In her capacity as enunciator she does however have knowledge. Indeed, what Kundry can tell Parsifal is his past, his provenance. This happens immediately after her call to him and her translation of his name. It turns out, in fact, in Kundry's narrative of Parsifal's genealogy, that it was his dying father who had named his as yet unborn son. Named by his father, it is however Parsifal's mother, Herzeleide, who makes him into his name—that is, into a fool who is to remain ignorant of the male world of strife and fury. Under Herzeleide's maternal law of kisses and embraces, whose desire Kundry calls "*wütend* [furious]," Parsifal learns how not to know, how to forget. Wagner thus posits two kinds of law here: the law of men who name and make war; and a maternal, furious law, a law of the operatic voice that like the voice is constituted as lack, as loss. Kundry's (and Herzeleide's) law, this Law of the Lady, of the cruel woman, is fundamentally arbitrary and capricious and has the sole purpose of making the man cry out.[47] Kundry is the diva par excellence: in her many disguises, her capricious appearances, and her namelessness, she is divine and demonic at once. In the words of Michel Poizat: "what is new in the appellation 'diva' is that now it is the female singer and she alone who is accorded divine status, as though it were her power to transform herself into pure voice, inasmuch as she is *one* incarnation of *many* successive roles, that allowed her to be characterized as divine." But as Poizat points out, the diva is always slated for a sacrificial death. To be a diva means to be undone.[48]

Indeed, Herzeleide's maternal lessons are dangerous to her own identity, for when Parsifal obediently forgets his mother and wanders off, she dies of a broken heart. It is here that Kundry first asks Parsifal whether he did not hear her cry or lament (*Klage*) before she finally fell silent. Parsifal agonizes over his role in Herzeleide's death (musically a variant of the Love-Feast theme appears here) and wonders what else he might possibly have forgotten. Kundry's answer is that it will be knowledge (*Kunde*) that will provide the answer to that question, and she offers herself to him by taking on his mother's role, by becoming his mother so that he may repeat both that which he had forgotten and that which made him forget. Kundry thus offers Parsifal knowledge: "Bekenntnis wird Schuld in Reue enden, Erkenntnis in Sinn die Torheit wenden [Confession will end guilt in remorse, understanding changes folly into sense.]." She offers this knowledge as the acting-out of incest: "Die Leib und Leben einst dir gegeben, der Tod und Torheit weichen muß, sie beut dir heut, als Muttersegens letzten Gruß, der Liebe—ersten Kuß [She who once gave you life and being, to subdue death and folly sends you this day, as a last token of a mother's blessing, the first kiss of love.]." The imperative to learn love is followed by the famous kiss, which, Wagner specifies, is initiated by Kundry, the enactor of a furious maternal law of desire.

What happens at this moment of oral communication? Standard interpretations of Parsifal's reaction to Kundry's kiss claim it is here that Parsifal begins to identify with Amfortas, to feel the latter's wound in and on his own body, to comprehend the nature of sin as deriving from sexual pleasure, at which point he is able to reject women for a chaste and holy existence, an existence that will resolve the crisis of the Grail order and redeem the fount of holiness. I have found only one alternative reading to this scenario: Barry Emslie describes *Parsifal* as an "unconsciously dishonest work whose real—though hidden—agenda is a rationale for masculine sexual and social freedom without loss of the dominant male's high moral and social status."[49] Thus, while posing as holiness and purity, the work in fact enacts pornography and blasphemy, a fact disguised by Wagner's musical *Rausch*.

I agree both with Emslie's general assertion that in the opera the taboos against incest and cannibalism are violated in the name of religious devotion and with his more specific claim that what happens in the seduction scene is more than simple sexual renunciation. He quite correctly asks how the "boy-redeemer" Parsifal will attain knowledge without suffering the same fate as Amfortas, whether it is possible to enjoy the fruit of knowledge without expulsion, and whether Parsifal does not in fact find a way to have incest without guilt and shame. And yet to the explicit question posed by Wagner regarding the interrelationship between male identity, mother love, and sexual desire, Emslie's answer is the double standard. After the anything but chaste kiss (which Emslie describes as one of the Wagnerian stagings that comes closest to penetration), Parsifal tears away from his prostrate position and sings of that other great moment of penetration, Amfortas's laceration by the spear— that is, of a combination of sexual penetration/gratification and religious stigmata. Emslie comments, "Yet Parsifal has not sinned: his virginity is not violated. Unlike Amfortas he has, as it were, pulled up short. Yet we are entitled to wonder whether this is not an artistic swindle. . . . It is as if Parsifal 'enjoys' a complete sexual experience without that experience completely taking place." In other words, Emslie understands the kiss as reflecting not only a (disavowed) process of secularization but a secularization that, due to its basis in sexual inequality, is always itself a swindle. Through Kundry's kiss, the Oedipal drive is made sublime: "Kundry can . . . carry the Oedipal wish into the terrain of the most sacred Christian notions, so that the sexual possessing of the mother by the son can symbolically be linked to the one of Man and the Mother of God. If this can be accomplished, has not the male artist in bourgeois, nominally Christian society totally appropriated the chief instruments of cultural control and denial?"[50]

The novelty of Emslie's reading lies in the fact that he sees Parsifal as a sexual being, one furthermore who does not "cede on his desire," as Lacan would describe it. The question nevertheless remains how Parsifal, or Wagner, pulls this off—how, in other words, can the act of renunciation nevertheless remain a way to create and hold onto one's sexual identity? We find ourselves here at the very crux of masochistic subjectivity. The masochistic subject-position is determined by the expulsion of the father's symbolic universe, submission to the cruel maternal order, and the disavowal and suspense of genital sexual desire in favor of a sexualization of guilt and punishment. I have also argued that within this universe, the woman must be sacrificed, even though she may be formally dominant. The result of such a scenario is the positing of a phallic mother whose power is simultaneously denied, thereby making possible a self-engendering or self-creation as an aesthetic or sublime/sublimated act.

In the seduction scene, Parsifal is not redeemed by a woman but through a woman. This redemption demands her death or self-sacrifice. How, specifically, does Parsifal react to Kundry's kiss? His first words, and this will be confirmed intermittently by the music, signal his recognition of and identification with Amfortas's pain: "Amfortas!—Die Wunde!—Die Wunde!—Sie brennt mir hier zur Seite! [Amfortas!—The wound!—the wound!—it burns here on my side!]." He immediately follows this with: "O, Klage! Klage! Furchtbare Klage! Aus tiefstem Herzen schreit sie mir auf." The German word *Klage* bears a variety of translations; it means grief, anguish, or sorrow, but this is always an *oral* pain, in the sense of lament, complaint, or grievance, and therefore has also the legal meaning of bringing a grievance to adjudication. It is oral pain brought to trial before a judge and thus by its very nature must be heard by someone. Parsifal describes this *Klage* as calling out from the depths of his heart. He returns to Amfortas's wound again in order to feel it on himself, but this time *in order to reject this identification*: "Nein! Nein! Nicht die Wunde ist es. Fließe ihr Blut in Strömen dahin! [No, no! It is not the wound. May its blood flow in streams!]." It is this point that constitutes Parsifal's distinctive subject-position; it is here rather than in his act of renunciation that he differs from Amfortas. It is not the bleeding wound that is at issue but the voice that bears witness to this wound. More specifically, I hold, it is the operatic voice that is at stake insofar as it is the object of an eroticized invocatory drive that Parsifal seeks to introject. Parsifal continues thus:

Hier! Hier, im Herzen der Brand! Das Sehnen, das furchtbare Sehnen, das alle Sinne mir faßt und zwingt! O!—Qual der Liebe!—Wie alles schauert, bebt und zuckt in sündigem Verlangen! Es starrt der Blick dumpf auf das Heilgefäß—das heil'ge Blut erglüht:—Erlösungswonne, göttlich mild, durchzittert weithin alle Seelen: nur hier, im Herzen, will die Qual nicht weichen. Des Heilands Klage da vernehm ich, die Klage, ach! die Klage um das entweihte Heiligtum:—"Erlöse, rette mich aus schuldbefleckten Händen!" So rief die Gottesklage furchtbar laut mir in die Seele.

[Here! Here in my heart is the flame! The longing, the terrible longing that grips and compels my senses! O torment of love! How everything trembles, quakes and quivers in sinful desire! The dull gaze is fixed on the sacred vessel; the holy blood glows:—the bliss of redemption, divinely mild, continues to make all souls tremble: only here, in my heart, will the pangs not be stilled. The Savior's lament I hear there, the lament, ah! the lament from his profaned sanctuary: "Redeem me, rescue me from hands defiled by sin!" Thus rang the divine lament loudly in my soul.]

Sexual desire is here united with and sublimated as the voice that commands a hearing; sublimated desire becomes the voice within him that not only demands redemption but also gives it. Whereas Amfortas can only dully fix his gaze at the holy vessel, Parsifal can hear its cry. While Amfortas stares directly and thus monstrously at the Grail and at Woman, and thus loses his masculinity as the voice of law and the law of voice, Parsifal and the audience learn how to look at the object of desire anamorphically, from the side. This look of disavowal, this enactment of an invisible seeing, sustains and is sustained by his capturing Kundry's voice: what is visible becomes invisible and thus audible. The voice becomes immanent and present, the cry of the past can be completely absorbed into Parsifal's knowledge of the Now, allowing him not to run away, not to renounce his love as torture.[51] In a truly Lacanian gesture, Parsifal can have a sexual relationship precisely because it is structured as prohibition, as unattainable object. Parsifal's sublimatory strategy in the form of music puts guilt and sin on exhibit, and in that move he guarantees for himself a masochistically structured sexual pleasure.

Parsifal takes music from Kundry through the kiss. After the second act, Kundry sings one more word, twice repeated: "Dienen, dienen [to serve, to serve]." What had been his mother's *Klage*, which had been silenced through her death, has now been transmitted to Parsifal orally through Kundry's kiss. There is always a certain kind of sexual indeterminacy or hermaphroditism about a kiss (mouth/tongue),[52] as well as a certain invisibility, an anamorphic quality that Parsifal is able to capture for himself and that is reflected in the music of Parsifal's lament. The opera as a whole is built on the opposition between chromaticism and diatonicism, whereby, for instance, the music evoking Klingsor or Amfortas's pain is chromatic, Parsifal's innocence and the sublimity of the Grail are diatonic. Parsifal's lament is first chromatic (beginning with "Amfortas!"), then again chromatic in the second part ("Nein! Nein!"), and at the end diatonic when it quotes the Grail theme ("Es starrt der Blick"). Yet this opposition is always a mediated one, conveying not simply an "art of transition" but, perhaps more strongly, a sense of indeterminacy.[53] In his film version of *Parsifal*, Syberberg underscores this ambiguity by exchanging the previously male actor for a woman while retaining the male voice. Parsifal becomes a man/woman: he takes the maternal voice or music; the death of his father is replayed in Titurel's and Klingsor's death; Amfortas is identified with and yet displaced. Like Amfortas, Parsifal has heard the maternal voice ("Ja! diese Stimme! So rief sie ihm [Yes! that voice! thus she called to him])," but his kiss has a different flow from Amfortas's otherwise identical experience: "Mit aller Schmerzen Qual im Bunde, das Heil der Seele entküßte ihm der Mund! [In league with the pangs of every torment, her lips kissed away his soul's salvation!]." While Amfortas lost it all in being kissed, Parsifal gets it all by kissing. He quite literally sucks the Wagnerian world-breath out of her ("Ha!—Dieser Kuss!"), leaving her to faithfully assist him in his ascent to hermaphroditic kingship, and then to die.

Parsifal in his victoriously failed seduction becomes feminized—and thus self-begotten—in order to have access to a form of enjoyment that is not overtly phallically organized. Parsifal is penetrated while retaining the phallus. Indeed, it is because he lets himself be seduced, because he consents to this penetration, that he can have the phallus. The phallic signifier functions here as the signifier of castration, setting to work a fundamental economic paradox: how, as Žižek asks, "can the subject be made to renounce enjoyment not for another, higher Cause but simply in order to gain access to it?"[54] And how does the subject attain his identity only if he loses it? The solution posited by Lacan is that the phallus must function in this situation as signifier both of enjoyment and of castration and loss. Such a construction is at once demystifying and fantasmatic: it is demystifying insofar as it subverts "the ideology of 'femininity as masquerade' according to which man is 'man as such,' the embodiment of the human genus, whereas woman is a man from whom something is missing (who is 'castrated') and who resorts to masquerade in order to conceal this lack: it is on the contrary the phallus, the phallic predicate, whose status is that of a semblance, so that when we throw off the mask, a woman appears."[55]

This realm beyond the phallus no doubt constitutes one of the forces behind Wagner's politics of visibility, his desire to lay bare, to strip off the mask in order to find underneath the possibility of pure enjoyment. And yet this demystification remains always fantasmatic insofar as it creates Parsifal's subjectivity, both as self-possession (as imaginary identification) and as a form of self-objectivization, as an instrument of enjoyment for the law (as symbolic identification).[56] Between these two forms of subjectivization lies a gap or wound, an open mouth that is opera's object of desire and which bespeaks the moment of indecision that generates and upholds Wagnerian fantasy. This fantasy is both that which allows for the creation of mother-substitutes and that which simultaneously permits a certain distanciation from the maternal order. Kristeva speaks of just such a fantasmatic structure as an in-between or reflexive voice, a voice that "cuts short the temptation to return, with abjection and jouissance, to that passivity status within the symbolic function, where the subject, fluctuation between inside and outside, pleasure and pain, word and deed, would find death along with nirvana."[57] Fantasy not only makes Parsifal's interpellation into the symbolic order possible, it enables his response to the call to do his duty and yet points to the moment when that interpellation fails, when the subject is torn apart by the voice of maternal desire.[58]

For Wagner, claims Gutman, the first kiss always gives way to panic because it marks the end of individuality. Whereas Parsifal is able to capture the law of music through this kiss and thus to usurp the power of woman's seductiveness, in itself this is clearly not enough. Wagner does offer the promise of a renewed masculinity if one only consents to giving in to his music, but this consent has its dangers if it is not also in command of the word.[59] The proof of this lies in the fate of Klingsor, who had sought redemption through self-castration; he is evidence of the fact, as Emslie points out, that purity and power do not derive from chastity. The spear in Klingsor's possession is clearly out of place; it belongs to Parsifal, who is not only a holy but also a sexual being. Yet why is the spear so out of place with Klingsor? What is the specific nature of Klingsor's misunderstanding?

In his essay "The Modern," Wagner criticizes modernity for what he perceives as its essentially Jewish origins. Or rather, it is precisely the fact that the modern always lacks origins and originality that makes it Jewish. Wagner sees the origin of non-originality as arising in the written word; there is nothing original, he states, in the "power of the quill." The quill, that instrument of etching and piercing, generates nothing but superficial decorativeness and hence a distortion of authentic German culture. Such decorativeness not only leads to a kind of mechanical parroting (Jewish *mauscheln*) but is always a form of false *naming*: "With foreign plumes one may *decorate* oneself, as much as with the exquisite names under which our new Jewish fellow-citizens now present themselves no less to our astonishment than our delight, whilst we poor old burgher and peasant families have to content us with a paltry 'Smith' or 'Miller,' 'Weaver,' 'Wainright [Wagner]' etc., for all futurity. Foreign names must have grown from our own skin if we do not merely want to deck ourselves, but to write from our heart from them, and so to write as thereby to gain the victory over a whole world."[60] The ruin of Germany lies in its willingness to take on foreign names or let others usurp good German names for themselves. Yet, as with the act of naming Parsifal (itself always in a state of translation), the separation between German and all other languages is unstable. In seeking the authentic German voice as compelling inner command, Wagner cites Luther's translation of Paul's epistle to the Corinthians (14:11): "If I know not the meaning [Deutung] of the voice, I shall be *undeutsch* [barbaros] to him that speaketh, and he that speaketh will be *undeutsch* to me." Wagner sees a fundamental connection between *Deutung* (meaning) and *Deutsch*, a connection that had become severed but that could be reestablished once Germany was able to hear the voice as imperative again: "what *must be* will shew itself when everybody must-s for once; though, to be sure, it then will appear as an outward obligation, whereas the inner Must can only dawn on a very great mind and sympathetically productive heart, such as our world brings forth no longer."[61] The power of the German

Must, a power felt in Parsifal's heart as the sound of music, must elicit active consent from the public, a consent based not on a popularity contest (Wagner sees universal suffrage as never the result of the Parsifalian inner Must but as the result of a fake, foreign freedom that generates only passivity, never active consent) but on a notion of the public good that simply stands on its own ground. Like music, the public good is "für sich selbst da." Good art has no intention, whereas bad art is only there to please. The first art creates a public of the (Wagnerian) theater; the second, a public that reads.

Klingsor represents this second public, a public that has come under the spell of the quill. To have possession of the spear only as a way to engage in the business of words and thus to subdue the seduction of music is a form of fake chastity, a self-castration that is un-German. It furthermore reflects an aestheticism that is merely decorative, that is, the production of art as modern writing or as classical, effete opera. What Wagner offers as alternative is a marriage, both for German art and for Woman. The first is to be reflected in his *Gesamtkunstwerk*, where "in the marriage to beget the grand United Artwork the poet's work is the masculine principle, and music the feminine."[62] In the second case, marriage between woman and man is to be redeemed not under the law of universal suffrage but precisely by taking the vote, the voice, away from woman.[63] "The process of emancipation," Wagner states in a marginal note to his last piece of writing, entitled "The Human Womanly," "takes place amid ecstatic throes. Love—Tragedy."[64] Žižek has articulated the logic of such a marriage in a very useful manner: Wagnerian (male) subjectivity is attained by the conversion of autonomous subjectivity into the predicate of some higher cause or power, whereby the subject operates like a ventriloquist of that higher power. What is crucial here is that this logic is gendered in such a way that a feminine ground functions as the support for masculine assertion. Two translations may be derived from this in Wagner's work. On the one hand, a political translation whereby a political leader adopts a passive stance, feminizing himself vis-à-vis the people: "his very subordination to the transcendent notion of the people . . . legitimizes him in acting as the 'formative power' and exerting full authority over empirically existing, actual people."[65] On the other hand, there is a musical, aesthetic translation that is effected: music drama is music made fecund by poetry but only to the extent that music, like woman and the people, is subordinated to poetry, the man, and the leader. This structure of the ground being subordinated to the figure stands behind Wagner's sexualization of music, a sexualization that guarantees its control and its containment.

Ultimately, Wagner's solution is a psychotic one, however, for such containment can only be brought about by the denial of symbolic castration. In his last opera, Wagner creates a hero or leader who is no longer bound by the symbolic universe of exchange—this is the true meaning of Parsifal's foolishness—for he has chosen *love*, a love of pure *jouissance* that transcends the Law. Parsifal refuses the legitimacy of the old order when he replaces both Titurel and Amfortas, but paradoxically he thereby also becomes Klingsor's true subject.[66] Parsifal sets himself up as a new Law, one no longer limited by the symbolic order of the classical bourgeois subject who had perceived the exercise of power to be possible only by its limitation and who had understood love only as viable if and when its absolute demands and immediate urges were subordinated to the necessities of social exchange via the prohibition of incest. Wagner's new man, on the other hand, takes within himself both music and poetry, thereby mastering his desire, his natural incestuous inclinations, in sublimated form. Woman is made to serve this process: "although transfigured by his ideal towards her individuality, she preserves a greater kinship to that nature-force than the man, whose passion now mates the fettered mother-love by turning to fidelity."[67] Parsifal steals her voice and, strengthened by this theft, at the end of the second act captures the spear from Klingsor, who along with his castle disintegrates into nothingness. In the third act Parsifal will complete the process of redeeming Germany as *Gesamtkunstwerk*: Grail and spear will be reunited as one; all difference will have turned to dust; Parsifal will now speak from the sole position of authority and power as a Bavarian *Weibjünglein*. Parsifal, whose predecessors had been Tannhäuser, Tristan, and Amfortas, no longer vacillates between radical rejection of woman and complete submission to her: he no longer needs her, since he first had her and then embodied her in the second act, and he thus can bring the opera, indeed all opera, to a close.[68]

4

SAVING LOVE:
IS SIGMUND FREUD'S
LEADER A MAN?

> The comparison with the way in which the skull of a newly born child is shaped springs to mind at this point: after a protracted labour it always takes the form of a cast of the narrow part of the mother's pelvis.
> —Freud, "A Special Type of Choice of Object Made by Men"

In March 1876 Freud traveled to Trieste on an ichthyological mission for his teacher Carl Craus, to confirm the existence of male eels. His attempt to counter the ancient belief that this particular water creature was hermaphroditic failed, since all the fish he cut open revealed themselves to be of the "tender sex."[1] Almost fifty years later, Freud sought for a similar clarity on issues of gender, this time as they pertained not to eels but to the leader of human social groups—as if a Parsifalian, hermaphroditic kingship, too, were something of an ancient belief. The leader, Freud states in *Group Psychology and the Analysis of the Ego*, is the purest form of subjectivity, the most perfect form of individual existence; the leader is a model for the masses, is authoritative precisely to the extent that the leader may embody what he calls individual psychology, that is, the subject as a coherent psychological entity. *Group Psychology* opposes this individual psychology to mass or group psychology and seeks the mechanisms by which the masses may be transformed into individuals. There must, Freud claims, be a way of scientifically discover-

ing the conditions under which mass psychology is transformed into individual psychology. The conditions for such a transformation should
have the necessity of the laws of science, laws that are, however, more
easily realized in the animal world: "it is possible," Freud writes, "for bees
in case of necessity to turn a larva into a queen bee instead of into a
worker."[2]

Freud appears to have had a liking for this apiary metaphor of leadership as the transformation of common man into a queen bee. In a 1913
letter to Sandor Ferenczi, Freud proposed that the psychoanalytic movement encourage and nurture Jung as the future leader of psychoanalysis.
He ordered Ferenczi to "feed the pupa (chrysalis) so that it can become
a queen bee."[3] The image of Jung turning into a queen bee is certainly
an amusing one, but it also points to a fundamental instability in Freud's
argument, an argument located at the intersection between his psychoanalytic and his political thought, his "individual" and his "group" psychology. This instability has two connected sources: the leader's gender,
and the fact that the leader is loved. In the pages that follow I trace this
double uncertainty in Freud's thought. Is the leader a mother or a father
substitute, and by what precise mechanisms do people willingly, indeed
lovingly, submit to power or authority? Freud calls these mechanisms
object-love (the prototype of which is man's overvaluation of woman)
and identification (man's introjection of the killed father as ego-ideal).

The three Freudian texts I discuss here—"On Narcissism: An Introduction" (1914), *Group Psychology and the Analysis of the Ego* (1921), and
Civilization and Its Discontents (1930)—share this concern about how the
leader is loved, as well as who the leader is in the first place—mother or
father?—and all three texts ultimately articulate a form of male subjectivity as masochistic. In addition, however, as a series they constitute
a particular form of historical narrative, that is, a melancholic narrative
of decline—the decline of modern subjectivity, of democratic liberalism, of self-sufficient masculinity.

On Narcissism

For Freud, there are two types of narcissists: the woman and the primal
father. Though the two most unsocial of all subject-positions, they provide for Freud the key to an understanding of the social group: they are
fundamental to the group because they are also the site where the social

bond shows itself in its most pathological form. Narcissism in Freud is, paradoxically, the site where the social bond is born and dies.

The aim of Freud's essay "On Narcissism: An Introduction" (1914) is to show how narcissism, rather than simply being a perversion or a constitutive feature of homosexuality and schizophrenia, works "far more extensively," operating in the regular sexual development of all human beings. Thus narcissism may also be found in "the mental life of children and primitive peoples," and it is on the basis of this evidence that Freud postulates a *primary narcissism*, "an original libidinal cathexis of the ego, from which some is later given off to objects, but which fundamentally persists and is related to the object-cathexes much as the body of an amoeba is related to the pseudopodia which it puts out."[4]

Now, the relationship between ego-libido or narcissism and object-libido is an extremely complex one, and Freud struggles not only with the question of primacy—which comes first, ego-libido or object-libido?—but also with keeping the two types of loving apart in the first place. It appears, for instance, that neither narcissism nor love of the other is really primary, for what precedes both is autoerotism; it is the latter that is primordial, there before a self even exists. Narcissism, if it means the libidinal investment of the ego, presupposes the existence of precisely that ego and is thus neither inherent nor constitutive of the ego. Moreover, it is impossible to tell narcissism and object-libido apart, for narcissism—like the death-drive later—is observable only when it is object-libido. From the outset, object-libido and ego-libido exist side by side (the German word Freud uses is *beisammen*, more accurately translated as "together"), and instinct theory is as of yet "too coarse to distinguish between them; not until there is object-cathexis is it possible to discriminate a sexual energy—the libido—from an energy of the ego-instincts." In addition, the two types of libidinal instincts also appear to operate in a relationship of a certain reciprocity.[5] The more there is of one, the less there will be of the other. It is where narcissism is at its lowest that Freud, paradoxically, proposes to study the phenomenon: where ego-libido is concealed by object-libido, it is also most visible—precisely because ego-libido is concealed. One can observe narcissism, Freud says, neither in itself nor, for that matter, in pure object-libido: one can observe it in the kind of object-*choice* people make when they love. Freud thus distinguishes between two types of object-choice: the anaclitic type where the mother, as the child's first sexual object, becomes the model for all later object-choices, and the narcissistic type where the model for object-choice is the self. Freud thus draws up the following well-known table of choices.

A person loves according to the narcissistic type (Type I):

a) what he is himself;
b) what he once was;
c) what he would like to be;
d) someone who was once part of himself.

A person loves according to the anaclitic type (Type II):

a) the woman who tends;
b) the man who protects.

In both cases, then, the libido is directed *outward*, toward an object—both anaclitic and narcissistic object-choices describe relations to an *other*. What the distinction determines, therefore, is not differences between egoism and altruism, or between non-love and love, but the method by which any person might choose one object as opposed to another. Narcissism does not indicate the refusal to choose an object (such refusal would point to an absence of desire, of choice), but instead signifies the preference for the self as object and thus cannot be distinguished from any other object-choice. And since Freud does not believe that one can really distinguish between people who love according to the anaclitic type and those who love according to the narcissistic type—both kinds of object-choice usually appear as a mixture of each other—we must assume that most individuals have not one but two original objects of love, the mother and the self, and furthermore that a sharp distinction between hetero- and homosexuality is impossible since everybody would love according to the models of both mother and self.

This, however, turns out not to be the case: there are indeed two types of people in the world, types that result from the two possible object-choices. They are man and woman. Object-love of the anaclitic type is what determines man's love, which explains his tendency to overvalue his object of love, namely woman. Yet this overvaluation, this depletion of the ego, Freud tells us, derives from and feeds off his original, childish narcissism, now transferred to the sexual object. Woman, on the other hand, loves according to the narcissistic type. She, too, begins from a position of original narcissism, but instead of transferring this narcissism to an object, or rather instead of choosing her object in ways more in line with men, she intensifies her original narcissism. In a woman, childish narcissism becomes even more childish, and indeed, Freud compares her to all those other narcissistic beings that exercise such fascination upon men: children, animals (especially cats and animals of prey), great criminals, and humorists. Women, particularly if they are beautiful, do not love, and they most certainly do not overvalue their men. And yet they do love—themselves. They embody a "certain self-contentment" because "it is only themselves that such women love with an intensity comparable to that of the man's love for them," and because their need lies not "in the direction of loving, but of being loved."[6]

The incongruity, as Freud calls it, between these two types of object-choice, and the fact they are gendered, does not bode well for the propagation of the species; but it does bode well for unhappy love, or—as Denis de Rougemont has called it—for the marriage of passion and death.[7] According to Freud, however, two factors intervene to produce a happy ending, and both involve some gender bending or crossing-over from one type of object-choice to the other. On the man's side, his slavish admiration of woman, his fascination with her narcissistic self-sufficiency, has its origins in the man's own narcissism, which he now sees reflected in the woman he loves: what man loves in woman is not woman but man. "It is as if we envied them for maintaining a blissful state of mind—an unassailable libidinal position which we ourselves have since abandoned." On the woman's side, on the other hand, there seem to be several options. If she has held on to her masculinity complex—which, given her narcissism, is something she is apt to do—she can "love according to the masculine type" and thus develop an overvaluation of man, that is, anaclitic object-love. Yet, such object-choice cannot be distinguished from her narcissism, since "the capacity of longing for a masculine ideal" is actually a survival of the "boyish nature" that she herself once possessed.[8] Second, Freud understands narcissistic love as, and perhaps confuses it with, the need to be loved. In other words, a woman loves a man who loves her. Her cruel indifference is, as Mikkel Borch-Jacobsen interprets it, only a trap laid for man's credulity: "She chooses the one whom she can lead to believe that she is not choosing." The woman, in other words, does make an object-choice (even if she does so only to renounce it), which means she loves like a man, or, "she loves like the man who loves a woman who loves like a man does—in order to be loved."[9] We are confronted here with a situation in which a man never chooses "happy love"—that is, a woman who loves him like a man—because what a man is really looking for is an untainted femininity: a woman capable of mirroring back to him his own renounced narcissism. Woman, on the other hand, constantly chooses that man who loves her but only in order to renounce him, and it is through her (masculine) choice of masculine renunciation or renunciatory masculinity that her femininity is established.

Freud has arrived at a paradoxical place of radical symmetry. Narcissism appears to have destroyed all sexual differences. Man and woman's positions end up, as Borch-Jacobsen comments, in a perfectly symmetrical relation by virtue of both their narcissisms, rendering the distinction between object-libido and ego-libido an impossibility. And yet this symmetry is not a shared position since there can only ever be one narcissist. An imperfect narcissism would immediately signal a joint renunciation of it, and thus a loving according to the anaclitic type. But then neither partner would be able to regain his or her originary narcissism. The femme fatale, the desiring woman, Borch-Jacobsen remarks, would indeed be fatal to man: only the cruel lady can give him what he once was. The symmetry created by narcissism—the latter's ability to act as the great equalizer—is in fact a violent confrontation, and in the ensuing battle narcissism triumphs over the defeat of love. Narcissism, according to Borch-Jacobsen's reading of Freud, produces a radical equality, understood as the destruction of difference, but an equality that finds satisfaction only in a voluntary servitude to the cruel woman. Borch-Jacobsen insists that Freud participates in this "dialectic of mistress and slave," that Freud writes his theory of love from the point of view of the slave who actually believes in the narcissism of the woman, and who thus refuses to see that this narcissism is always his own.

Deadbeat Fathers

Nevertheless, Freud's picture of narcissism is considerably more complicated, a complexity that arises from its very unrepresentability. Freud's fantastic schema of anaclitic and narcissistic love in fact takes place only in the form of a displacement. How does this displacement function in "On Narcissism"? First, Freud in fact speaks of two original objects of love—the ego and the mother—and these two objects cannot be collapsed into one another without the entire essay becoming totally incoherent, or without, quite simply, denying the fact of birth. Second,

Freud inscribes into his structural schema a time, or *developmental*, element—namely, history—and he does this, quite paradoxically, on the side of narcissism. Narcissism, for Freud, is always a non-original origin, or alternatively, an original non-origin.

Let us return to Freud's schema (see page 119), but this time in order to take seriously Freud's insistence that the distinction between anaclitic and narcissistic love is gendered. Continuing to assume Freud's ideal types, we arrive at a very interesting configuration.

Man loves narcissistically (Type I):

b) what he once was, namely, himself as a child, and he does this according to the model of identification;
c) what he would like to be, namely, his ego ideal, and this he does as overvaluation.

Man loves anaclitically (Type II):

a) the woman who tends, namely, his mother and all the maternal prototypes that follow her, and he does this always in terms of overvaluation, the pure state of being in love.

Woman loves narcissistically (Type I):

a) what she is herself (she loves herself), and she does this in the form of overvaluation; and
d) what is/was part of herself (her child), according to identificatory attachment (penis = child).

Woman loves anaclitically (Type II):

a) the woman who tends, and instead of substituting the mother with other maternal prototypes, she switches from overvaluation to identification with her.

What is striking in this classification is that *no one loves the father anaclitically*. In Freud's enumeration of Type II, the space for the father who protects (b) is always left vacant, and indeed—if one takes Freud at his word—anaclitic cathexis of II(b) by men and women is a structural impossibility. In the second part of the essay, where Freud draws the distinction between anaclitic and narcissistic love, the father is neither mentioned nor discussed—he appears only in the table of choices. Why?

Several possible answers present themselves. First, one may say that the father's place is Freud's blind spot in the system and that it is occupied by Freud himself: he cannot see the father because he is speaking from his place—he *is* the father. Borch-Jacobsen would thus be incorrect in holding that Freud in "On Narcissism" is speaking from the servile position of the mother's son; he would, on the contrary, be speaking from the position of absolute mastery. Second, if the father is there but crossed out, he appears only as dead father, or as Lacan would say, pure signifier; the father is here a *point de capiton* that allows for the classification of love by his simultaneous presence and absence. The mother "rules" here as absolute primary object of love. It is to her that one is subservient; it is she that is overvalued, but only to the extent that the always dead father stands behind this rule. Third, the position of narcissism—as also Freud's text "On Narcissism"—functions only when the family scenario is ruled by a headless head, when we have a leader who has been beheaded. Narcissism is this headlessness: its very possibility depends on a certain democratic element—the killing of the father of the primal horde and the occupation of the father's place by the son; conversely, this democratic structure depends fundamentally on the son's narcissistic subject-position. Fourth, though the system depends on but also creates the death of the father and thus a democratic rule of the brothers, power does not thereby disappear. The dead father remains the *agency of repression* in the narcissistic system, but only insofar as he does not directly partake in the system—that is, insofar as the father is placed on the side of anaclitic love. Repression works here to the extent that it is loved blindly.

It is the love of authority, the anaclitic, sexualized love of the agency of repression—indeed, this masochism—that Freud points to but represses in "On Narcissism" and that makes its return in his 1919 essay which addresses infantile fantasies of being beaten by the loved father.[10] Here too Freud makes a similar remarkable move: he shows that the origin of the beating fantasies for both boys and girls lies in an incestuous attachment to the father. And yet, at the end of the essay, he insists that in psychoanalytic theory, the agency or motive forces of repression can never themselves be sexualized. This is an extraordinary statement in an essay dedicated to masochism, for what defines the latter phenomenon is precisely the libidinal investment in the repressive agency—the beating, punishing father.

Is the father loved, then? And where does he take his place in the Freudian schema? These two questions are always linked in Freud's thought in a kind of inverse relationship, a relationship that is in an odd manner connected to the (in)visibility of the mother. In "A Child is Being Beaten," the boy loves his father but only as mother, for the boy adopts "a feminine attitude without a homosexual object-choice."[11] The girl, for her part, may keep the father in place but only to the extent that he is not loved—that is, to the extent that the daughter forfeits her sexual life, desexualizing herself. There is no trace in this essay, writes Kaja Silverman, "whether male of female, of the wish to be loved by the father."[12] This, I believe, is the secret of woman's narcissism. No one loves the father anaclitically because the woman is a narcissist; or, the woman is a narcissist because no one loves the father anaclitically. Therefore, both the woman and the (primal) father are excluded from the game of love. It is this exclusion that determines their role in Freud's social thought, indeed, makes his thinking about the social possible.

Social Psychology

The relationship between libido and its object constitutes the essence of psychoanalysis, Freud tells us at the beginning of *Group Psychology and the Analysis of the Ego*.[13] The analysis of the ego is always already a group (*Massen-*) psychology, for the individual embodies from the outset some kind of fusion, understood both as a connection with the other—this is what defines libido or object-oriented drive—and as an admixture or supplementarity (*Zumischung* or *Zusatz*) of conflicting instincts. Freud is uncertain about the absolute desirability of such fusion, for object-orientation and the admixture of instincts create a functioning ego, but also social bondage. Although Freud makes repeated changes to the theory of drives, in the very mutability of his theory, he will consistently adhere to one claim—namely, that of the inconstancy, adaptability, indeed the *freedom* of the instinctual drives to substitute objects. Instincts are capable of substituting, displacing, condensing, sublimating: this was the great discovery Freud had made by interpreting dreams. Instincts are defined by a fundamental faithlessness or plasticity, a plasticity that is nevertheless limited because instincts are always caught in a network. Ever since his earliest metapsychological formulations in the *Project*, Freud had conceived of this network as a system of *Bahnungen*, paths of desire through which and by which desire remains always deferred: "we must bear in mind that the sexual instinctual impulses in particular are extraordinarily *plastic*, if I may so express it. One of them can take the place of another, one of them can take over another's intensity; if the satisfaction of one of them is frustrated by reality, the satisfaction of another can afford complete compensation. They are related to one another like a network. . . ."[14]

The instincts find satisfaction in their very displaceability, though as Freud always insists, this satisfaction will inevitably be problematic not only because instinctual substitution is imperfect—the new object of desire is never the original, lost object—but also because all objects of desire are created in and through a system of production—a network of collectively or socially accepted objects. But sublimation is the love and production of such objects. In fact, sublimation constitutes more than a valuation of socially accepted objects; it is always at the same time an *over-valuation* or idealization of those same objects. Overvaluation lies at the very center both of the ego ideal and of the definition of sexual object-love. Instinctual fusion refers then both to a process whereby instincts substitute for one another and to the tendency of the instincts to make substitute objects their own. These objects in turn are the result of a collective valuation, a common ideal which itself is an overvaluation precisely to the extent that it is an ideal. Freud speaks here of "*eine starke Gemeinsamkeit*," a strong, a powerful if not violent commonality that is common, hence subject to laws of equal distribution, and yet already off balance, an unbalanced budget insofar as it is based in a fundamental overvaluation.[15] From here derive the constant economic problems that the libido will have to confront in the social network of object-production: the libido tends both toward a general defusion, expenditure or displacement of itself and toward becoming fixed onto one object.

Group Psychology and the Analysis of the Ego is the text that thematizes this "*starke Gemeinsamkeit*" most explicitly. There is something in people, Freud asserts, that binds them as a group even when they seem to have nothing in common. This common element does not derive from a social instinct, that is, a drive that could be perceived as original, primitive, and "insusceptible to dissection."[16] Freud had already ensured the impossibility of such a drive by proving that individual psychology must always entail a social psychology, provided that this individual psychology is approached psychoanalytically, that is, at the level of the individual in his relationship to the other. Psychoanalysis always already takes the social into account. As Mikkel Borch-Jacobsen points out, Freud thus equates the social bond to object-cathexis: *any* relation to another individual is a social relation, a political relation, and therefore a relation of power.[17] Two consequences follow from this reduction. First, Freud does not understand the private and the public domains as subject to separate laws: "it may be possible to discover the beginnings of [social] development in a narrower circle, such as that of the family" (70). Second, by recreating the opposition between individual psychology and social psychology within psychoanalysis as that between narcissism and love for the other, Freud transforms the problem of the social bond into an intra-psychoanalytic problem of narcissism.[18]

If there is no such thing as a primitive group instinct, what then is the crowd, the *Masse*? Following Gustave Le Bon's analysis of the *foule* or *Masse*, it turns out that the crowd exhibits all the same characteristics of the individual in his most primitive, uncontrolled state: the crowd acts like the Freudian unconscious. When the individual is part of a crowd, he gives up all those qualities that are characteristic of him qua individual: his unconscious life takes over; heterogeneity is submerged in homogeneity—a condition akin to Freud's later "oceanic feeling." Individual responsibility vanishes in this sea of indifferentiation and is replaced by a feeling of omnipotence and invincibility—by those affects that define narcissism. All repressions are abandoned, and the member of the crowd becomes incapable of perseverance, of delay in the fulfillment of desire, of exercising his critical faculty. Not critical judgment, but imitation or suggestion is what determines his relation to others. The member of the crowd tends toward extremes, toward spontaneity and violence. The individual becomes an automaton, giving up all will; the cultivated individual regresses to the barbarism of primitive people, obeying only the dictates of instinct, not those of the intellect. Because the member of a crowd has given up all will—and this is crucial—he can respect only force; he wants to be ruled by a master. In its thirst for submission, the crowd is like a primitive people: it subjects itself to the master's power of words, it never thirsts for truth but demands instead magic and illusion.

The relationship between the unconscious and the crowd is not, for Freud, one of mere analogy. It entails from the very beginning the question of *historical* primacy, a question that dominates the entirety of the text. At stake is not only the (theoretical) viability of the psychoanalytically conceived subject of desire but also the viability of a psychoanalytic explanation of that subject's historical existence, or, if you will, the subject's entry into history—indeed, the birth of the subject as the birth of history tout court. Freud is faced here with a dilemma: if the crowd is primary, then the notion of self-sacrifice of desire makes no sense, for there was never a desiring self to be sacrificed. We must remember that if there was to be desire at all, it had to be located in the individual, for Freud had excluded a social instinct from the beginning. But if the individual is primary, Freud cannot hold to the primacy (both historical and theoretical) of the unconscious and of desire. Thus, either there is a subject or self without desire, or there is desire without a subject.

It is in the person/subject of the leader that this dilemma comes to a head: for Freud, the crowd is never acephalous.[19] The failure of Le Bon's analysis, according to Freud, was that he had not explained how a leader arises out of the crowd, which is another way of saying that he had not explained how an individual arises out of the crowd, nor determined the individual's implication with desire. The entire Freudian text is dedicated to establishing just this: the desiring, loving subject, conceived as a social being with all the characteristics of an individual. But since this individual is bound to the leader, both analytically and historically, the text remains haunted by the problem of authority, by the possibility, that is, that subjectivity or individuality can only ever exist as a function of leadership. Either the leader is the only true subject-position possible, or subjectivity can only be conceived properly as a desire for the leader. What haunts the text is the relationship between power, desire, and subjectivity.

Freud attempts to control the spectral quality of this relationship through a series of translations. We have witnessed the first: the translation of individual and social psychology into psychoanalytic discourse, with the consequent effacement of the distinction between individual psychology and social or political psychology. A second translation is effected through the shift from the crowd to the organized group,[20] the paradigm from which Freud seeks to draw the contours of the relationship between power and subjectivity, since the main goal of any *stable* group must be the acquisition by its members of the characteristics of individuality. A third translation takes place in the move from the phenomenon of suggestion to that of libido or love, from power to that of freely chosen love, and it is to this translation that Freud turns first.

Two features, above all, describe the dynamics of a group: the intensification of affects and the inhibition of the intellect ("There is no doubt that something exists in us which, when we become aware of signs of an emotion in someone else, tends to make us fall into the same emotion" [89]). There is then in groups a coercive power of empathy or imitation, and this power inhibits normal thinking. Social psychologists explain this strange power as the power of *suggestion*. Freud rejects this term precisely because it is already deeply implicated with power; it is itself a "tyrannical power," for two reason. First—and here Freud refers back to psychoanalysis's own violent origins in Bernheim's practice of suggestion and Charcot's use of hypnosis—he recalls "even then" experiencing a "muffled hostility to this tyranny of suggestion" (89). Suggestion and hypnosis as medical practices subjected the patient, exercising a violence over him because it rendered him without will. In this context, Freud's practice of "free association," as Borch-Jacobsen has noted, is not just a therapeutic innovation but carries with it a wider ethico-political project grounded in the rights of free subjectivity.[21] Second, Freud's "resistance took the direction of protesting against the view that suggestion, which explained everything, was itself to be exempt from explanation" (89). The danger in the term suggestion, "which explained everything," was not only that it in fact explained nothing, but also that as a theoretical concept, it had strange capacities of contagion: "the word is acquiring a more and more extended use and a looser and looser meaning, and will soon come to designate any sort of influence whatever" (90). Freud proposes to furnish a logical foundation for suggestion with the psychoanalytic concept of libido, by which he means the quantitative magnitude of the instincts that everyday language calls "love." Love must be the basis of our scientific discussions and expositions, even if this leads to aggression and criticisms by the opponents of psychoanalysis. Freud could have spared himself much heartache, he says, if he had refused to give suggestion its true translation—namely, that of love—but he had denied himself such "concessions to faintheartedness." For who could say where that would lead? Thus, "one gives way first in words, and then little by little in substance too. I cannot see any merit in being ashamed of sex; the Greek word 'Eros,' which is so often the affront, is in the end nothing more than our German word *Liebe* [love]; and finally, he who knows how to wait need make no concessions" (91). For love's sake, Freud refuses faintheartedness, suggestion. He will not be ashamed and know how to wait, thus defer his own pleasure. Oddly enough, the act of translation itself seems to fall under the spell of suggestion: while there is legitimacy, indeed scientific authority, behind Freud's act of translating "suggestion" into "libido" or "love," too much translation, as the giving away first on words and then on substance, signifies giving way to social pressure, to the spell of the social bond, to the crowd. It is by holding onto love that Freud can refuse concessions to the group and thus assert his own theoretical independence, and yet it is precisely this same love that binds, that holds the group together. Love both brings the crowd together *and* furnishes a brake on its seductive power. Love may play this role in Freud's analysis because it is allowed here to speak for itself: what distinguishes the Freudian translation from Bernheim's theory of suggestion, Charcot's theory of hypnosis, and Le Bon's theory of the crowd is that it allows the patient or the mass to speak for itself—to speak, in fact, as a lover. Freud articulates here very rudimentarily a notion of *consensual* submission, a submission made out of love, a paradoxical movement where individuality depends for its existence on its simultaneous renunciation.[22]

Having established that all groups are held together by the binding function of love, Freud can now direct his attention at their organization. Although he raises the possibility of groups without leaders, he immediately sidesteps the issue by choosing, "in complete opposition to usual practice" (93), the (Prussian) army and the (Catholic) Church as exemplary groups: they are artificial and thus stable, highly organized, their membership is compulsory, and they have strong leaders. What interests Freud above all is this leadership, but quite perplexingly because it generates an important illusion: namely, the illusion that the leader loves all its members with equal love.[23]

The illusion of love shows itself in different ways in the Church and the army. The illusory love of the Catholic Church has two features. First, though the Church clearly has a leader, this leadership is somewhat ambiguous. Christ is both a substitute father and an elder brother. The Church is defined by a "democratic strain" of love which considerably complicates the leader's position: he is both a leader (father) and an equal (brother). Second, this democratic love is unequivocally embodied in the figure of Christ; he himself bears no substitution. What characterizes the Church, then, is both an equal distribution of love and a surfeit of *personal* love. The army differs from the Church in both these respects. It is not democratic: there is no question that the commander in chief is a brother to the soldier; he remains a far less ambiguous father substitute. Although one may certainly detect hierarchies in the Church, "[love] does not play the same part in it economically [here Freud adds in a footnote: 'i.e. in the quantitative distribution of the psychical forces involved']; for more knowledge and care about individuals may be attributed to Christ than to a human Commander-in-Chief" (94). It is the absence of these libidinal ties in the army that gives ground to the question of the role of ideals in groups: whereas Christ's love is always a personal, embodied love, the army may very well be held together by such ideals as national glory or country. In the army, Freud tells us in the postscript, the soldier puts the commander in chief in the place of his ego ideal and identifies with the other soldiers; he would make himself ridiculous if he tried to identify with his leader. The Christian Churches, in contrast, require much more from their members, who must both identify with Christ and love all other Christians as Christ loves them. It is in this sense that one must understand Christ's double position as father and son/brother, for the Church demands a supplement: "Identification has to be added where object-choice has taken place, and object-love where there is identification" (134).[24]

This double attachment takes the form of a double bind. Freud's reading of the Christian command to love requires both an identification with the leader and the simultaneous prohibition of this identification—a command that recalls Freud's discussion of the superego, which is the product of the Oedipus complex. What the superego commands is that the individual be like the father and not like the father, take his place and always give way to him. The problem, as Borch-Jacobsen has remarked, is that the law that forbids identification with the rival is uttered by that same rival with whom one is identifying, and it thus has no legal authority: "As a result, there is no choice but to identify with the law that says one must not identify; there is no choice but to imitate (or 'internalize,' or introject) the model that says one must not imitate it."[25] The law can be obeyed only insofar as one transgresses it. This, for Freud, lies at the heart of Christianity's claim that it has in some sense transcended the law and reached a higher ethical level of existence, to the extent that this supplementary demand must always exceed the requirements of the group. The social bond of love created by the Christian Church always already exceeds itself.

In the army, the situation of command appears to be more straightforward: the soldier does not identify with his leader but puts him in the place of his ego ideal. This raises the question of whether a group could in fact be held together by a substitute of the father's substitute, by a leading idea that would dispense with the need for a leader. It appears that the army fails to create such a substitution because it suffers from a dearth of the libidinal factor: the "neglect of the libidinal factor in an army," it seems, is "not merely a theoretical omission but also a practical danger. Prussian militarism, which was just as unpsychological as German science, may have had to suffer the consequences of this in the [first] World War." The war neuroses in the German army were a direct result of the harsh treatment of soldiers by their superiors. It was the need for love that the superiors had failed to recognize—a love of the leader in the form of a valid ego ideal. The absence of love produced a generalized castration, thereby losing the war for Germany and handing victory to the United States: "If the importance of the libido's claims on this score had been appreciated, the fantastic promises of the American President's Fourteen Points would probably not have been believed so easily, and the splendid instrument would not have broken in the hands of the German leaders" (95).

There is thus too much love in the Church and not enough in the army. Freud's two exemplary groups are both somewhat "unpsychological," with disastrous consequences for the individual and the group. Love is always a function of some quantitative factor—a situation that puts love dangerously close to panic. Panic arises in a group when the bonds of love disintegrate, when the individual is "only solicitous on his own account," and when a gigantic fear is set loose. Freud is explicit that this fear arises not because of any real danger but because libidinal cathexes are broken, which means that "ruthless and hostile impulses towards other people make their appearance" (98). The example Freud furnishes of this outbreak of violence is where one would least expect it: in the religion of love. The Christian Church forbids all expressions of hostility within its own confines, but it can only achieve this because it "must be hard and unloving to those who do not belong to it" (98). The surfeit of love for Christ in the Church and the dearth of love for the commander in chief in the army both lead to violence; the moment of greatest love and the moment of non-love appear to be the same thing. In the case of the Church, the individual's lack of freedom derives from the strong emotional bonds he retains with both the leader and the other members of the group. Freud insists throughout that love—which certainly binds and often blinds—is nevertheless also the source of freedom; this was the essence of his critique of the theory of suggestion and of his condemnation of the Prussian army. Nonetheless, in both cases, love seems to hide or carry within itself some other emotion: its own seed of destruction that renders love an illusion.

What then would be ideal leadership for Freud? What would destroy love as illusion? I would hypothesize that it is precisely the presence of an adequate amount of libido in the group that constitutes Freud's own ideal, his leading idea, and that this ideal can only be achieved through the act of its theorization, through the return of intellect into the group as *the sublimation of love*: the leader can and should be substituted with a theory of leadership. In this sense, I disagree with Borch-Jacobsen's reading of the same passages. He claims that ultimately there is no way of distinguishing between regressive identification (the murder of the father and the devouring of him) and identification with the ego ideal, a lack of distinction that leads to massive identification or mimetic rivalry that in the process devours the other. It is just this kind of identification that Freud is criticizing. The loss of the individual's freedom, his "alteration and limitation," can only be countered by the working through of that loss in the act of formulating a theory of the leader. It is that, and only that, which will allow for the eventual replacement of the leader with an intellectual ideal. This is how one must read those remarks of Freud that follow his description of the army and the Church. He voices "a mild reproach against earlier writers for not having sufficiently appreciated the importance of the leader in the psychology of the group, while our own choice of this as *a first subject* for investigation has brought us into *a more favourable position*" (95; emphases added). Is it possible, he asks, that groups with leaders are not simply a more primitive form of highly evolved groups that are bound together by the force of an abstract ideal? This ideal would serve as a substitute for the substitute father, and it would even be possible that this ideal in turn may be embodied in "secondary leaders," who would substitute for the substitute ideals. Such a situation would lead to "interesting varieties" in the relationship between leaders and ideals, and to "other questions besides" (100).[26]

Groups are held together by libidinal bonds, both between the group's members and between those members and its leader. Furthermore, the ideal form of leadership would be that which is able to manage this libidinal economy: it would be able to establish a situation of adequacy of love between the leader and the group members as well as between individuals. Such adequacy appears possible only if the leader is always a secondary leader, a leader who substitutes a leading idea that in turn has its origin in some original leader. But who is this original leader? And what is the precise nature of the libidinal attachments between members and between the group and the leader? What, finally, intervenes to undermine this ideal situation?

Queen Bees

Schopenhauer's fable about the dilemma of the freezing porcupines, according to Freud, best describes his ideal of adequate distance. In order to avoid freezing on a cold day, a company of porcupines huddles together, but the animals are immediately driven apart by their quills. They are pulled together again by the cold, and this process continues until they find an adequate enough distance from each other in order to tolerably exist. No one, Freud asserts, "can tolerate a too intimate approach to his neighbour" (101). What the intolerable intimacy reveals is both a quantitative and qualitative factor in the mental life of human beings. The quantitative factor resides in what Freud calls the phenomenon of "minor differences"; the qualitative factor is explained by the so-called ambivalence of feeling. The ambivalence of feeling is the most important expression of the fusion or admixture of the instincts, though the components of this admixture seem to vary: "some instinctual impulses make their appearance almost from the first in pairs of opposites—a very remarkable phenomenon . . . which is termed 'ambivalence of feeling.' The most easily observed and comprehensible instance of this is the fact that intense love and intense hatred are so often to be found together in the same person. Psycho-analysis adds that the two opposed feelings not infrequently have the same person for their object." It is the coexistence of love and hatred that leads to their transformation. The instincts submit to an internal factor where ego instincts are influenced by erotic instincts, in other words, by the human need for love. This admixture (*Zumischung*) creates social instincts, and egoism is transformed into altruism: "We learn to value being loved as an advantage for which we are willing to sacrifice other advantages."[27] This internal factor is thus not quite internal, for it involves a certain economic calculation, a measuring of advantages that themselves derive from the second factor contributing to this admixture: the "*Zwang der Erziehung*"—the compulsion exercised by education and upbringing, by the pressures of civilization. Civilization demands from individuals the renunciation of instinctual satisfaction—though Freud does not tell us *which* instinctual satisfactions must be renounced here, whether egoistic or erotic ones.[28] More important, these instincts must be displaced; they must deny themselves satisfaction and thereby be changed.

Freud calls this process the susceptibility to culture (*Kultureignung*): "Throughout an individual's life there is a constant replacement of external by internal compulsion. The influences of civilization cause an ever-increasing transformation of egoistic trends into altruistic and social ones by an admixture of erotic elements. In the last resort it may be assumed that every internal compulsion which makes itself felt in the development of human beings was originally—that is, in the *history of mankind*—only an external one."[29] Cultural adaptability requires educational practices that, as Eric Santner has remarked in his discussion of Moritz Schreber's child-rearing manual, not only "instill certain behaviors in a child; they aim also to convert these behaviors elicited in *heteronomous* fashion (i.e., by means of external commands and pressures) into behaviors willed by the child *autonomously*, of its own volition." The goal of rote and repetition is to sublimate obedience to an external authority and thereby become an act of free will.[30]

The replacement of external compulsion for internal compulsion is, however, always a displacement. As Freud was to insist time and again, the primitive emotions never die. The conversion of heteronomy into autonomy is never perfect, for the resultant autonomy both falls short and produces an excess. Displacement is expensive: instinctual renunciation requires of the civilized human being that he live, "psychologically speaking, beyond his means." And since the instincts do not die, it is precisely in the confrontation with death—the ultimate narcissistic wound—that the primitive feelings of egoism and hatred are (re)born: faced with the death of the loved other, "in his pain, [primitive man] was forced to learn that one can die, too, oneself, and his whole being revolted against the admission; for each of these loved ones was, after all, a part of his own beloved self. But, on the other hand, deaths such as these pleased him as well, since in each of the loved persons there was also something of the stranger."[31]

The displacement of instincts introduces time or history into the psychic apparatus, both as the deferral of pleasure and as the confrontation with the reality of death. This entry of time expresses itself in the form of permanent social bonds. Relations with the other can be, Freud tells us, of two types: momentary or lasting. Momentary relations would be those founded in the sexual instincts alone, relations that are devoid of affection. They are temporary not just because of the nature of the sexual drive—when satisfied, the latter ceases to exist for the time being—but also because the *value* of desire is reduced when it can be immediately gratified. In the immediacy of exchange, love becomes worthless and life empty and meaningless.[32] Man becomes psychically impotent. Love requires obstacles or barriers for it to have any value, a high demand of love and a low supply of it will inevitably raise its price, thereby creating permanent relationships: love at a high price creates a (social) bond—indeed, a form of bondage.

All permanent bonds require the overvaluation of the object: the object must be socially valued; in effect, the sexual instinct directed at the object must undergo transformation; it must be sublimated.[33] Such sublimation does not come easy: "The instincts of love are hard to educate; education of them achieves now too much, now too little."[34] Whether too much or too little renunciation is demanded, the result is inevitably the same: the ego is depleted when the cost of love is too high, for the object is overvalued at the cost of the ego; when it is too low, the ego is depleted in its constant and high expenditures of libidinal cathexes. Permanent social bonds are created then through an adequate degree of sublimation—and if necessary also repression—of the sexual instincts through the turning of desire into affection. Furthermore, this affection must combine with residual sexual desire to create loving or consensual dependence. This dependence must be fused in turn with what Freud variously calls the instinct of self-preservation, ambition, aggression, aversion, narcissism, the ego-instinct, and the death drive.

All lasting relations between two people are profoundly ambivalent in character because they are relations of dependence and thus a challenge to the individual's libidinal cathexes onto his own self, that is, a challenge to his narcissism. "In the undisguised antipathies and aversions which people feel towards strangers with whom they have to do," Freud recognizes "the expression of self-love—of narcissism" (102). When a group is formed, this aggression disappears because narcissism is limited in the toleration of difference. Narcissism is limited by love because it "knows only one barrier—love for others, love for objects" (102). There is one relationship, however, that is exceptional, though Freud merely remarks on it in a footnote: "the relation of a mother to her son, which is based on narcissism, is not disturbed by subsequent rivalry, and is reinforced by a rudimentary attempt at sexual object-choice" (101). Love, which is the great civilizing force, and which thus forces a change from egoism to altruism, constitutes both a limit and an excess, for it must entail "desexualized, sublimated homosexual love for other men, which springs from work in common" (103) and a "sexual love for women, with all the obligations which it involves of not harming the things that are dear to women" (103).

Later I will address what it is that women hold so dear; meanwhile, this discussion has approached, in the violent conversion of egoism into altruism, hate into love, but also love into hate, a moment of horror born at the same time as love. Freud names this horror the *narcissism of small differences*—the calling forth of difference in a context of identity—which he defines as "the hostility which in every human relation we see fighting successfully against feelings of fellowship and overpowering the commandment that all men should love one another."[35] This narcissism of small differences is paradoxical if not traversed by an inherent and violent contradiction, for it appears to arise precisely when altruism is at its height, in those feelings of fellowship and in the commandment to love all human beings *equally*.[36] Freud articulates here a kind of panic, a massive and mass panic that threatens the group with a lack of differentiation, with self-loss. By the end of chapter 6 of *Group Psychology*, Freud in essence proposes that the social bond can be understood only as that which also constitutes its greatest threat: group psychology always functions according to two mechanisms of attachment (*Bindung*)—the love bond to woman, and bonds of identification ("those insufficiently-known processes and hard to describe" [104])—that name homosexual love. This double process of binding and unbinding provides Freud with his formula for the constitution of groups: "A primary group . . . is a number of individuals who have put one and the same object in the place of their ego ideal [this is the love bond for woman] and have consequently identified themselves with one another [this is homosexual identification] in their ego" (116).

It is woman who makes the social bond possible while she also undermines its existence. She is a threat because she is an object of desire and at the same time a potential source of identification. Man's anxiety of becoming feminized, of losing his self or individuality, is due to the fact that the social bond simultaneously binds (as object love) and unbinds (as identification). The German word Freud uses for "unbinding" is *Entbindung*, which has two meanings: to come apart, and to give birth. That woman seems to have some operative function—behind the scenes, as it were—may be gleaned from one detail of Freud's formula for a *Massenpsychologie* that must immediately strike his readers as extremely puzzling. This detail is quite obvious, though Freud himself never seems to notice it: the leader of a group *is not a woman*. Yet he insists on theorizing leadership according to man's love for woman—a love that is always an overvaluation, an idealization, a love that has (social) value, a sublimation. One must ask, then, whether Freud's leader is not really a dominatrix; or alternatively, whether the lady loved by man is not really a political authority, a substitute of the substitute father of the group. Freud consistently sidesteps the issue in the text by changing the gender of his exemplary groups: whereas the army and the Church function as the prototypes of organized groups—groups, furthermore, as Freud points out, that have no space for women, his discussion of the libidinal and identificatory bonds always turns on girls' boarding schools and female spectators who jointly adore the dashing virtuoso pianist.[37] A fundamental transformation seems at stake, a sexual transformation that serves as a foundation for both subjectivity and the principle of leadership:

"There must therefore be a possibility of transforming group psychology [into individual psychology]; a condition must be discovered under which such a transformation is easily accomplished, just as it is possible for bees in case of necessity to turn a larva into a queen instead of into a worker" (124).

The first result of this uncertainty in the leader's gender is that Freud cannot keep object-love and identification apart. Thus, not only does there appear to be a problem with the object of attachment, but the mechanism by which the subject is bound to the object of desire is also unclear. If the leader is a man, or occupies a male subject-position, then by rights the relationship between group members and leader should be one of *identification*, in other words, it should follow the classic Oedipal scenario of identification with the father. However, this would create virtually insoluble political and theoretical problems for Freud. Politically speaking, and Freud shares here one of the basic dilemmas of liberalism, if members of the group identify with the leader, it becomes impossible to distinguish the father from the brother.[38] After all, as Freud tells us, identification begins in the nursery and with sibling rivalry.[39] If the father cannot be distinguished from the brother, if identification—like narcissism—works as the great equalizer, then the basis for the leader's authority must be seriously questioned.[40] Furthermore, the confusion between father and brother threatens Freud's theory of the inherent dualism of the drives because such identification would leave no space for love, for object-cathexes.[41] Who then is this leader, and is this leader in reality a woman disguised as a man?

Dead Fathers

The father makes his appearance in the Freudian schema in two ways: as the absolutely narcissistic father at the beginning of history and, once killed, as the ego-ideal in modern civilization. The absolutely narcissistic woman is matched, if not outdone and done away with, by the absolutely narcissistic father of the primal horde. Chapter 10 of *Group Psychology* narrates Freud's "scientific myth" of this father. The primal horde, we are told, is a small band ruled by a despotic, powerful male and whose members (the sons) are essentially without will. It is only after the killing of the father that these will-less men are transformed into a community of brothers—namely, individuals or subjects. It would follow, Freud remarks, that "the psychology of groups [*Massenpsychologie*] is the *oldest* human psychology; what we have isolated as individual psychology, by neglecting all traces of the group, has only since come into prominence out of the old group psychology, by a gradual process which may still, perhaps, be described as incomplete" (123; emphasis added). Thus, first comes the group, then the individual—and this must mean that a group without a leader (an individual) is at least a theoretical possibility. This is, however, not the case: the individual must precede the group, for the latter is born from the father of the horde, who is absolutely free insofar as he is absolutely narcissistic. The primal father loves no one; his love, as Freud repeatedly stresses, is nothing but an illusion. He loves no one but himself, and it is with this awakening to the illusion that the sons kill the father. But, as we know, the death of the father is what gives rise to love, a love born from the father's grave. The sons' guilt over their crime enables love; it puts a check on narcissism which in turn makes civilization possible.

What happens to the individual once the father is dead? Have the sons not just killed the father but with it individualism? How can the group psychology of the sons be transformed into individual psychology? While the father was alive, he monopolized individual psychology for himself: "He forced [the sons], so to speak, into group psychology. His sexual jealousy and intolerance became in the last resort the causes of group psychology" (124). Here the sons were prohibited to play the game of love. Their forced sexual abstinence took the form of a sublimated love for the father, an ultimately illusory love, for what it disguised was the equal submission to the father's persecution. Sublimation here *hinders* the development of individuality, precisely to the extent that it inhibits not simply object-cathexis but also ego-cathexis: "The fixation of the libido to woman and the possibility of satisfaction without any need for delay or accumulation made an end of the importance of those of his sexual impulsions that were inhibited in their aim, and allowed his narcissism always to rise to its full height" (124). The individual is therefore he who through the love of woman can make himself into a narcissist— that is, occupy the place of the primal father. This individual thus recreates the old scene: the individual forces the sons' masochistic submission to himself; he keeps them in group psychology.

Freud has thus proven the simultaneous birth of individual and group psychology, and therefore the fact that groups can never exist without a leader. He has done so through his hypothesis of the first, original, and primary narcissistic father. He has also accomplished this by the *exclu-*

sion of the mother, that other absolute narcissist. The scientific myth of the primal horde is an affair between men: between father and sons. For though access to women is important, this is an Oedipal scenario that has as its *primary* goal the achievement of the position of absolute narcissism—that is, not love of woman but love of self as love of no one.

And yet, a problem remains, for woman has not quite been written out of the process. She appears, as already noted, in the form of a queen bee, a matriarch, once the father has been killed. In the postscript to *Group Psychology*, Freud again narrates the scientific myth of the birth of the hero. The hero's fantasy of ambition encounters here a certain blockage, an obstacle met with in the passing on of the father's heritage. At what point, Freud asks, is there an advance from group psychology to individual psychology for *all* members of the group? It would seem that the killing of the father produces two possibilities: either his place is filled by a successor or his place *remains vacant*, in which case the father's heritage is not passed on. While the latter solution is what makes civilization possible, it is not a happy one for the totemic community of brothers. It produces a certain dissatisfaction, an *Unruhe*. Freud gives two reasons for this *Unruhe*: society is fatherless, and this lack is compensated for by the establishment of a gynaecocracy, ruled by goddesses whose priests had been castrated for the mother's protection, "after the example that had been given by the father of the primal horde" (135). A castrating primal mother has apparently succeeded the castrating primal father, and the sons—in defense—return to the "old state of things at a new level" (135). But "the new family was only a shadow of the old one; there were numbers of fathers and each one was limited by the rights of the others" (135). It is here, with the rebirth of the father, that he is finally displaced and replaced. The individual is born "in the exigency of his longing" by freeing himself from woman and from the group; and the name for this first individual is the *poet*. The individual—in the "advanced," civilized sense—is achieved in imagination: he invents the heroic myth. The hero, who Freud tells us is the mother's favorite son, kills the father/monster and gives birth to a new father out of himself: "the poet now created the first ego-ideal" (136). It is through myth, in fantasy, that the poet-individual steps out of group psychology, joined by his listeners who identify with him because they recognize themselves in the story. Both individual psychology and social consensus are born as a fraternal community of artistic men.

It is as ego-ideal that the father makes himself felt and is recognized.

This occurs always *within* the son or individual, both because this ideal is fantasmatic and because it requires a subject that is always split in its structure and in its development. Structurally speaking, all relations that psychoanalysis had studied between ego and object, Freud tells us in the last chapter of *Group Psychology*, replay themselves within the individual or the ego in its relationship to the ego ideal. And this relationship always constitutes a historical displacement—a sublimation on the one hand and a disenchantment on the other—where visibility or embodiment is relinquished in favor of the pleasures of a certain interiority, a new relationship to the real and to history: "in human history the recognition of the function of the Father is a sublimation that is essential to the opening up of a spirituality that represents something new, a step forward in the apprehension of reality as such." As Lacan has rightly noted, to introduce the primordial function of the father itself represents a sublimation; to put it more exactly, one could say that though Freud realizes that the hypothesis of the primordial father is a myth, sublimation can only occur by means of the myth to which Freud has recourse. Sublimation, idealization, the establishment of the ego ideal, of the superego—it is toward these that the myth of the death of the father moves, creating thereby not simply a brake on instinctual drives but "the originary possibility of a function like the poetic function in the form of a structure within a social consensus."[42]

No one, I have said, loves the father anaclitically, but everyone, at least in the case of men, loves him narcissistically, that is, as an interiorized ego ideal, as that which one would like to be. Once in the realm of the ego ideal, all men are narcissists. Part III of "On Narcissism" has this dead but idealized father as its focus of analysis. The ego ideal represents both a projection of the ego's desire for or return to an original omnipotence and self-sufficiency and a projection of an external authority who takes on all those qualities of original narcissism. The ego ideal becomes thus the source of repression, and the ego submits humbly, like all lovers, to its demands. The problem, of course, is that it is impossible to distinguish between the love of the ego ideal (which is a displaced love for the father) and the overvaluation produced by an anaclitic attachment to woman (whose origins lie in a primary attachment to the mother). Who is really loved in the ego ideal: the father or the mother? This, it seems to me, is the real question that stands behind Freud's *Group Psychology*: The text hinges on a fundamental distinction, to wit, between identification and object-love, and if we accept Freud's word that narcissism is itself a form of object-choice, we must assume that identification and narcissism are not reducible one to the other. Like narcissism, identification is, however, "hard to describe" (104).

Identification, Freud tells us right away, is the *earliest* expression of an emotional bond with another person, and contrary to all expectation, this bond, in the case of the boy, is not with the mother but with the father. A son wants to be like his father. This desire, however, does not connote a feminine attitude toward him: it is, Freud says, typically masculine. At the same time, the son also develops object-cathexes toward the mother whereby he follows the now familiar anaclitic model. The son is thus doubly bound to objects: through a sexual tie to the mother and an identificatory tie to the father. These two ties exist side by side without interference until, due to the "irresistible advance towards unification of mental life," they become wedded, and from this unification is born the Oedipus complex. Feelings of identification with the father turn hostile—the son wants to substitute the father with himself. Yet, Freud insists, identification is ambivalent from the beginning: it may express both a feeling of tenderness and a desire to remove the rival, since identification has its origin in the oral stage where what is loved is eaten and thereby destroyed.

Freud arrives here at what he perceives as the fundamental distinction between identification and object-love: identification expresses what one would like to *be* (how is this different from certain forms of narcissism, one may ask?) while object-choice expresses what one would like to *have*. The distinction depends on, he says, whether the bond attaches to the subject or the object of the ego. The bond to the subject is "already possible before any object-choice has been made"; however, he realizes it is extremely "difficult to give a clear metapsychological representation of the distinction. We can only see that identification endeavors to mold a person's own ego after the fashion of the one that has been taken as a model" (106).

Identification is thus a mode of *being*, not *having*, since the latter would describe object-love, and yet identification is being precisely what one is *not*: the subject seeks to mold his ego according to another, according to a model that is presumably different. Otherwise, identification would simply describe narcissistic object-choice. Identification thus takes place as the creation of sameness or identity in the context of difference. Freud, however, has difficulty with this, for he must insist that identification signifies an attachment to the subject—the self, the same—prior to all attachments to an object. Freud proposes to disentangle identification from object-choice, from difference, by studying the neurotic symptom, and therefore *women*. This constitutes an interesting but cru-cial shift in his argument and indeed repeats the transformation into the queen bee: he places his theory of identification in the context of sexual difference by moving away from the "straightforward" situation of the boy to the hysterical situation of the girl, a shift that is fundamental to Freud's argument about the male leader.

It appears—as with the boy—that if the girl establishes a relationship of identity (*eine starke Gemeinsamkeit*), with the same-sex parent—if the girl identifies with her mother—then all is well: her eventual feminine position will be guaranteed. If on the other hand she identifies with her father—and this was Dora's problem—difficulties must always arise; in-deed, Freud views such identification as inevitably hysterical. All signs of transsexual identification are signs of something having gone wrong: "In that case we can only describe the state of things by saying *that identifica-tion has appeared instead of object-choice, and that object-choice has regressed to identification*" (106–7). Regressive identification thus means not merely identifying with an object; even prior to that, it signifies identifying with an object-*choice*. Regressive identification means that *one becomes one's own object-choice*, whereas primary identification means becoming one's object of choice. This distinction is gendered—that is, primary identifi-cation assumes sexual sameness, whereas regressive identification de-pends on sexual difference. The question that immediately arises, of course, is how the child—and later, by extension, the analyst—reads the signs of sexual difference. Does primary identification not already pre-suppose a knowledge of difference? How does the child know whom to identify with? Who is his/her model? How can primary and regressive identification be kept apart? Why, for instance, would Dora's identi-ficatory cough with her father be hysterical? Why would not *any* symp-tom of sameness be hysterical? How is it possible to distinguish between identification with an object and identification with an object-choice? And finally, where is libidinal love in this system?

It appears that identification can in fact occur in such a way that the rule of love is completely avoided. This is Freud's third type of iden-tification; it describes a kind of identification where the object-relation to the person is absent. Here, identification may arise as a consequence of a common quality shared with another person who is not an object of the sexual instinct. This desexualized sharing of a common quality is what constitutes the social bond, that is, the relationship that members within a group have with each other. Freud gives a nonsexual but hardly innocent example of identification based on sharing:

Supposing, for instance, that one of the girls in a boarding school has had a letter from someone with whom she is secretly in love which arouses her jealousy, and that she reacts to it with a fit of hysterics; then some of her friends who know about it will catch the fit, as we say, by mental infection. The mechanism is that of identification based upon the possibility or desire of putting oneself in the same situation. The other girls who would like to have a secret love affair too, and under the influence of a sense of guilt, they also accept the suffering involved in it. (107)

This is indeed a peculiar little story.[43] It is hardly nonsexual, of course, for what it seeks to prove is that all groups depend on a shared quality—the libidinal attachment to the leader—in this instance, an amorous male letter-writer. Yet the tale exhibits rather strange characteristics. First of all, it assumes that the writer of the letter is indeed male or, more broadly speaking, that the leader is libidinally cathected as male, and that the members of the group are of the same sex, and thus can nonsexually identify with one another.[44] Second, it is not at all clear why the recipient of the letter—let us suppose her name is Dora—should have a fit of hysterics in the first place. Why does the letter arouse *jealousy* in her? Is she not in fact getting what she wants? What exactly is the content of the letter? Third, why is the ensuing infection of hysterical fits *not* libidinal when Freud had already shown that behind contagion stands love? Why is this identification necessarily rivalrous or aggressive in origin? How can love and aggression be held apart? Sharing, it would appear, is constitutive of the social bond, and yet such identification seems based in its opposite: "social feeling is based upon the *reversal* of what was first a hostile feeling into a positively-toned tie in the nature of identification" (121; emphasis added).

Two other forms of identification—homosexuality and melancholy—end Freud's chapter on the subject. Like the other forms of identification, homosexuality and melancholy appear indispensable to the formation of groups, while at the same time they also contribute to the group's undoing. If we return to Freud's organized or artificial groups, the army and the Church, we will remember that their stability, their leadership, had to founder on their constant tendency toward two extremes: either insufficient or too much love. Both the army and the Church face the choice of either homosexually loving a male leader or heterosexually loving a leader who stands in for the mother. The latter option is simply foreclosed by Freud's analysis: when the possibility actually arises as a question, he changes the gender of the group and transports us to girls' boarding schools. But the former option, homosexual love, also undermines leadership because it destroys the distinctive nature of the members' relation to the leader: it is a form of identification and thus is identical to the bond between brothers. Homosexuality is uncontrollable: "The striking thing about this identification," Freud tells us, "is its ample scale" (108). If all bonds are bonds of identification, true object-love is destroyed along with the leader, and violence inevitably ensues.

Group Psychology is ultimately unable to solve this problem of rampant identification and cross-gendering. The text seems to perpetually succumb to the power of its own suggestion, to reproduce the kind of commonality it had sought to destroy. Freud himself was unhappy with the results. As he later wrote to Sandor Ferenczi, he considered the text "banal, lacking in clarity and badly written";[45] and perhaps it was for these reasons that he would return to the same questions ten years later in *Civilization and Its Discontents*.

The Love of Common Man

Civilization and Its Discontents (1930) is without doubt Freud's greatest piece of cultural writing, an extraordinarily complex text that has suffered from almost universal misreading and simplistic reduction. And yet its central theme is concerned precisely with the difficulty, if not impossibility, of making universal judgments, in particular about politics and about love. For Freud, these two judgments come together in the evaluation, or indeed *overvaluation*, of the Other, of the neighbor, be he friend or enemy. What Freud calls common judgment is continuously played off against some other form of judgment, the mechanisms of which he spells out in the final chapters of the text.

The very first paragraph of the first chapter begins with the problem of formulating a general judgment (*allgemeines Urteil*)—namely, the judgment people make of themselves and others. General judgment is invariably a false standard of measurement for two reasons: it disregards "how variegated the human world and its mental life are";[46] and the *content* of such judgment—that people see "power, success and wealth for themselves and admire them in others" (64)—leads to an underestimation of the true value of life. The concept of "great men" is thus a complicated affair: they may be created by a common judgment that is always a misjudgment, or they may be great without this judgment, without the need for a certain overvaluation.

Freud seemingly makes these comments as a way to introduce a great man of the latter type, Romain Rolland, who calls himself Freud's friend but who nevertheless has caused Freud some difficulty with his theory that all religion has its origin in a feeling of "eternity," in something that is limitless, unbounded, oceanic. It is in the meeting place between general judgment as misjudgment and the oceanic feeling that the entire text takes its place. Freud's response to the oceanic is now famous: "I cannot discover this 'oceanic' feeling in myself" (65). Furthermore, it is not comfortable (*bequem*), he continues, to work *feelings* over scientifically; one can trace their physiological signs back to the body's functioning, or return to their ideational content (*Vorstellungsinhalt*), which is connected to the feeling in question. This latter move is Freud's: he gives the oceanic a representation and in that move reformulates it into its opposite. The limitless oceanic transforms, through his scientific working-over, into "a feeling of an *indissoluble bond*, of being one with the external world as a whole" (65; emphasis added).

This feeling of an original bondedness to the world goes against all psychoanalytic insight. As Freud had already proven in *Group Psychology and the Analysis of the Ego*, no such thing as an originary, unanalyzable social instinct exists; the latter can always be referred back to the individual ego. Freud makes just this move here. Unboundedness is grounded in a bond, not with the other or the world but with the self: "there is nothing of which we are more certain than the feeling of our self, of our own ego" (65). However, it turns out that this certainty, too, is a deception (*Trug*), for what psychoanalysis has shown is that the ego is in fact a facade: toward its inside the ego has a relationship to the unconscious, the id, a relationship characterized by a lack of sharp delimitation (*ohne scharfe Grenze*). It is only toward the outside that the ego *appears* to maintain clear lines of demarcation. Yet here too the ego's boundaries are not constant: overvaluation by a man in love is the most frequent cause of fusion with an object; pathological states, such as paranoia, is another.

The state of being in love as well as pathological fusion with an object are not, however, originary. They themselves derive from the fact that originally the infantile ego includes the entire world within itself, and only later separates itself from the world at large. Two factors compel the ego to become but a "shrunken residue" of its former self: the withdrawal of the most desired of all objects—the mother's breast—and the experience of pain by and because of which the ego throws *out* of its own

contours everything that causes this pain. Although a defensive structure, the ego sets itself up as a "pure pleasure-ego which is confronted by
a strange and threatening 'outside'" (67). The reality principle comes
into being and asserts itself when the ego must cede on its own existence
as pure pleasure-ego. Here the ego recognizes that pleasure lies not solely
inside itself, whereas unpleasure is always located in the outside, but that,
in fact, pleasure may be derived from an object, just as unpleasure may
originate from within.

Freud now feels he is in a position to explain the oceanic. It is a residue
of the old infantile ego-feeling, which is incapable of distinguishing between inside and outside, between self and other. The oceanic feeling
cannot, however, explain religious sentiment because a "feeling can only
be a source of energy if it is itself the expression of a strong need" (72).
What is this need, and what is its strength? One would have expected
Freud to say the mother's breast—that is, the originally most desired of
all objects. This is not his answer, however, for there seems to be an even
stronger desire: *Vatersehnsucht*, longing for the father. What had been
left unformulated in the earlier "On Narcissism" is now made explicit:
Freud "cannot think of any need in childhood as strong as the need for a
father's protection" (72), and therefore, he continues, the oceanic feeling
has been "ousted from a place in the foreground," though, Freud hesitates, there *could* be something further that "for the present . . . is wrapped
in obscurity" (72).

We find here again Freud's oscillating movement between mother and
father. The movement here, as in *Group Psychology*, is the inverse of that
in "On Narcissism." The mother, along with feeling, love, and desire, is
ousted from a place in the foreground and replaced by the father as the
source of need—a move that propels Freud's analysis into the economic
domain of demand and supply, of needs and their satisfactions. And yet
this is the male world of common man (*gemeine Mann*) and common
judgment. The desire for the father, *Vatersehnsucht*, is the result of a
common judgment and therefore of a misjudgment, and chapter 2 is
dedicated to an analysis of this economy. Why, Freud asks, does the
common man hold so tenaciously, so against evidence, to this nostalgia
for the exalted father? Freud's answer comprises an extended analysis of
the utilitarian structure of need and desire, of the economy of pain and
pleasure.

Common man sticks to his common, religious judgment because life
is full of pain. Although other ways of dealing with pain (through deflec-
tion, substitute satisfaction, intoxication) are available, the specifically

religious solution—the need for the father—also answers the purpose of life. For what do men demand of and hope to achieve in life? They strive after happiness, and therefore the purpose of life "is simply the programme of the pleasure-principle" (76). Since the pleasure principle is always in conflict with the reality principle, however, life's striving must be both positive and negative: it seeks happiness and more commonly tries to avoid unhappiness. Freud thus quite commonsensically equates the pleasure principle with the pursuit of happiness, though only imperfectly so, and this imperfect equation propels his argument onto a very different path. What is the nature of this imperfect equation, what disturbs the economy of pleasure from the very beginning? It is, as always with Freud, a disturbance of both a positive and a negative sign, a too much and a too little. Positive happiness means "the experiencing of strong feelings of pleasure" (76), and it is only in this narrow sense that we may understand true happiness. People try to achieve this happiness and keep it, but by its nature it is a perishable good; it is only an episodic phenomenon, for it stems from "the (preferably sudden) satisfaction of needs which have been dammed up to a high degree" (76). Continuous pleasure is impossible; it only provides a mild contentment: we derive enjoyment only from contrast or difference, considerably less from "a state of things" (76). The pleasure derived from sating an instinct that has been tamed, Freud writes later in the chapter, is considerably less than the violent satisfaction of an untamed instinctual impulse. Happiness in a wider sense, however, appears as an absence of unhappiness, and since unhappiness is so pervasive (it may come from our body, from the natural world, or from our relations with others), "the general task of avoiding suffering pushes that of obtaining pleasure into the background" (77). We have here another background, then: the pursuit of happiness in its wider, more general sense prevents true pleasure; it does away with the mother's breast and condemns man to pursue his *Vatersehnsucht* in order to gain protection both from pain and from the most untamed of pleasures.

The greatest source of unhappiness comes from our relations with others, since in those relations we are compelled to regulate our desires and needs. The regulation of instinctual impulses—through repression and sublimation—condemns men to the simple management of unhappiness. This management of unhappiness, this happiness understood as the absence or limitation of unhappiness, is "a problem of the economics of the libido" (83). It describes an economy that lacks a golden rule that may be applicable to everyone, and therefore this approach to unhappiness leaves man essentially alone. The economy of the libido—and this economy is what describes civilization—is one where choices must be made, where too much investment in one area of the "techniques of avoiding unhappiness" will inevitably lead to poverty. The libidinal economy of happiness is inherently capitalistic: "Just as a cautious businessman avoids tying up all his capital in one concern, so, perhaps, worldly wisdom will advise us not to look for the whole of our satisfaction from a single aspiration" (84). Religion as the search for the exalted father is just such a bad capitalist, for it insists on the presence of a golden rule. It restricts the possibilities of multiple aspirations, imposing on everyone to an equal extent the same path to happiness and the same protection from suffering. Religion intimidates intelligence and prescribes a delusional picture of the world; it may spare individuals a certain amount of neurosis but at a high price, for it forces people into psychic infantilism and draws them into mass delusion (*Massenwahn*). It takes individuals back to mass psychology, in other words. Unconditional submission becomes here both the final consolation and the ultimate source of unhappiness.

Freud, by the end of the second chapter, has dispensed with religious sentiment and thus with *Vatersehnsucht*. In its place he has put something else, another technique of living that has a considerably more complicated relationship with the capitalist economy of pleasure. This technique does not turn away from the world, it refuses the resignation involved in the simple avoidance of pain and instead strives for a positive fulfillment of happiness: it is "the way of life which makes love the center of everything, which looks for all satisfaction in loving and being loved" (82). Freud understands this love in a wide sense. He includes in it the sublimating activities of aesthetic life, the life led in pursuit of beauty, which is a "perfect example of an impulse inhibited in its aims" (83), for it constitutes a displacement of excitation from the genitals to the admiration of secondary sexual characteristics.

Freud mentions that psychoanalysis must fall silent when faced with beauty, and yet one must wonder if this is not in itself a displacement of silence imposed on psychoanalysis by the question that stands at its own center, its own *Mittelpunkt*, namely the problem of love and, metonymically, the problem of woman. This *Mittelpunkt* is problematic for several reasons. Whereas love strives for fulfillment in the narrow sense—that is, seeks a kind of wild, asocial satisfaction in the form of impermanent ties—it is also the foundation of the ego, who is the one most capable of creating permanent social bonds and thus managing happiness in the wider sense. This reintroduces the problem of narcissism, for the strong ego is Freud's wise capitalist, the one who can stand alone and make decisions. In a footnote added in 1931, Freud states, "No discussion of the possibilities of human happiness should omit to take into consideration the relation between narcissism and object-libido. We require to know what being essentially self-dependent signifies for the economics of the libido" (84, n. 2). The self-dependence alluded to here, the independent capitalist who can pick and choose his way through the economy, is the figure Freud sees as most threatened by the power of love. But at the same time, the inverse relationship is equally true: the capitalist who distributes his libidinal investments equally is also the figure most responsible for debasing the value of love. The rest of the text will address precisely this threat, marking in this move the specifically political dangers involved in giving either too much love or too little, in concentrating love too much in one place or of spreading it too thin, with the consequent result of the debasement of the value of love. The second part of Freud's text thus deconstructs his original, commonsensical definition of love as the pursuit of pleasure or happiness. Freud provides, in other words, a critique of the utilitarian conception of pleasure and pain, or happiness and unhappiness.

It is this deconstruction that requires emphasis. Freud's thesis that civilization is the greatest source of man's unhappiness is now famous and generally misunderstood. In referring to his belief that while civilization has given us a measure of security against physical disease, against the forces of nature and the intrusions of our neighbor, it has also turned us into "prosthetic gods" and has demanded tremendous instinctual renunciations, Freud states repeatedly that he had arrived at this belief by allowing "common feeling to be our guide." Such an understanding of civilization provides a *general* picture of civilization (and we have seen that such general pictures must be distrusted); in fact, "we have discovered nothing that is not universally known" (96). In light of his repeated insistence on the essential valuelessness of this belief, it is quite extraordinary that the common reading of Freud's text has been to state this belief as its central thesis. Such reading has in this sense fallen precisely into the trap Freud himself wants to avoid. Freud is clearly searching for a new direction: he wants to go somewhere else. At stake then is the familiar, the common, the general, and its relationship to something different: "The development of civilization appears to us as a peculiar process which mankind undergoes, and in which several things strike us as familiar. We may characterize this process with reference to the changes which it brings about in the familiar dispositions of human beings, to satisfy which is, after all, the economic task of our lives" (96).

Freud's new direction is consonant with the redirection of drives; his new theory is new precisely to the extent that it not only takes drives into consideration but itself participates in their redirection. "A few of these instincts are used up in such a manner that something appears in their place which, in an individual, we describe as character-trait" (96). It is here that a new conception imposes itself (*aufdrängen*): the similarity between the process of civilization and the development of the individual. The social economy and the psychic economy function in a fundamentally analogous way: they engage in sublimation and in repression; both, that is, demand the substitution, displacement, and renunciation of instincts. Civilization is saddled with the same burdens of having to absorb or neutralize all the hostility and frustration that results from such renunciation; it faces an economic problem of either compensating for this loss or dealing with the dangerous consequences of continuous frustration.

Having determined two analogous economies, Freud is now ready to rewrite again his scientific myth of the original slaying of the father and the consequent establishment of the totemic community by his sons. Although the sons have killed the father, they find themselves with two parents, the generators, if you will, of civilization: Eros and Ananke. In the period after the father, man is compelled by two drives—the need to work and the power of love. Why, Freud asks, did this situation not provide a stable solution to social existence? What interfered in this family romance?

Before he can address the nature of this interference in social progress, Freud directs himself to another interference: a "digression" that must be excused by the recognition of love's power. All of chapter 4 is dedicated to this digression, and it appears that it is one of the most important sources for the lack of progress in civilization. The problem and the power of love is that it affords the greatest of instinctual satisfaction and at the same time generates the greatest of dependence on the object of love. In response to this, many humans either displace "what they mainly value from being loved on to loving" (102), that is, they redirect libidinal instinct from passivity to activity; they distribute their love evenly to many objects (this is the wise capitalist again); or they sublimate their instincts and produce "a state of evenly suspended, steadfast, affectionate feeling" (102). It is this universal love of mankind—considered by many the highest of ethical achievements—that will become the focus of Freud's critique. Here he immediately objects to it on two grounds: a nondiscriminating love forfeits its value by doing injustice to its object; and, not all men are worthy of love. Such universal, general love of mankind is uneconomical in a double sense, for it spreads itself too thin, loving all objects, some of which do not receive enough love, while others receive love without deserving it. The wise capitalist is not a desirable figure after all.

The devaluation of love already finds its symptomatic expression in the inflated, overvalued use of the word itself. Nevertheless, and Freud must say this, given the constant attacks on psychoanalysis for its supposed pansexual reductionism, the application of the word to all sorts of relationships has a "genetic justification" in that the social bond has its origins in sexual love, though "*we* [psychoanalysts] are obliged to describe this as 'aim-inhibited love' or 'affection'" (102). The pervasiveness of love is what ultimately enters into conflict with the goals of civilization: though the latter requires libidinal bonds for social cohesion, love must eventually enter into conflict with the interests of civilization, since the latter imposes substantial restrictions on love's movement.

The evidence for such a conflict lies with woman, and Freud finds this evidence already at the dawn of history. He in fact narrates another scientific myth—another, second origin of civilization. In the beginning, Freud states, women "laid the foundations of civilization by the claims [*Forderungen*] of their love" (103). Like the claims for love made by the Church, this demanding love is excessive and therefore in need of control. Women represent the interests of the family and of sexual life, interests that must necessarily take second place to civilization's later more important, more manly, claims. The work of civilization must eventually require greater sublimations from man, sublimations "of which women are little capable" (103). Sublimation forces man into economic existence, into a kind of calculation of his relative strengths and weaknesses: "Since a man does not have unlimited quantities of psychical energy at his disposal [something woman apparently does have], he has to accomplish his tasks by making an expedient distribution of his libido. What he employs for cultural aims he to a great extent withdraws from women and sexual life" (103–4). Woman is yet again forced into the background, and she therefore adopts a hostile attitude toward civilization; she retards and restrains the civilizing project.

Like man, civilization obeys the same laws of economic necessity when it withdraws sexual energy and uses it for its own purposes. It imposes heavy restrictions on man, however, by paradoxically demanding what man had apparently already chosen for himself: the first and most painful prohibition of incestuous object-choice. As in the case of man, sexuality is civilization's greatest natural resource, and civilization behaves, Freud states, in the same way imperialist nations behave toward underdeveloped nations: it mercilessly exploits these natural resources for its own benefit and never pays its bills. What Freud does not say here, of course, is that such a comparison could also be applied to man's relationship with woman, that other natural resource that never gets paid.

Yet sexual renunciation is not the only demand imposed by civilization; it also requires the creation of strong bonds between members of society through the establishment of bonds of identification. Here Freud departs significantly from his analysis in *Group Psychology* a decade earlier, for he now reads these identificatory ties as a "disturbing factor." Identification is an ideal demand and is summarized in the commandment "Thou shall love thy neighbour as thyself." Freud chooses to refuse his own identification with this commandment and instead to adopt a "naive attitude" toward it: "Why should we do it? What good will it do us? But above all, how shall we achieve it?" (109). Freud's naive stance is easily recognizable as that of the common man, the man who always asks the question of utility. There must be use and there must be value. My love, Freud insists, is something valuable and should not be wasted or thrown away; if I love someone, he must deserve it. To love the undeserving would be an injustice to those who do deserve it. And who deserves my love? He, according to the naive Freud, who is so like me that I can love myself in him; and he who is so much more perfect than me that I can love my ideal of myself in him. Both of these loves, we will immediately recognize, are narcissistic forms of love, founded in either specular identification or idealization. The commandment thus appears to demand love of the other, but what it actually disguises is nothing but narcissistic love of the self.

An additional problem raised by the commandment will become central to Freud's analysis. Just as the commandment to love the other as one loves oneself disguises narcissistic love, so it also refuses to acknowledge aggression. In all likelihood my neighbor bears aggressive feelings toward me—and I know this because I feel them for him—so that loving that aggressive neighbor would be tantamount to putting a premium on his being bad. This aggression is in fact the element of truth that is disguised in the universal commandment to love: the latter points to an inherent human aggression that must always disturb "our relations with our neighbour and which forces civilization into such a high expenditure" (112). Civilization incites people into relations of identification in order to hold man's aggression in check; it represses them and deflects them into bonds of identity and sameness. This is ultimately why libidinal object-love must also be suppressed by the forces of civilization: they too have their basis in man's aggression, in man's desire to possess and destroy the other.[47]

If the commandment of universal love only existed to counter human aggression, then it should by all rights be supported and sustained. But for Freud such an understanding—the common understanding—must be a misreading. Universal love, which has its reason in aggression, must *itself* always lead to aggression and violence. Although already hinted at in *Group Psychology*, this explicit account of narcissistic identification is new in Freud's analysis. Universal love leads to violence for two reasons. First, it always depends on some form of exclusion or scapegoating. This is what he had earlier called the narcissism of small differences: in universal love there are always "other people left over" who are excluded from the commandment of love. What makes a social bond cohesive is this remnant: "the Jewish people, scattered everywhere, have rendered most useful services to the civilization of the countries that have been their hosts" (114). This service is performed not by the discourse of assimilation but by the ancient yet dramatically new one of persecution. Christianity and its intolerance for other religions, Germanic imperialism and its historical need for anti-Semitism, and Soviet Russia and its persecution of the bourgeoisie are all examples of such scapegoating mechanisms, where interiority or selfhood depend on an exteriority, an Other, that is excluded. But Freud at the end of chapter 5, after having shown the need for exclusion in universal love, also hints at another form of violence required by the universalization or generalization of love. This second form of violence—which he names the "psychological poverty of groups"—takes place at the very center of the social group; it marks an interiority that in its essence is the most profoundly disturbing factor, for it makes the other form of violence possible. Freud names here a specifically modern form of power. Man, he says, has exchanged a piece of happiness for a modicum of security, and yet this economic exchange has not been at a fair price. Modern society has become leaderless. The killing of the father, the subsequent compromise formation of love and guilt that called forth God, the ensuing death even of that God, and society's secularization have led to a security that has eliminated the ancient happiness of love. Secular society is founded on strong bonds of identification that may well have eliminated the authoritarian, narcissistic father but have also forfeited all claims to differences *within* the group. Modern society has destroyed difference and, consequently, privacy—a privacy Freud views as the place that makes possible a free, autonomous subjectivity.[48] The psychological poverty of groups and of subjects, founded in a love that is spread equally until it loses all value, finds its most developed expression in America—the place Freud loved to call "Dollar country" but whose further analysis he refuses, mysteriously, for fear that he himself might appear to be employing American methods of criticism.[49]

The New Masochistic Man

Chapter 4 of *Civilization* opens with two concerns. First, Freud worries that he is still in the realm of common knowledge, that he and his readers are wasting their energies. Second, and as a consequence of the first, he must hurry to show that the recognition of an independent aggressive instinct does not constitute a change in or threat to the psychoanalytic theory of the drives. He gives a rapid overview of the history of drive theory in psychoanalytic thought, showing how the original opposition between hunger and love had to be modified once psychoanalysis redirected its attention away from the repressed forces, from the object-instincts, and moved toward a closer analysis of the repressing forces located within the ego. The analysis of power and the analysis of the ego are thus closely linked, and it is the concept of narcissism that provided this link. Narcissism, which made the ego into the libido's headquarters, was decisive, Freud states, for the rethinking of drive theory; it eventually forced him into postulation of the death drive, whose existence was evidenced by sadism and masochism, both of which were created by the fusion of libidinal and death drives. The fusion of these instincts had been difficult enough to accept, but what Freud had hitherto resisted was the possibility that aggression could show itself on its own in an undiluted state. The analysis of what produces but also hinders civilization had made this pure death drive a theoretical necessity, and it is from this basis that all social analysis must begin.

Undiluted aggression, the purest form of the death drive, is what most threatens civilization, and it is precisely the latter's task to throw up barriers against this violence. How does society, then, curb this innate aggression? The model, Freud states, for a social response to individual violence may be found in individual development, and it is here that we may note, he continues, something quite peculiar. Human aggression in individual psychic development is introjected, internalized, sent back to where it came from: it is returned to the ego. Aggression is set up *within* the ego but *against* it as the superego, and the latter's action we register within the psychic economy as conscience. The tension between the ego and the superego we call a feeling of guilt, which expresses itself as the need for punishment.

The superego, it would appear, functions like an internalized state: civilization, Freud remarks, "obtains mastery over the individual's dangerous desire for aggression by weakening and disarming it and by setting up an agency within him to watch over it, like a garrison in a conquered city" (123–24). The superego's function is thus *always* political, and therefore it makes little sense to say, as Freud appears to, that society's methods for curbing aggression follow those of individual development. The introjection of aggression is that moment by which individuals are constituted as individuals *and* as members of a social group. This is a very different conception of the social bond from the one articulated in *Group Psychology*. In the latter, we will recall, the social bond depended on a love relation to an *exterior authority figure* and on the consequent identificatory bonds with other members; here that exteriority is undone in favor of an interiority that has lost its own cohesion and unity and that cannot, in essence, ever be distinguished from relationships to other members of the group.

What has happened to Freud's leader? Why, Freud wonders, would the individual obey or subject himself to this interior authority? What does he have to lose? Why does he feel guilty, in need of punishment? The superego derives its power from what appear to be two sources, sources that closely parallel those from which cultural adaptability derive. First, there is an *exterior* source: the individual fears a loss of love, whether from the father, the mother, or society at large. A person will renounce aggression if he fears retribution in the form of not being loved. And yet, Freud insists, this is not really the origin of conscience and guilt; their actual birth can only be dated to the moment when that exterior threat becomes part of the self. This is the second source of the superego's power: conscience and guilt are always subject to a peculiar *interior* economy where action and desire can no longer be distinguished. This is their defining characteristic: whether the individual has committed an aggressive act or simply desired or imagined it makes no difference to the superego; indeed, the superego will act all the harsher, the more the ego obeys its commands.

The two sources of guilt, its exterior and interior origins, follow each other chronologically; they in fact describe a wider political history of leadership. First comes the fear of an external authority that forces on the individual the renunciation of instinctual satisfaction; its method is repression. This absolutist power is itself capable of experiencing and even giving a certain amount of satisfaction: when the required renunciation has been made, the accounts between self and other, individual and state, are closed; a relation of a certain parity has been established. This form of power is followed by the fear of the interiorized superego, a kind of panoptic power: since act and desire cannot be distinguished, repression does not work, and punishment is in any case inevitable. Given that desire never vanishes and cannot be hidden from the superego, the "aggressiveness of conscience keeps up the aggressiveness of the authority" (128). This produces not a relationship of exchange but a rather bizarre arithmetic; it "constitutes a great economic disadvantage in the erection of a superego, or, as we may put it, in the formation of a conscience. Instinctual renunciation now no longer has a completely liberating effect; *virtuous continence is no longer rewarded with the assurance of love*" (127–28; my emphasis). This is for Freud a particularly modern form of power, a power that may have no direct visible signs or embodiments, such as a leader. What this force destroys are the possibilities of love and of interiority and privacy, precisely *to the extent* that it sets itself up in the interior of the subject. It furthermore makes power unreadable, for while it may appear as a situation where the primal father or absolute leader has been done away with, a situation where the individual now becomes completely self-dependent, it in fact makes political power worse. This new form of power is absolute and authoritarian; it is inescapable and in its inescapability will eventually lead to a call for a return of a "real" absolute leader. Whereas the first form of power constituted a *threat* to the individual's happiness (in the form of a fear of the loss of love), the second form has transformed this threat into a *real and permanent* internal unhappiness.

The transformation of threat into real event recalls Freud's understanding of the castration complex and its resolution into the Oedipus complex. It also assumes a situation where trauma is real and permanent, a constitutive factor of all modern subjectivity. We will remember that the castration complex for boys is always a threat, one that is resolved by the boy as he passes through the Oedipal configuration: masculinity results from this threat and its eventual active displacement. For a girl, castration is never a threat but a fact, and its acceptance as a permanent state of being is what allows her eventual acceptance of the feminine, passive position. Modern power—one might say, power as exercised through the superego—castrates man; it feminizes him and thus makes him incapable of loving. Via a direct encounter with or introjection of power, men might be individuals, but they thereby inevitably become narcissists. They are incapable of love, for they have given up on their desire, renounced their drives. In a strange way, and to the extent that the superegoic function replaces repression, it has also destroyed *drive theory*.

Nevertheless, it is this strange economy of the superego—an economy that institutes castration as the condition for masculinity—that is the proper object of psychoanalysis; this economy is that which the common man cannot think and is thus the only thought capable of transcending religious thought. Freud is very clear on this point. What does psychoanalytic thought show? It shows that in the civilization process, the relationship between conscience and renunciation has been *reversed*: "Every renunciation of instinct now becomes a dynamic source of conscience and every fresh renunciation increases the latter's severity and intolerance" (128). Freud arrives at the "paradoxical statement that conscience is the result of instinctual renunciation, or that instinctual renunciation (imposed on us from without) creates conscience, which demands further instinctual renunciation" (129).

How does this paradox work? Freud illustrates its mechanism by taking aggression as an example, though this aggression must in reality be exemplary. When a child renounces aggression, this aggression is taken up by the superego, which in turn increases the latter's aggressiveness against the ego. There are, then, two original sources of aggression, which parallel Freud's previously distinguished sources of power: the *father's* aggression that is interiorized, and the son's *own* aggression, produced in turn by the father's aggression—namely, by the fact that the father is the authority who can prohibit. The son deals with this "economically difficult situation" (129) by identifying with the unattackable authority; he introjects it as superego. And thus, the "relationship between the superego and the ego is a return, distorted by a wish, of the relationships, as yet undivided, and an external object" (129). This distortion, it seems, wrecks representation, for the severity of the superego does not reflect the real severity of the father but one's own aggression toward the father. It is a representation distorted by the wish to kill the father.

But from whence does this distorted wish originate? Why would the son want to *misrepresent* the father? It turns out that the son is following another model—the phylogenetic one. The son is responding to the original, primal, narcissistic father against whom a real act of aggression was actually carried out. The question is, of course, where did the guilt by the murderous sons come from? From love, Freud answers, from the fact that the sons both loved and hated the father. It is love and not aggression or hate, Freud states by the end of chapter 7, that founds conscience, for it forces identification with the now dead father who is identified with as ego-ideal and interiorized as superego.

Guilt—which for Freud is "the most important problem in the development of civilization" (134)—has its origins in love and at the same time is nothing but a "topographical variety of anxiety" (135). Indeed, guilt seems to coincide completely with the fear of the superego. Since guilt and anxiety are virtually synonymous, the former follows the same rules as that of the latter: it may be conscious or unconscious. The guilt that lies at the foundation of civilization is generally unconscious and is perceived at best as a kind of malaise, as the *Unbehagen* of culture; it is felt as the general dissatisfaction that is so associated with the lack of happiness in civilized life.

The fear of the superego on the part of the ego, the latter's sense that it is being constantly watched over, the ego's need for punishment, has turned this ego into a masochistic ego. The relationship between ego and superego is characterized by what Foucault calls "*perpetual spirals of power and pleasure.*"[50] Fear of the superego is an instinctual manifestation that is "employed for forming an erotic attachment to the super-ego" (136). Yet Freud is not clear why this attachment is an erotic one, for Freud makes a clear distinction between the vicissitudes of the erotic drives and the aggressive drives: "When an instinctual trend undergoes repression, its libidinal elements are turned into symptoms, and its aggressive components into a sense of guilt" (139). On the one hand, then, he distinguishes between aggression and libidinal ties; on the other hand, he insists that the sense of guilt has its origins in the love for authority and in the fear of losing that authority's love.

The Fort/Da Game of Political Power

What explains this double origin of guilt in both love and aggression? The explanation must lie—though Freud does not make this connection explicit—in the fact that though individual and social development are analogous, they are not identical: individual development describes "the integration of a separate individual into a human group," whereas social development describes "the creation of a unified group out of many individuals" (140). In some sense, Freud must insist on this difference, on the possibility that the individual is not completely subsumed by the social bond. Individual development is always subject to the program of the pleasure principle, namely, the drive of a human being to find satisfaction for his libidinal impulses: the individual wants to be happy insofar as he loves. Such happiness finds satisfaction through two contradictory drives: the egoistic drive for personal satisfaction, and the latter's achievement through altruistic urges of fusion or union with other human beings. With the process of civilization, however, happiness is pushed into the background: the most important goal of civilization is to create unity, and it can achieve this only by curbing aggression.

Though individual and social psychology are often in conflict with one another, though they constitute "a dispute within the economics of the libido" (141), they do admit of some accommodation. Paradoxically, Freud states at the end of *Civilization and Its Discontents*, such accommodation is afforded by the superego, but this superego is a very special kind of superego: it is cultural. This cultural superego is "based on the impression left behind by the personalities of great leaders" (141). We have returned to Freud's theory of the leader, the leader as sublimation, as theory. The existence or memory of great leaders and the figure of the father interlock: they create ideals, set up demands, and articulate what is generally referred to as ethics. What the cultural and individual superegos jointly achieve is the conversion of aggression into love—and the clearest expression of this conversion is the command to love one's neighbor as oneself.

Yet, as we have seen, it is precisely this conversion that Freud views as dangerous. It inflates the value of love and thereby debases it and consequently feeds violence. To love universally means for Freud to destroy the other, the *Nebenmensch*, for such love is ultimately narcissistic. This narcissism leads not only to the false establishment of difference through exclusion (Freud's "narcissism of small differences")—that is, to an absence of love for what is different—but also to the creation of identity as the destruction of difference. This latter situation describes "Americanism," the psychological poverty of the masses, and is always characterized by a surfeit of love, a process of overidentification. In opposition to this universal love, Freud places psychoanalytic theory, a theory that seeks to create an adequate love as a theory of the subject and as a theory of the leader. What he seeks to find is a love that is authoritative and an authority that is loving and loved.

Yet Freud encounters fundamental problems in formulating such a theory of adequate love and adequate leadership. The first concerns Freud's continuing problems in articulating and maintaining a theory of the drives (his theory of the libido) without undoing the fundamental presuppositions of psychoanalysis. The second problem is a political one, for one is required to ask whether Freud is not, in his critique of modern civilization, engaging in a major *Vatersehnsucht* of his own, and whether, as a consequence, he is demanding an authoritarian state. The two problems come together in the universal validity of the Oedipus complex, a requirement not only for the primacy of libidinal drives but also for the continued primacy of the father. The difficulty lies in the heir to that Oedipal father, an heir that, Freud increasingly fears, might completely displace the father's role both in the theory of drives and in the institution of authority. How, Freud is increasingly compelled to ask, can the father's authority be maintained without him thereby sliding into his old, primal, authoritarian habits? What, furthermore, interferes in the control of this father? Why has he lost control, and what sets him loose?

As we learn from Freud—and this marks his ambiguous relation to the superego—that which controls the father is simultaneously what feeds his unbounded power.[51] What the superego demands is total identification. Pure identification without love is always melancholic and narcissistic; it produces, paradoxically, a situation of "too much love," an *intrusion* into the privacy of the subject, and a situation of "too little love," an *abandonment* of the subject. We may recognize here both the melancholic subject who yearns to bring an end to the fatherless society, and Schreber's universe of paranoid power. The two scenarios describe what for Freud is a specifically modern form of authoritarianism that reduces the members of a group to a passivity that, as Freud had narrated in his scientific myth, forced individuals back into group psychology. The superego is always an authoritarian leader to the extent that he exists in a form of constant oscillation; he is, one might say, the greatest player of the Fort/Da game: he is never quite the father, for behind him lurks the danger of the mother, behind whom in turn stands again the father—ad infinitum. The leader stands both outside and inside the subject, imposing his impossible demands of identification and the latter's transgression on the now passive, feminized son, who refinds the disavowed mother in his identification with her. What is perverse about authoritarian power is this double placelessness: its exterior power is interiorized and thereby loved—it draws on narcissistic libido for this—and thus forces a love of repression and, by extension, a love for the father; yet the resultant interiority created by the father's intrusion is itself placeless because it identifies with or occupies a place that has already been excluded: the place of the mother or of woman. Authoritarian power is thus perverse precisely to the extent that it is utopian.

Freud does not say any of this, of course. He adumbrates a theory of power and leadership but stops short of a profounder critique when he encounters the problem of the mother. *Group Psychology and the Analysis of the Ego* and *Civilization and Its Discontents* are in some very significant sense mirror images, and narcissistic mirror images at that, of his earlier essay on narcissism. While in the earlier essay the mother takes a primary place as the central object of love to the extent that this maternal space is constituted by the blind spot of the father, in *Group Psychology* and in *Civilization*, the father as leader and as central object of love can exist only if the role of the mother is in turn disavowed. This does not lead us to the conclusion that Freud's figure of authority (the figure that commands love or obedience) is hermaphroditic. Freud founders on the problem of sexual difference, but he never collapses that difference into identity. For sure, the superego's gender remains ambiguous—it is, Freud states vaguely, the introjection of *one or both* parents.[52] Yet the greater ambiguity stems from a feeling, as Alice Yaeger Kaplan has correctly pointed out, "that Freud simply can't keep track of the place of both parents at once." Kaplan continues that this visual play of "now you see him/her, now you don't" reproduces Freud's real world: "father-child relationship goes to work in the analogies between man and society, mother-child is left at home."[53]

Yet, as I hope to have shown in my reading of the three Freudian texts, things are considerably more complicated for Freud. Not only can the distinction between society and home not be maintained, but it is never quite clear who stands for the leader (who is him- or herself always a stand-in) and with whom exactly the child is left at home. Kaplan furthermore accuses Freud of constructing a structural Oedipal drama between an abstract mother and a "cultural" but equally abstract father whose power is passed on between generations through tradition, an abstraction that nevertheless is condemned to reproduce Freud's real world. Freud's are undoubtedly cultural constructions. And just as surely, one of his greatest theoretical failures lies in his inability to come to terms with the role of the mother in psychic development. To some extent, he was forced to acknowledge as much, as he once told the symbolist poet H. D. in her personal analysis with him, "I do not like to be the mother in transference—it always surprises and shocks me a little."[54] The mother occupies for Freud a site of the greatest anxiety and is always closely associated with seething masses, the concept of the uncanny, feelings of the oceanic.[55] At the same time, however, there is something incontrovertible, material, irreducibly bodily about the mother. Maternity, he writes, "is proved by the evidence of the senses while paternity is a hypothesis, based on an inference and a premise."[56] And again, the child "realizes that *'pater semper incertus est,'* while the mother is *'certissima.'*"[57] The role of the father is a hypothesis, a hypothesis whose name was bestowed by Freud. He called it psychoanalysis, or more specifically, the theory of drives. Psychoanalytic language was to be a language of authority, a paternal language of love that would guarantee the birth and life of the subject. But given the uncertainty of the father, indeed his uncanniness, Freud was never quite sure whether the father would turn out good or bad.[58] Furthermore, that this language may have forced Freud to speak from the position of the mother, as psychoanalysis set out to nurture the autonomous subject, caused him considerable anxiety and doubts as to whether psychoanalytic theory itself would be capable of mastering or passing beyond the Oedipus complex.

The difficulty lies precisely in this passing, first of all in the ambiguity of what it means to smash the Oedipus complex: how can the castration of the castration complex (for that is ultimately what the Oedipus complex signifies), how can this act of violence and inhibition of masculinity lead to masculinity and the inhibition of violence, and thus to the construction of the loving social bond? How can this love be anything else but the introjection of repression? How can this love ever be *free* and not always a love for and before power? The problem springs from this internalization of repression, for in some sense the creation of the superego leaves no remainders—it destroys external authority conceived as the good father. Ultimately, there is something quite monstrous about the superego: while Freud designates it as the rightful heir to the Oedipus complex, he nevertheless perceives in it a threat to the Oedipal scenario and the latter's eventual resolution. The superego is a threat to the Oedipal son, for the superego cannot guarantee a peaceful resolution precisely to the extent that it cannot guarantee the continued existence of an *exterior* authority. What Freud seeks to articulate is an ethical space that cannot be reduced to the paradoxical and relentless demands of the superego, which ignores the subject's demand for freedom and love.

Yet Freud has difficulty in determining the precise nature of the super-ego's threat to the psychic economy. There are two reasons for this. First, the superego is heir both to the good and to the bad father: the internalization of authority creates a Kantian subject of culture and autonomy *and* the persecutory, narcissistic father of the primal horde. Freud's ideal leader is a sublimated one, a "secondary leader" who represents ideas and ideals. And yet the process of sublimation can go too far: it can demand a love that generates its own violence, a love that does away with all difference and creates men that masochistically submit to the love of everyone as the love of repression and violence. Second, such sublime love always depends on an overvaluation, and this overvaluation always has the structure of the ego's submission to woman—man will always bear, as the epigraph to this chapter states, the form of a cast of the maternal pelvis. In the end, Freud cannot keep the problem of the uncanny father and the powerful mother apart: put more concretely, Freud becomes increasingly unsure whether the Oedipus complex is threatened by the mother, woman in general, or by historical developments, that is, by those forces that he called cultural adaptability. Freud never gives a straightforward answer to the question whether political threats can only ever be conceived as sexual threats or whether the threat to sexuality always has its source in a political crisis. In a very important sense, a decision on this matter already constitutes a political position, a judgment, that is, on the viability of democratic liberalism. When Freud opts for the first possibility, he is forced to read man's insertion into a social order as inevitably castrating; subjectivity, democracy, and love are nothing here but dreams of the impossible. When he opts for the second possibility, his critique becomes a political critique of liberalism in crisis and of rising authoritarianism. In the end, of course, we are compelled to read Freud at both levels—that is, as a pessimism that was itself constituted by a specifically modern crisis of the subject.

5

THE RHETORIC
OF
POWERLESSNESS

Eine dumme Geschichte, Part III:
The History of the Dominated Woman

The normal woman, when she is overcome by passion, commits suicide rather than a crime, according to Cesare Lombroso. Indeed, the woman in the masochistic fantasy is committed to some form of death in order to redeem the self-sacrificing male. Whether she does this quite literally, as in Wagner's *Parsifal*, or metaphorically by being increasingly replaced by decorative furs and fixed into a painting, as she is in Sacher-Masoch's *Venus in Furs*, does not ultimately matter. What does matter is the difference between female suicide and male masochism. As Barbara Johnson has stated, "when men employ the rhetoric of self-torture, it is *read* as rhetoric. When women employ it, it is confession."[1]

The product of this rhetoric, the Cruel Woman who is erotically loaded but nevertheless cannot be touched, has its source in the phantasmatic creation of the good/bad mother as well as in her inevitable double, the common or vulgar woman as prostitute. This fantasy is given in the nineteenth century the consistency and the scope of a general history of civilization whose ebbs and tides may be read in the face of woman. Johann Bachofen, whose *Mother Right* was published eight years before

Venus in Furs, not only asserted the historical existence of matriarchal forms but understood this past as the very poesis of history itself. Matriarchy constitutes the poetry of history; all fantasy, Bachofen insisted, is concentrated in woman, who thus becomes the marker by which history may be periodized and understood. The first stage of history is that of the uterine mother. She represents natural law, chaos, and the swamps. Aphrodite as the goddess of life and death rules supreme at this stage. During the second stage, the swamps are drained, agriculture becomes the predominant mode of production, marriage is instituted under matriarchal law, and society is ruled by Demeter, the oral goddess of fertility who institutes a strict gynocratic order. The third stage finally establishes patriarchy. This is the properly Oedipal situation where the mother becomes the simultaneous victim and accomplice of the sadistic father. As such an accomplice, the woman turns mean; she is now nothing but a common or vulgar slut.[2]

All three of these women have their counterparts in the cultural fantasy at large. Thus, the uterine woman of the swamps turns up as a creature who is so closely connected to nature that she becomes virtually indistinguishable from it. Like Kundry in Act I, she is the missing link between animal and man on the evolutionary scale and is in constant danger of sliding back on this great chain of being. When woman comes to be identified with Nature, she is condemned to take on the physical attributes of animals or plants. Nineteenth-century iconography is full of such associations: women are represented as or at least in close company with various animals—such as snakes, cats (Sacher-Masoch's personal favorite), or birds (like Freud's vulture)—or in some in-between stage of evolution, and then most likely represented as sphinx.[3] Baudelaire's flowers of evil are distinctly feminine, and so are the syphilitic flowers in Huysmans's nightmare in *Against Nature*. Parsifal comes dangerously close to perdition when flower maidens attempt to seduce him, and Zola in *The Sin of Father Mouret* can placidly state, "At night, this ardent country assumed the tortured arch of a woman consumed by lust." When Nature thus comes to be associated not only with woman (an old association) but, more pointedly, with her sexuality, and when Nature is then viewed as that which must be transcended, as that which is chancy, wasteful, and dangerous, the consequences for women are disastrous. "Nature has had her day," the hero of *Against Nature* announces. Woman in her animal- or plantlike existence seeks to draw man back down the evolutionary scale and make him forget what he is doing. He is supposed to become subservient to her physical needs and thus drain himself of all his energy: "woman became a nightmare emanation from man's distant, pre-evolutionary past, ready at any moment to use the animal attraction of her physical beauty to waylay the late nineteenth-century male in his quest for spiritual perfection. . . . she was a veritable siphon of regression ready to gorge herself on that 'great clot of seminal fluid' of man's brain."[4]

The common, vulgar woman is another favorite construction, and like her natural counterpart, she too is intent on wasting man's brain and seminal fluid. The problem with the prostitute is not only that she has entered into a despicable alliance with the sadistic father, she has also let herself be paid for it. The customer certainly makes a contract with the prostitute—he receives her services for his money—but the commodity has become more powerful than her buyer; she is now a commodity that knows her price. The prostitute is both the site where lust originates and the site of its commodification. In speaking of traitorous armies of prostitutes, nineteenth-century males detected in these women the uncanny ability to destroy fortunes, the arts, and idealist beliefs. One observer notes that in one such incarnation, "Venus-Pandemos triumphed over idealistic aspirations; she ridiculed chastity, the family, the fatherland, the future life, drama and the world of dreams."[5] What the prostitute undermines then is the distinction between work and sexuality, and she thereby threatens the male work of civilization. To make matters worse, the prostitute is allied to the patriarchal order and thus can no longer be distinguished from the wife at home. Ultimately all women are behind the search for gold: "The goods-consuming middle-class wife who spent her husband's hard-earned money and the life-consuming prostitute who took what he had left in exchange for sharply punished dreams of Eros thus blended in the fin-de-siècle male's fantasies to form the primal woman, incessantly voracious in her hunger for gold."[6]

The department store, Rita Felski has argued, became a paradigmatic form of public space that represented and created mass consumption but that linked this consumption with specifically feminine desire. Such mass consumption was figured as feminine and required a new form of subjectivity, one that was "antithetical to old forms of rigid authoritarian masculinity."[7] The "salesman" as the representative of such a new public space turned into the slave of woman's voracious desire. He responded with anxiety to the castrating effects of increasing commodification, a commodification that was leading to the blurring of distinctions between public virtue and private desire. Masochism reflects the attack on and dissolution of the nuclear family in the last years of the nineteenth century; it registers the distance created between family members by compulsive desire and stages the dissolution of family intimacy at the very heart of that intimacy: love is nothing but a war between the sexes; marriage, a trap; and children, simply another means by which women dominate and imprison men.[8]

Poised between the uterine, swamplike woman of nature, on the one hand, and the prostitute and voracious housewife, on the other, stands the product of such staging: the Cruel Woman. She is clearly linked to her sisters in the fast-growing Woman's Movement and will eventually take on an even more spectral existence when she becomes associated with the phantasmatic but ever-dangerous New Woman. This Cruel Woman is in no way an endorsement of women's rights, then. When Sacher-Masoch or Wagner trace her contours, they simply desire to find their erotic place within these historical configurations, an eroticization that derives from an attempt at keeping the woman in their picture in order to prevent her from sliding either into nature or onto the streets.

In the case of Sacher-Masoch, the Cruel Woman must function as the mythical blank screen on which the gazing and gazed at male can project his desire, and she must do so by becoming the embodiment of the gaze. Sacher-Masoch's act of sublimation—his "supersensuality"—creates a cultural but highly sexualized object in the Cruel Woman, the result of which is a suspension of both the possibility of sexuality (there is a remarkable absence of sexuality in *Venus in Furs*) and, paradoxically, a suspension of the creative act: painting can only take place as a non-painting. Ultimately, this paradoxical structure guarantees the masochist's male to have an erection and thus to produce, for he can in this act take for himself the position of man and of woman. The Cruel Woman is therefore neither a phallic substitute for the absent father nor the usurper of the father's phallus.[9] The gaze that Sacher-Masoch seeks to occupy is always an aesthetic gaze, one he conceives as the icily cruel Ideal whose goal it is to bring about a new birth of male subjectivity independently of the mother, to initiate a kind of parthenogenesis. The act of male self-creation always works to the benefit of the son; Sacher-Masoch rewrites the idea of brotherhood by disavowing the father and killing the mother, and he does this rewriting under the sign of a historically predetermined violence. The history of the brotherhood of man is the history of fraternal conflict: *Venus in Furs* constitutes, not coincidentally, a small part of Sacher-Masoch's much more grandly conceived but never completed cycle, *The Legacy of Cain*.[10]

Wagner is in some sense more direct insofar as Parsifal, in order to be both redeemer and redeemed, requires Kundry's death. Nature as Woman has no part in the process of redemption: "Ihn selbst am Kreuze kann sie nicht erschauen: da blickt sie zum erlösten Menschen auf; der fühlt sich frei von Sündenlast und Grauen [She cannot see Him on the Cross: she sees him in redeemed mankind; mankind that is freed from sin's great weight and terror]." The redemption of nature/woman leads to her inevitable but thanked-for death: "Das dankt dann alle Krea- tur, was all da blüht und bald erstirbt, da die entsündigte Natur heut ih- ren Unschuldstag erwirbt [All creatures then give thanks, all that there blooms and soon is to die; for now redeemed nature lives today its day of innocence]." As with Sacher-Masoch, however, sexual desire and aes- thetic production are founded on disavowal and suspense: the sexual act is always posited as nonsexual (Wanda and Severin appear to be having sex, though they are not; Kundry and Parsifal appear to be renouncing the sexual act and thereby have it), while the production of cultural or aesthetic objects is always posited in terms of their impossibility or sus- pension (Sacher-Masoch's men seem no longer able to paint; Wagner's Parsifal brings about a redemption through music but only to the extent that this redemption becomes a simultaneous reassertion of its capacity to inflict wounds). It is through such disavowal and suspense that woman can be finally eliminated from the redemptive process, and man can give birth to himself and his art. The moment of Parsifal's final redemptive sinfulness, his moment of becoming king, is musically expressed as the beautifully painful and yearning "Karfreitagsmusik," said by Wagner to have been the moment of his own act of giving birth to his last opera. In April 1865, Wagner wrote to Ludwig, "Today is Good Friday, again. . . . Most meaningful day in the world! Day of redemption! God's suffer- ing! . . . A warm, sunny Good Friday inspired me by its sacred mood to write the Parsifal which since then has lived and grown inside me like a child in its mother's womb." Man on Good Friday can become both man and woman, and in that act take possession over life and death.

The Blindness of the Gaze

Carl Schorske, in tracing the filaments of the "politics in a new key" of fin-de-siècle Vienna, invites us to imagine "St. Augustine weaving his *Confessions* into *The City of God*, or Rousseau integrating his *Confessions* as a subliminal plot into *The Origins of Inequality*."[11] What constitutes the essence of the new structures of late-nineteenth-century relations of power is just this inscription. Thus, Freud's *Interpretation of Dreams* must, insists Schorske, be read as reflecting its dual nature of both scientific work and personal self-therapy. Although Schorske ultimately, and mistakenly, separates these two levels into surface layer and deeper layer, he has pointed to a crucial aspect of the reorganization of power and culture: the fact that power can now only be read through personal experience or inscription and that personal experience, in turn, can only be made sense of by virtue of its inextricable enmeshment with dominant cultural and political constructions. But the claim is in fact even more radical: Freud was to state, in *The Interpretation of Dreams* as well as in other works, that the very peculiarity of psychoanalysis is constituted by the fact that it is impossible to separate out its subject and object of analysis, that observer and observed came to occupy within psychoanalysis the same position.

As Jonathan Crary has shown, the conflation of subject- and object-position in scientific analysis as well as in cultural or aesthetic practices dates from the beginning of the nineteenth century when the "camera obscura" model of vision, of knowledge, and of representational practices was abandoned in favor of analyses that made vision itself, in the very materiality of the bodily eye, the primary target of investigation. Schopenhauer, for example, rejected models of "the observer as passive receiver of sensation" and posited "a subject who was both the site and producer of sensation."[12] Thus, the postulation of an aesthetic subject who is freed from the demands of both the body and the will, a subject who may occupy the transcendental position of pure perception, of a pure eye, cannot be separated from Schopenhauer's placing this pure perception in the bodily, physiological mechanism of the brain's and the eye's functions. Whereas Schopenhauer places pure aesthetic perception in *physiological* functions in order to avoid the body's instinctual life of ceaseless pulses and desire,[13] Freud places those same aesthetic practices just there, in the *psychological* mechanisms by which all representation (political, aesthetic, and epistemological) comes about. What is novel in such an understanding is not simply such a psychological explanation but the fact that the latter founds itself on a representation of representation—on a language that is at once symptomatic and diagnostic and that, as a consequence, produces a certain unrepresentability.

I have been arguing that the refocus of, if not the challenge to, representation must, when it constructs this challenge in masochistic terms, rely on a very specific gender politics. Nowhere is this made clearer than in a truly amazing analogy Freud makes in "Creative Writers and Day Dreaming," wherein he seeks to show the role of the drives in artistic creation. This analogy is, I hold, a perfect allegory for the masochistic fantasy. The male child, Freud tells us, has two desires: to be like his father (these are identificatory desires of ambition) and to possess his mother (these are erotic desires). But, he continues, not too much emphasis should be given to the opposition between these two desires, for in fact they constitute a unity of desire. He then explains this unity in terms of an analogy: "Just as, in many altar-pieces, the portrait of the donor is to be seen in a corner of the picture, so, in the majority of ambitious phantasies, we can discover in some corner or other the lady for whom the creator of the phantasy [der Phantast] performs all his heroic deeds and at whose feet all his triumphs are laid."[14]

Freud describes then the unity (Vereinigung) of identification and sexual desire not with one picture but with two, and these two pictures are not in themselves identical. I will begin with the altar piece. As Freud tells us, the painting is clearly a religious one: at the center of the painting, elevated above all, stands the deity—let us say, for hypothetical purposes, this deity is embodied in Christ. The donor, by paying for the painting, has put himself into the picture (this is his ambition) in order both to love the deity and to identify himself with the other believers who in all probability are also represented in the painting as a crowd. The second picture, on the other hand—the one created by the daydreamer—requires for its purposes only two people: the hero (the self) and the woman lurking in the corner. Another difference between these two pictures is, however, even more important. Whereas the donor of the first painting is placed in the corner, that is, in the position of an adorer, with his position explicitly marginalized and in a posture of subjection vis-à-vis the god of love, in the second picture the creator of the fantasy *replaces* the deity and stands at the fantasy's center.

This is obviously and clearly a fantasy of ambition, but where is love in this representation? It stands in the corner in the shape of the Lady who presumably adores the hero. However, this is not what Freud says. The hero's centrality is in fact decentered; it succumbs to love, lays its dreams of ambition at the feet of the Lady. The Lady's marginality is actually central, for it is her good will, her position as the giver or donor of favors and mercy, that forces the hero to prostrate himself at her feet. What Freud is describing here is a scene of courtly love as man's submission to narcissistic woman. Here the Lady does not love at all except in her graciousness to accept the lover's love. Man may be ambitious but only to the extent that he submits to the rules of love; the first painting says so explicitly, putting the lover into a marginal position but disguising the gendering of the relation; the second picture disguises man's marginalization but makes explicit its gendering. In the first painting God is alive and well; in the second, God is dead and has been replaced by man himself, but man who is always already castrated in his ambitious desire for self-sufficiency as he is brought to his knees before love's game.

Ambition and love are thus united in a double move: just as the first picture is read by Freud as a representation of love, but a representation that nevertheless has ambition inscribed in it, so also is the second image conceived as a representation of ambition, but one already decentered by the demands of love. In other words, the *Vereinigung* thus established is one not of equality but of power. Why does Freud not recognize this obvious imbalance? Why does he not recognize that the pictures are in fact not analogous and that the analogy he has created is off balance?

Freud practices a certain elision here that centers on the question of who produces these images. In the first, religious painting, it is the donor, not the painter himself, who is included in the painting and in Freud's discussion. Freud provides, in essence, a *description* of a painting that depends on the lack of involvement, or the exclusion, of the images' producer; in other words, it depends on the possibility of perspective. In the case of the daydream, however, we witness a collapse of perspective: the object represented in the image (the daydream's hero) is also the subject who creates the fantasy. The painter is now, if you will, in the painting. But so are its viewers, and this means that we, as these viewers, cannot see the daydream, precisely to the extent that we are participants to it. Descriptive language founders on this paradox. If Freud had described the picture of the daydream, we would see a hero at the center with a woman in the corner at the *man's* feet. If he had placed the man at the woman's feet, he would have had to put the hero in the corner, which is precisely what Freud does not want to show. The second image, that of the daydream or fantasy, is in fact unrepresentable.

What holds Freud's unrepresentable perspective in place? Two limitations, two sources of blindness, are in fact necessary for his analogy to work. First, though the woman, like her predecessor Wanda, is the one adored, she never has the paintbrush in her hands. She always remains an object represented, never the creator of representation. Though the hero may dedicate all his ambitions to her, this dedication is of necessity limited: he cannot so dedicate the fantasy of heroism itself, for this too would take her out of the corner and into the center of the picture. The second limitation depends on a displacement—namely, the fact that between the two pictures, the paintbrush has been exchanged for the pen—the creative writer's and Freud's. The representability of the second image depends on the introduction of a narrative, of a historical dimension; it is a text, not a frozen image. What Freud in fact provides is a historical narrative of both the creation and the simultaneous displacement of male subjectivity, a history that begins with God and with man in the submissive, feminized position of adorer and ends with an ambitious fantasy of the male subject who has taken the place of God but who in that same move finds himself woman's vassal. The dream can continue, however, only if the woman is deprived of both the paintbrush and the pen. Man's castrated existence can only be denied by its simultaneous assertion and its displacement onto woman; his ambition, paradoxically, asserts itself in its submission to the love of woman.

This is the strange unity of ambition and love marked out by Freud, a unity that depends on a peculiar hierarchy that places man at a marginal center and woman into a central, crucial marginality. Sexual bondage is what Freud calls this marginal centrality of man in "The Taboo of Virginity."[15] He takes the term from Krafft-Ebing, who defines it as the conjunction of love and will-lessness in one partner and unbounded narcissism in the other. It would stand to reason that women must on the whole occupy the position of sexual bondage; but this, Freud tells us, is belied by the experience of psychoanalytic practice. Sexual bondage is on the rise in man, and is the result of the *victory* over psychic impotence—that is, the presence of sexual bondage signifies that man has successfully combined affection and sexual desire and produced a lasting love-relation with a woman to whom he is now bound. In effect, it is the marriage contract that creates sexual bondage. Man fears his own dedication to woman. He dreads her not simply because of her mysterious and inexplicable nature, but because a real danger is somewhere present, a danger whose prototype lies in the aftereffect of coitus that produces flaccidity.[16] Man fears that his strength will be taken from him by woman. He dreads being infected by her femininity and thus proving himself a weakling. Freud's analogy both represents this fear and disguises it at the same time; it is disguised as the dream of ambition, whose dangers are displaced on to woman. Woman in this analogy is a truly Lacanian symptom of man: she stands in for and displaces not only man's ambitions but also his own marginality as producer of cultural images.

A similar structure holds for Sacher-Masoch's work as well. By virtue

of their active passivity, his literary heroes are both observer and observed of their own perversions, and it is within this dual structure that
Sacher-Masoch binds himself to his literary creations: both he or his
texts alternately occupy the position of a perversely passive object or an
actively gazing subject who transforms this object into a sublimely aesthetic one. The result is a dizzying display of mirroring between real
life—always already heavily mediated through its presentation—and
the resultant work of art, as well as a peculiar medicalization of his own
condition. Thus, Sacher-Masoch could write into his diary in 1872, "*Venus in Furs* most effectively shows my mode of approach. Used my passions in order to demonstrate by them where pleasure leads when a man
makes himself the victim of a woman; I describe this not as desire, but
condemn it. Furthermore, I too am moral in life; have always conquered
these inclinations because have not found a woman into whose hands I
could confidently commit myself."[17] Although Sacher-Masoch invites a
reductive reading of his texts to his own life and to the historical context
in general, he can only achieve this as long as the Cruel Woman remains
a wish or a myth. Yet myths or cultural fantasies gain and retain their
own truth or consistency, and Sacher-Masoch is both compelled by the
truth of this wider cultural fantasy—he remains its slavish, transferentially bound object,[18] engaging in a mirroring of his life and his history—and actively participates in its making *as* passive mirroring.

Sacher-Masoch cannot conceive of the history of power and passion
without this history being deeply implicated in his own personal, sexual
history. He thus *cultivates* his private obsessions, in both senses of the
term: not only are they a literary event, but they form part of everyday
private and public language. The results of such a strategy are ambiguous. As Koschorke has shown, Sacher-Masoch writes his own life history as inseparable from his most successful literary character, Severin
(Sacher-Masoch invents Severin in order to live his own life according
to the libretto spelled out in *Venus in Furs*). Sacher-Masoch presents his
life as a series of dramatic episodes that come to be indistinguishable
from his narration of historical events. Adjectives like "sumptuous" come
to equally cover women's wardrobes, private, social, and natural events,
as well as the cruelty of women, of social injustices, or of revolutions.
This results in a string of clichés that describe both his family life with
its consonant traumas and fixations, as well as the structures of power
that mark the transition to capitalism in his native Galicia and the political instabilities of the Habsburg Empire. Sacher-Masoch constructs a

conflation of the personal and the public spheres, of sexual and revolutionary passion, where the storming of enemy barracks and the storming of the woman constitute one single event. The following passage comes from one of his first novels:

> [Donski] suddenly however felt a great weight on his shoulders, and with his hands he reached up and felt Wanda's stockings. He looked up and saw her perched on his shoulders while laughing; and as he looked again, he noticed that she had a large mustache and that she was very pale. He stopped short and noticed that his shirt was stuck to him in anxious perspiration. Then suddenly he felt two spurs digging into his sides, he jumped up, rolled over panting. Now he believed to hear his gun explode.[19]

Politics and sexuality, reality and dream, man and woman are semantically so closely intertwined here that "the war logic of passion and the eroticization of political struggle cannot be wrenched apart."[20] Catastrophe inevitably ensues, and the insurrection ends when Wanda is thrown off her horse and cruelly dragged to her death. Although Donski may have dreams of erotic submission, the woman pays for this ambiguous insurrection of the phallus by herself having to die for it passively, literally thrown out of her saddle and out of her role as despotic ruler.

Yet the close enmeshment of private and public life results also in a form of history writing that points to the ever greater difficulty of recognizing a form of law free from the arbitrariness of an unreadable structure of patriarchal power: "I spent my childhood in the house of the police. Very few people remember what this signified in pre-1848 Austria: military police who brought in vagabonds and handcuffed criminals; grim-looking officials; a thin, sneaky censor; spies who dared not look anyone straight in the eye; the flogging bench; barred windows through which peeked here laughing, made-up tarts, there pale, melancholy Polish conspirators. God knows, that was not a happy environment!" Thus Sacher-Masoch describes his childhood memories in the house of his father, the Police Chief of Lemberg.[21] Sacher-Masoch père represented the Austrian absolutist regime of the *Vormärz* years (1840–1848) that became synonymous with the name of Metternich and implied the ruthless suppression of democratic and nationalist elements in Galicia, restrictions on the freedoms of association and of the press, and the infiltration of the police in the private lives of citizens. Sacher-Masoch described the creation of this police network in *Soziale Schatten-*

bilder: Aus den Memoiren eines österreichischen Polizeibeamten (1873) and *Das schwarze Kabinett* (1882), which were probably among his more successful writings. Both the later novella and the earlier collection of short stories rely heavily on his own father's memoirs, *The Polish Revolution* (1863), which described the latter's involvement in the radical suppression of the Polish nationalist movement.

Sacher-Masoch's indictment of his father is never direct but may be inferred from the son's description of a totalitarian world where public and private cannot be kept apart. One of the stories from the *Soziale Schattenbilder* (Social Silhouettes, or Social Phantoms), "The Demented Count," is particularly noteworthy, not only because it follows closely and in condensed form the plot of *Venus in Furs* but also because its masochistic scenario is embedded in an explicitly political context that is perceived as producing this masochistic subject-position and simultaneously leading to its undoing. The story narrates how the cruelty of the law (whose representatives are both the Cruel Woman and the intrusive father) fails to protect the individual and his rights—that is, to the extent this law takes the masochist at his word and cannot allow for a private space of fantasy.

In the tale, a handsome count is married to a good but plain woman whom he wedded on the rebound, having been previously betrayed by a beautiful and highly intelligent woman. Although it is stressed that the count is himself an excellent father and actively involved in his children's education, he has nevertheless developed some peculiar habits that result from the fact he has divided women into two groups: women who, like his wife, are good but without charm and intelligence, and women who are beautiful and intelligent but evil. What he requires of the latter type is "honesty in sin," that is, the courage to be domineering and cruel in their relationships with men. From this fantasy, the count develops a secret preference for furs, "best explained by the electricity of the latter," and in this manner his "fantasy ideal turned into a very specific wardrobe." Needless to say, the count's ideal materializes in the shape of Bella Hartmann, the children's new governess, a woman "perfectly innocent in the eyes of the world but hardly in those of the psychologist." The ensuing events are predictable: the count falls in love with the dominatrix Bella, leaves his wife and children, and marries the Cruel Woman. Life with this Messalina follows the pattern of life with Wanda: the count signs over his life and his property to her and suffers from her betrayals.

The denouement closely resembles the scene with the Greek in *Venus in Furs*, though the political implications are here more explicitly stated, for the other man is a representative of the new disciplinary power. Bella has brought in the director of a mental institution, who hides behind the curtains of her boudoir and is allowed to witness a whipping scene. The count is declared mentally unstable and taken off to the asylum. The final paragraph links the masochism of the story directly with the failure of the legal system to provide justice. One year after the "catastrophe," rumors spread that the count's fate had been the result of a crime. An investigation ensues, but the police, having arrived at the mental asylum, find the count now truly insane. "The straight-jacket and the cruel whippings at the hand of his torturers, which obviously caused him less pleasure than those of the beautiful Bella, had made him indeed insane. It was one of those not rare cases where punitive justice recognized itself as completely impotent and where it had to leave retribution to other, higher powers."[22]

The construction of the masochistic subject as one that embodies an active passivity in the form of an identity between observer and observed, or between patient and clinician, has a concrete, specific place within the history of modern male subjectivity. Fin-de-siècle culture constructs male subjectivity as one where desire and law come to be inextricably entwined, where pleasure is only conceivable in terms of one's relationship and involvement with power. Two interrelated consequences follow from this new connection between pleasure and power. First, desire becomes both continuous with and beyond cultural norms— the desire to subvert the law is itself a form of lawfulness;[23] second, this new relationship between desire and law is reinscribed in patriarchal terms, though these terms are no longer unambiguously structured according to Oedipal logic. The male offspring of liberalism only imperfectly occupies the place left vacant by the dead father. Male subjectivity can only be conceived as one that is fundamentally traumatized, and the origin of that trauma is the Cruel Woman in all her possible variations: mother, prostitute, saint, vampire, sphinx. What emerges is a tragically incomplete or mutilated masculinity whose very center is his self-punishment: "the image of a neurotic father burdened by his own authority, tormented as well by his unfulfilled dreams and aspirations . . . became the central metaphor for the production of culture. That image refigured identity in terms of a new kind of selfhood rooted paradoxically in a desire for selflessness, in a kind of death wish."[24]

The nineteenth century rescinds on the postulation of a free, autonomous subject by formulating relentless natural laws of evolution and by insisting that culture and society demand acts of renunciation. Self-determination is thus transformed into self-renunciation or self-sacrifice as the primary mode by which the social subject is constituted; and political guilt, as Pascal Bruckner has remarked, is transformed into metaphysical guilt.[25] The bourgeois subject comes to be defined as both mover and victim of social relations; he is the subject of his own submission and must suffer on his own body his self-created laws that have the force of a cosmic determination. The bourgeois male thus comes to know his subjectivity in terms of his own marginalization. Within this process of marginalization, history—as it traumatically creates and disrupts this new subjectivity—is not that which must be worked through but indeed constitutes the moment of the subject's salvation.

Crucial to the constitution of the marginal male is a reworking of the masochistic contract, which has a structure similar to that of the Freudian superego; indeed, one may argue that the superego is Freud's own formulation of this new contract. Thus, like the superego, the masochistic contract reverses the relationship between guilt and punishment, between pleasure and punishment. Transgression here has always already happened vis-à-vis a law that must remain indeterminate and where guilt is inevitably present before the act. It is this punishment that is erotically cathected; it comes to stand for what Lacan has termed *jouissance*. Punishment in the masochistic universe does not prohibit or prevent erections but, as Deleuze has remarked, guarantees them.[26] What the contract stages, therefore, is not the transition from violence to legality but a law that moves back to its origins in violence. Most fundamentally, the masochistic contract lends the traumatic insertion of the subject into the symbolic order a language by which to represent this violence. Catastrophe, as Koschorke puts it, gains a contractual form; anxiety or fear, by an act of pure decision, is transformed into order. In this sense, the contract acts as a parody of relations of power, constituting a parody in a double sense: it both exposes the relentlessness of the law and the impossibility of a nontraumatized existence, and it stages this trauma as willing consent; on the other hand, it must simultaneously present itself as rhetorical gesture: the masochist must seem to be held by real chains but may be bound only by his words. The words of the contract are experienced, as Victor Smirnoff has stated, not as a fatality but as a branding, since it is not by "the absolute power of the other, but by the fictitious power that he himself has bestowed on the executioner" that the contract is set into motion and is thus maintained.[27] The willed enslavement that the contract initiates may be never more than a verbal en-slavement; the contract can only work if it constitutes a form of role playing. This is the source of Sacher-Masoch's culturalism, of his move to aestheticize politics. Participation in this contract requires that the masochist occupy a double position: he must be the victim, the sacrifice or object of the contract, and yet he must always remain its originator as fully autonomous subject. In other words, the masochist must always be in the position of witnessing his own victimization.

This double position as both subject and object of the masochistic scenario leads, almost inevitably, to the masochist's undoing. Like Seve-rin, who must either die as a result of his own imposed conditions or break the contract with his executioner, Parsifal—the new, foolish hero, who is both redeemer and redeemed, both witness to and source of a generalized crisis in the symbolic order—is in the last act of Wagner's last opera reduced, like Kundry, into a paradoxical silence. Parsifal has usurped the woman's voice, but the price for this theft is a high one, for in the end, in the absence of all difference, what is left for Parsifal is an empty act of ritual consent, a "tautological performative" through which he takes on himself the symbolic mandate of an ultimately mute power.[28] "The corollary of a negation of otherness," writes Juliet Flower McCannell in a different context, "is an act of sacrificing the other to the benefit of the self, a self staged as an ethical sacrifice to society, and a so-ciety which is only a disguised form of the ego."[29] Redemption—like the masochistic contract—is a purely performative gesture, both because all resistance has been silenced and because, in its very emptiness, it can only ever be a repetition of the sin that it seeks to renounce. With the spear recaptured from Klingsor, Parsifal may reinflict the wound on Am-fortas and thus heal him. Redemption can only be instantiated as a re-wounding—and in that gesture Parsifal establishes himself as the new authority. Parsifal's deed of redemption is postulated as a non-deed—he again in the third act must lay down his weapons and recognize his own innocence in the form of his sinning nature. When Gurnemanz anoints Parsifal as the new king, Parsifal becomes a law unto himself, a law that is radically other but that also destroys all difference. The odd quality of *Parsifal*'s third act, its static character, is symptomatic of this silent dom-ination as rhetorical, repetitive gesture. Act III is fundamentally a repe-tition of the first act and thus does not provide anything dramatically new to what has preceded it. The game is already played out by the end of the second act.

The Silence of the Voice

Why then did Wagner compose a third act? How to explain the strange supplementarity of Wagner's final musical composition? It is possible to argue that Wagnerian opera is, along with the soprano, functionally dead by the end of the second act, and that the third act is thus either no longer opera or simply no longer necessary. Indeed, musically, the third act is much closer to oratorio than opera conceived either in traditional or in Wagnerian terms. The immediate comparison that this invites is Schoenberg's great "anti-*Parsifal*" opera, *Moses und Aron*. Like Wagner, Schoenberg was directly concerned with the problem of the relationship between music and words, and the questions that this relationship posed for the problem of (religious) representation. Schoenberg never composed music for his last act, and all that remains is the text: he thus, whether intentionally or not, ended with the assertion of the power of the word as the interdiction of representation, at which point music must fall silent.

Wagner, on the other hand, makes Parsifal quite literally into the mouthpiece of the sacred or the sublime, into the transsexually sublime object of desire: the voice of God. Paradoxically, however, Wagner could only do this through a Promethean theft of that which belonged to the gods, and while aspiring to bring about divine presence, what he assured was its ultimate undoing. The joys of self-division posited as the presence of sublime pain, the pleasures of the perverse body wounded and yet redeemed by the immediacy of sound—these in the end can generate only a cynical distanciation, a form of exhibitionism that plays at being seriously concerned with salvation. In his flight from the banal, from the secularization and commodification of art, he contributed to and guaranteed precisely its quality as commodity.

"Amfortas must yearn for the boon of that blood which erst flowed from the Saviour's like spear-wound, when, world-renouncing, world-redeeming, He pined world-suffering on the Cross! Blood for blood, wound for wound—but from here to there what a gulf between this blood, this wound!" Richard Wagner wrote these words to Mathilde Wesendonck almost a quarter of a century before the actual composition of *Parsifal*, and yet they capture the very essence of his last opera. *Parsifal* stages a crisis in the symbolic order, a rift or gulf—a wound—that has the fundamental structure of a paradox. Indeed, it is not simply that the existence of paradox wounds the integrity of a seemingly seamless symbolic universe but, perhaps more crucially, that the cure to the crisis generated by the paradox is the paradoxical nature of the crisis itself. Blood is the cure for blood, wound the cure for wound, a set of identical substitutions, and yet there exists a gulf—one that opens out onto an abyss of sacrificial substitutions and onto the space from within which Wagner will compose, twenty-five years later, its cure, its ground. The crisis of the symbolic order *Parsifal* stages is marked by the creation and undoing of a series of binary oppositions: between inside and outside, sign and referent, body and language, male and female, visibility and invisibility, self and other, sacred and profane, redemption and sin, law and transgression, activity and passivity, suspense and resolution. However, the creation and undoing of these oppositions is, within Wagner's particular brand of masochistic aesthetics, anything but subversive. Instead, it relies on, indeed generates, a crazed bloodletting or sacrificial mechanism that creates a new form of male subjectivity (the masochist) as well as a new community that is bound together by a repetitive, narcissistic identification with a leader who exacts a hypnotic spell over the community in the form of a re-embodied voice of conscience.

The "wound is healed only by the spear that caused it" is, as Adorno has said, the motto for Wagner's mode of composition. Yet it is the religious quality of *Parsifal* that demands filmlike techniques of transformation, and it is precisely the magic of the opera that conjures up its antithesis, to wit, the mechanical work of art. Wagner transposed masochistic subjectivity as the subjectivity that gives up all in order to gain all onto opera as an art form. In the name of worldly sensualism, he generated a physiological inscription of the body through sound; within the structure of what Kittler calls Wagner's respiratory erotics, acoustic effects replace the symbolic order whereby the unthinkable becomes audible: "Under such conditions, even the most hallucinatory and phantasmagorical claims come true, simply because they cannot be sung. . . . In the orchestra, the dead Tristan experiences an acoustic erection."[30]

Wagner's subject abdicates sovereignty and renounces the possibility of giving shape to time; he projects the "ground of Being as a metaphysical catastrophe."[31] The opera's characters lose their empirical existence in time (at Montsalvat, Gurnemanz tells Parsifal, time becomes space) and, like the Grail and the spear, are transferred to the realm of the sacred as universal symbols. Wagner's *Parsifal* is both secular and magical at the same time. The composer has brought us, insists Adorno, into the realm of myth, a secular myth that rejects both the transcendental and the empirical and that can posit a reconciliation of opposites only under the sign of an eternal ambiguity. Indeed, *Parsifal*'s music remains both fundamentally indeterminate, fully suspended, and yet completely resolved. It exhibits the narcissistic wound of subjectivity and claims this exhibition as its own resolution. Resolution is itself a form of suspension, a failed synthesis of expression and gesture where signifiers and signified remain exchangeable. Despite the claim to a total work of art, Wagner's music drama remains fragmented and disjointed, forever parading its wounds, which nevertheless gush forth a musical intensity designed to obliterate all resistance. This is where it also undoes itself: "The more triumphantly Wagner's music resounds," says Adorno, "the less capable it is of discovering an enemy to subdue within itself."[32] By usurping the operatic voice, *Parsifal* turns musical composition into love as torture and thereby, paradoxically, puts an end to opera.

In the end, of course, Wagner made larger claims than Sacher-Masoch had ever dreamed of. Whereas Sacher-Masoch perhaps sought to reduce history to a bedroom drama, Wagner's conflict between hammer and anvil was to forge the sword that would bring about national renewal and racial purity. In part this was because music, and Wagnerian music in particular, held a special place in the nineteenth-century quest not only for "great art" but for an art that was to have authority, that was, in other words, to be an official art. That music appeared to lend itself particularly to the displacement of religion into a "religion of art" not only was due to the secular need for lost emotions but also was related to music's historical connection with the unrepresentable expression of emotions—that is, to the sublime. Opera more than any other art form lent itself to combining what Kant had determined are the three ways of presenting the sublime: tragedy in verse, sacred oratorio, and the didactic or philosophical poem. There were also other, more historical reasons why opera or musical drama could function as a vehicle for religious displacements. As Lacoue-Labarthe has argued, musical drama owed its strength to what was also its greatest weakness: despite the constant claims that music was the recomposition of ancient music and drama, there were in fact no records of this music, and for that reason music, in total ignorance of these ancient models, was forever compelled to completely reinvent itself. Music had no predecessors and was thus immediately modern. The ideology of opera as an art form that is always already past or passé, as an art that seeks to (re)capture the voice already lost, is a symptom both of this modernity that insists on its own traditional foundations and of its constitutive desire, its quest for the divine, maternal voice. Furthermore, as the site of extraordinary technological innovation, both in its instrumentation and its application,[33] music was, as it developed during the nineteenth-century, the first mass art to be born, and it thus established, especially in Wagner, an inherently close connection to politics and to the latter's aestheticization.[34] In the form of a pure music, Wagner sought to create a form of expression that was at once entirely subjective and German *as well as* universal and supranational. Whereas music was to emerge from the isolated "nooks" of Germany, in the depth of the German soul, it was also to transcend all languages and become the spontaneous expression of feeling.[35] For Wagner, music "has the power to *conciliate*, to unify different forms, and that is why it dominates, why it is 'sovereign'; but it also has the power to *resolve* . . . , that is to say to *sublate* the mind—which is enslaved to language—in and through feeling, and that is why it provides the 'universal organ.'"[36] The paradox of Wagner's music drama is that it is at once intensely private or subjective but only insofar as it also demands a theater or a public staging of this privacy. His music drama becomes identical or identified with the constitution of a people-subject, of the constitution of the German political community as a work of art.

Wagner's self-obliterating individual, his "impotent petitioner" before the law,[37] who is both a result and a function of this new political order, rests therefore most comfortably within dominant relations of power: the goal for Wagner is always containment, both aesthetically and politically. That "each art demands, as soon as it reaches the limits of its power, to give a hand to the neighboring art" does not signify the radical critique of existing art forms but, as Lacoue-Labarthe has argued, the containment of their possible excesses. Yet Wagner achieved this containment precisely in the name of excess: he played the victim and invited others to do the same. He staged what Georges Bataille has called the three luxuries of nature—eating, death, and sexual (re)production—as a system of absolute expenditure that must nevertheless submit to the rigorous laws of his new aesthetic production.[38]

Ultimately, the *Schadenfreude* that is projected onto Kundry is Wagner's own. The language of the victim that Parsifal usurps from Kundry is a masochistically structured language of the new master, the language Bram Dijkstra has described as spoken by the executioner's assistant.[39] Masculine degradation and bankruptcy—"a bankruptcy of the father and manly authority"—along with the persecuting mother, unite in Wagner to create bureaucratic, technocratic man as the privileged subjectivity of what Kristeva calls post-Catholic destiny.[40] Ivan Nagel describes the law of this new technocratic man in the following terms:

The disabled self survives the annihilation of the autonomous subject, which it announces, by excepting itself (as a political theologian or mythologist) from the common fate: to be the self-appointed spokesman of mute domination. It prophesies, propagates a new world of sacrifice, whose murderous law is impenetrability—and whose murderous impenetrability will be called law. Soon, Franz Kafka's tales and Carl Schmitt's jurisprudence will mock the enlightened demand for clear and accessible laws as liberal hairsplitting; indeed such querulous claims of the individual will constitute, for the court of mythical willfulness, proof of his guilt, the very reason for his condemnation.[41]

Parsifal, the very quintessence of this new form of subjectivity, is one prototype of this new bureaucratic man. Parsifal not only mocks all liberal claims to just and clear laws as hairsplitting but finds it necessary, in the third act, to have his feet washed with that same hair. As Adorno has remarked, Wagner—and here, perhaps, lies his most radical difference from Freud—fundamentally distrusts the private realm that might possibly furnish a defense against the law's simultaneous impenetrability and persecutory nature. Wagner's creation of his *Gesamtkunstwerk* is inevitably totalitarian and administrative:

> He belongs to the first generation to realize that in a world that has been socialized through and through it is not possible for an individual to alter something that is determined over the heads of men. Nevertheless, it was not given to him to call the overarching totality by its real name. In consequence it is transformed for him into myth. The opacity and omnipotence of the social process is then celebrated as a metaphysical mystery by the individual who becomes conscious of it and yet ranges himself on the side of its dominant forces. Wagner has devised the ritual of permanent catastrophe. His unbridled individualism utters the death sentence on the individual and its order.[42]

Resistance with Wagner becomes identical to domination, and salvation can only ever be conceived as another form of destruction. This is the source of Wagner's ambiguity, an ambiguity that becomes the very principle of his style. Indetermination becomes the main form of aesthetic expression because it simultaneously insists on the inherent weakness and unfettered individuality of the subject. Wagner is the "prophet of indeterminacy," a fact that comes powerfully to the fore in his music for *Parsifal*:

The music of *Parsifal* reflects the greater concern with those more passive yet responsive states of mind that rituals encourage; . . . the dramatic theme of renunciation produces music in which the potential of the thematic material, whether chromatic or diatonic, is contemplated and explored with the greatest intensity, even if the music itself is often more reticent, more concentrated than is typical of the earlier works. . . . its music has most to offer to those who fully appreciate the structural strength as well as the expressive power of the "pure" music dramas which precede it and prepare for it . . . the most fundamental lesson to be learned from all the music dramas, though most specifically from *Parsifal*.[43]

Like Wagner, Sacher-Masoch participates in redefining this new male subjectivity, and it is noteworthy how ordinary he really is among the producers of late-nineteenth-century culture. Despite his own claims, he is neither particularly pathological nor particularly subversive when compared to the norm. In a rhetorical gesture, he, like Wagner, transforms a generally repressive climate into a theatrical act, the violence of power into the violence of aesthetic impressions, inviting his perversions to be read as fundamentally strategic. As the son of the Lemberg chief of police, who had witnessed public floggings and executions during his childhood, Sacher-Masoch succeeds in recoding the father's administrative gaze as an aesthetic one:

As Austrian centralism becomes increasingly weaker during the course of the nineteenth century, the state's political conduct comes to rely more and more on theatrical metaphors until finally the fin-de-siècle death dance transforms this rottenness and disintegration of the Empire into a pleasurable aesthetic object. The thinking of order has the schizophrenic ability to metaphorically incorporate pleasure in disorder, at least as long as this disorder remains within the realm of metaphor, as long as it does not transgress the picture frame.[44]

Although Wagner's and Sacher-Masoch's disabled self, their decentered, marginalized subjectivity, is rhetorical, it nonetheless constitutes a rhetoric in a new key, a key that now seeks to adjust itself to the rapidly changing economic and political relations of a mature but nevertheless crisis-ridden capitalism. These new relations were destroying the classic self-made man in order to make room for a far more depersonalized rule of finance capital. This new rhetoric does not disguise real power relations but reorganizes them in the form of an aestheticized politics. While Bram Dijkstra quite correctly places this new masochistic subjectivity squarely within the triad of class, gender, and race, he nevertheless tends to view this masochism as a new form of false consciousness, as a new installment of petty bourgeois ideology.[45] "Masochism is the opiate of the executioner's assistant," he paraphrases Marx, and the masochist is the "little man"—the typical representative of the lumpen proletariat, if you will, who has been excluded from real power relations but who usurps the position of victim while dreaming of having his master as his slave:[46]

> He has no personal being, feeding on defeat to turn his personal, parasitic existence into a secret mirror world of the executioner's values. In this realm of moonlight and looking-glass magic, of fantastic dreams and majestic feats of submission, he tries to make the executioner see him as the threat he very well knows he isn't by manipulating the master into dealing with his pointless servant as if he were a meaningful, threatening victim: for, at least so the executioner's assistant has come to believe, a victim has individual being in the eyes of the master, while the servant has none. Thus, in his fantasies the executioner's assistant becomes master over his boss by making his master be slave to his wishes.[47]

Dijkstra claims that the masochist, requiring a substitute for this boss, picks someone who will do his bidding and beat him—namely, women, particularly the masochist's wife. It is the construction of the Cruel Woman that allows the masochist to turn his marginalized existence into a mirror image of dominant power relations, thus making the masochist into the executioner's perfect assistant by ensuring the proper continuation of the rituals of power. Dijkstra thus posits what he calls an "imperial sadist," who continues to hold the reins of "real" power.

Yet this imperial sadist is an ever-receding figure who, instead of occupying the site of real power, functions like Lacan's *"point de capiton"*—that is, as the necessary hypothesis of power—in order to thereby construct the figure of the assistant. In this sense, masochism is less the ideology of the executioner's assistant than the ideology of the son who has executed the executioner. This would then be Kafka's world of assistants, where the master becomes ever more ephemeral and certainly more inscrutable, a symbolic structure of power constructed on the postulation of the phallus that does not really exist but which nevertheless founds this order. Power, in this new, dispersed, and discursive form, power as disciplinary or administrative practice, is experienced as a Schreberian rottenness in the system that nevertheless is acceded to as pleasurable aesthetic practice.[48] To no small measure this is due to the fact that the law is re-gendered, that is, rhetorically given over to the Cruel Woman. Within the masochistic universe, law is a capricious woman that can no longer guarantee either formal neutrality or a certain predictability in remaining aloof.[49] This law as a cruel maternal force exacts its ruthless persecution not in the form of a law to be obeyed but as a relentless gaze and a relentless voice against which even the forces of repression stand impotent.[50]

Great Men

Freud, too, was the author of a final third act, and like *Parsifal* it centered on the themes of the religious leader and the creation of a community of believers. Unlike Wagner, however, Freud harbored significant doubts regarding the text's publication. The essay in question—one of Freud's last—is "Moses, His People and Monotheistic Religion," written in 1938 after the appearance of two other essays that together with the third appeared as *Moses and Monotheism*. Freud's hesitations in publishing the final part of his book on Moses were largely political: fearing that his text may offend Catholic readers at a time when "progress" had "allied itself with barbarism," Freud believed it was the Catholic Church that had resisted the forces of National Socialism and that the Jews of Europe were therefore living under the Church's protection.[51] So he stated in the first preface to the text, written in Vienna prior to the *Anschluß*. Six months later, from London, Freud added a second preface and at last published his essay, the Catholic Church now proven "a broken reed" (57).

Freud's conviction as to the correctness of conclusions reached already in 1912 with the publication of *Totem and Taboo* is unwavering and repeatedly if not compulsively asserted in *Moses and Monotheism* (58, 130, 132). These conclusions refer specifically to Freud's myth of the slaying of the primal, narcissistic father by his sons as the foundation of subsequent social, religious, and cultural developments. *Moses and Monotheism*—especially "Moses, His People and Monotheistic Religion"—repeats this myth as it concerns the constitution of the Jewish people. As in his earlier cultural writings, Freud articulates the death of the primal father to the problematic political question of this father's successor: the band of the surviving sons, matriarchy, and leaders or "great men" of history. The great leader is what most occupies Freud in this late text; indeed, it constitutes the very essence of the "Moses problem": "How is it possible for a single man to evolve such extraordinary effectiveness that he can form a people out of random individuals and families, can stamp them with their definite character and determine their fate for thousands of years? Is not a hypothesis such as this a relapse into the mode of thought which led to myths of a creator and worship of heroes, into times in which the writing of history was nothing more than a report of the deeds and destinies of single individuals, of rulers or conquerors?" (107). Freud wonders then whether his own recuperation of the figure Moses could possibly be another form of *Vatersehnsucht*, a repetition in and as historiography of the religious dynamic itself. And yet Freud also announces his thesis as a denial of such a leader to the people: "To deprive a people of the man whom they take pride in as the greatest of their sons is not a thing to be gladly or carelessly undertaken," he states at the very beginning of *Moses and Monotheism* (7).

The first two sections of *Moses and Monotheism* had produced the now well-known but controversial thesis that the founding of the Jewish religion was based in a double structure:

> *two* groups of people who came together to form the nation, *two* kingdoms into which this nation fell apart, *two* gods' names in the documentary sources of the Bible . . . the foundation of *two* religions—the first repressed by the second but nevertheless later emerging victoriously behind it, and *two* religious founders, who are both called by the same name of Moses and whose personalities we have to distinguish from each other. All these dualities are the necessary consequence of the first one: the fact that one portion of the people had an experience which must be regarded as traumatic and which the other portion escaped. (52)

The traumatic experience undergone by part of the people was the slaying of Moses, their leader. And yet Freud, at the conclusion of Part II, feels that much has been left undone: though he has established the presence of a trauma at the foundation of history, he has not explained how, despite this trauma, leadership and a national tradition can nevertheless come into being. Thus he ends Part II: "What the real nature of a tradition resides in, and what its special power rests on, how impossible it is to dispute the personal influence upon world-history of individual great men, what sacrilege one commits against the splendid diversity of human life if one recognizes only those motives which arise from material needs, from what sources some ideas (and particularly religious ones) derive their power to subject both men and peoples to their yoke—to study all this in the special case of Jewish history would be an alluring task" (52–53). Freud succumbs to this alluring task by writing "Moses, His People and Monotheistic Religion," and what he seeks to establish is the specifically Jewish response to the memory of murder.

Although Freud was accused of having been the actual slayer of Moses, of having deprived the Jewish people of its great leader, he will, in fact, in the very moment of that repeated murder, see himself as recuperating that ideal as sublimated leadership. Freud's final version of the primal myth constitutes a return to but also a fuller elaboration of his earlier theory of the leader, a far more complicated articulation of the role of the superego in history and an attempt at taking national character traits into account as the moment where the leader (individual psychology) and the people (mass psychology) come together as the foundation for a specifically national tradition. Freud retells the myth of the slaying of the all-powerful, narcissistic father by the sons; the latter's cannibalistic incorporation of him; the consequent establishment of a social contract of common renunciation via the taboo of incest and the laws of exogamy; the mother's occupation of the dead father's now vacant place; the memory of the father expressed in totemism as the earliest form of religious sentiment; the humanization of the deities; and the replacement of the mother through a restitution of the patriarchal order. It is this last moment that initiates a "great social revolution" (83), both in history and in Freud's theory: "The male deities appear first as sons beside the great mothers and only later clearly assume the features of father-figures" (83). It is this new countenance of religious authority that brings about the next step in history, one not previously emphasized in Freud's narrative: the *return*, as the return of the repressed, of the omnipotent father.

Why does this father return? What gives him his power? The omnipotent father returns because "each portion [of memory] which returns from oblivion asserts itself with peculiar force, exercises an incomparably powerful influence on people in the mass," and because such a memory "raises an irresistible claim to truth against which logical objections remain powerless" (85). The father who returns is not the same primeval father: his authority is no longer inherent but given to him by his sons; the act of memory functions here as an act of investiture. The father returns as the force of memory, understood by Freud as the working of tradition and as a form of knowledge that properly belongs to the masses: "It seems, rather, as though there must have been something present in the ignorant masses, too, which was in some way akin to the knowledge of the few and went half way to meet it when it was uttered" (94); and "men have always known . . . that they once possessed a primal father and killed him" (101). The father comes back, then, in sublimated form, first as the *substitute* for or the embodiment of this memory of the people in the shape of the leader, and later, once the leader himself has been killed, as the bodiless monotheistic God of the Jews. The Mosaic God is the effect of the traumatic murder of the father, an effect that does its work retroactively as both sublimating and sublimated displacement and substitution.

Precisely because the Jewish God is a sublimation that gains its power from the strength of a repressed memory (the memory of the murder of the primal father, of the leader, of Moses), because it constitutes a specific form of knowledge, this God will demand and receive the molding of a people with definite national characteristics. Jewish monotheism constitutes the meeting point, the compromise formation, between the knowledge of the people and the knowledge of the few. It was, according to Freud, the great man Moses who forged this knowledge into a set of national character traits and into a coherent religious ethic: "it was the man Moses who imprinted" the Jewish people with a national character and made this character "a part of their religious faith" (106); "it was this one man Moses who created the Jews" (106). What is the character of the religiously constituted Jewish people? How was one single man able to create this people?

Moses was able in ways that had never occurred in history before to harness and absorb the desire and love for the father and make them his own. It was this love that then came to be reversed, transformed into his and God's love for the people, thus producing the first character trait of the Jews: their sense of having been chosen as the father's first object of love. Jews thus believe to have a singular relationship to God and consequently have produced a strong sense of self-confidence vis-à-vis other peoples. Nevertheless, this self-confidence had a price, for it was founded in a strict ethics of instinctual renunciation and a parallel articulation of God as more grandiose than any other deity. The bedrock of the greatness of God as ethical God was the prohibition against making any representation of him, the compulsion, that is, of worshiping an invisible God. For Freud this was crucial, for it signified the moment where sense perception was subordinated to an abstract idea: it was "a triumph of intellectuality over sensuality, or, strictly speaking, an instinctual renunciation accompanied with all its necessary psychological consequences" (113). This, "one of the most important stages on the path to hominization," created a realm of intellectuality where "ideas, memories and inferences" took priority over the immediate perceptions of the sense organs. The birth of intellectuality gave rise to the very possibility of the father, since "maternity is proved by the evidence of the senses while paternity is a hypothesis, based on an inference and a premiss" (113–14).[52] Intellectuality, as the victory over the senses in the form of both instinctual renunciation and intellectual sublimation, explains the Jewish sense of superiority vis-à-vis those who remain "under the spell of sensuality" (115), as well as the fact that "the scattered people" have been held together as an intellectual community gathered around the study of the Holy Writ.

To say, however, that Jewish self-confidence is a result of the subordination of the body to the mind is not in itself sufficient. Instinctual renunciation must be internalized. It must derive, states Freud, from inner motives; otherwise, Mosaic leadership would be nothing but another form of arbitrary and authoritarian rule that founds itself on the external act of prohibition. An agency is required that has as its specific function the capacity to observe, criticize, and prohibit. Freud of course names this agency the superego. It is the superego that provides the ego with a compensatory satisfaction: in order to counteract the unpleasure of instinctual renunciation, obedience and submission become pleasurable because they are felt to be morally and ethically uplifting. Under the hegemony of the superego, submission and instinctual renunciation become pleasurable. At the level of "mass psychology," this internalized agency of observation, reflection, deduction, memory, and prohibition nevertheless has a body—to wit, the leader or the "great man." The "great man is precisely the authority for whose sake the [ethical] achievement is carried out; and, since the great man himself operates by virtue of his similarity to the father, there is no need to feel surprise if in group psychology the role of superego falls to him" (117). The leader is a substitute for the superego, which in turn is a substitute for the original murdered father of the primeval horde. This original father is, however, never quite original, for he himself is the result of a *decision* "against direct sense-perception [maternity] in favour of what are known as the higher intellectual processes [paternity]" (117)—an inevitably arbitrary decision, since there is proof only for maternity. Hence Freud's extraordinary conclusion: "in the case of some advances in intellectuality—for instance, in the case of the victory of patriarchy—*we cannot point to the authority which lays down the standard which is to be regarded as higher. It cannot in this case be the father, since he is only elevated into being an authority by the advance itself*" (118; my emphasis).

This is the very essence of Freud's understanding of the victory of intellectuality over the body. The new authority founded by Moses and later taken over by the Prophets is one that by its very nature must be always displaced and replaced, though what it displaces and replaces is itself only ever a retroactive hypothesis. Its ethical nature requires it to be in a constant state of dissolution: "even the demand for belief in [God] seems to take second place in comparison with the seriousness of these ethical requirements" (119). The Jewish religion survives, paradoxically, the death of its own God. The fragility that pertains to Freud's hypothesis of paternity—a hypothesis that has the death of the father inscribed into it—is, however, also threatened by another instability. As Thomas Laqueur has correctly pointed out, the victory of mind over matter constitutes the essence of Freud's definition of hysteria: the hysteric exhibits symptoms that derive not from the body but from unconscious ideas that are somatically expressed. Female sexuality, for Freud, comes into being precisely on the basis of this same movement: the maturing woman transfers sexual excitation from the clitoris to the vagina, a hysterical cathexis "that works against the organic structures of the body. Like the missing-limb phenomenon, it involves feeling what is not there."[53] Woman, like the idea of fatherhood, is thus not a natural category but a social role imposed by the process of civilization. Ultimately, Freud's invention or hypothesis of vaginal orgasm is homologous to his hypothesis of the victory of intellectuality over both sense perception and the body—paternity is grounded in a kind of feminization, a form of hysterical renunciation and an investment of an imagined body with a new form of pleasure.

Freud cannot help feeling that his own hypothesis about the constitution of the Jewish people through the hypothesis of the father is "somehow or other unsatisfying" (123). A certain uneasiness lingers, linked as it is to the content of the repressed memory about the father. At the end of Freud's text, this repressed memory returns and is articulated not as an ambivalence of gender construction but as the essential ambivalence that pertains to the relationship between *father and son*. Although the mother as much as the father had been killed for the sake of the civilizing process, she never returns to haunt the son's memory. Moses himself apparently repressed one important factor in the father-son relationship: the Jewish religion of the father had not guaranteed a space for the "direct expression of the murderous hatred of the father. All that could come to light was a mighty reaction to it—a sense of guilt on account of that hostility, the bad conscience for having sinned against God and for not ceasing to sin" (134). The sadistic side of the superego, hitherto completely ignored in Freud's text, returns as a debt never paid: the Jewish "rapture of moral asceticism" is unable to disavow its "origin from the sense of guilt felt on account of a surpressed hostility to God." Ethical ideals "possess the characteristic—uncompleted and incapable of completion—of obsessional neurotic reaction-formation" (134–35). They find renewed expression in the words of Saul of Tarsus, a Roman citizen also known as Paul. Expiation of guilt through the sacrificial death of God *as* son replaced "the blissful sense of being chosen" with "the liberating sense of redemption" (135). The birth of Christianity is the most radical expression of the return of the repressed: "It was as though Egypt was taking vengeance once more on the heirs of Akhenaten" (136). Christianity posited a reconciliation between father and son while at the same time manifesting itself in the Son—that is, the son became the father and was condemned, in this very act of reconciliation, to kill the father once again: Christianity "has not escaped the fate of having to get rid of the Father" (136).

Christianity constitutes, for Freud, both a progression and a regression vis-à-vis Judaism. It marks a progress in the history of religion as it concerns the return of the repressed—Jewish religion became a "fossil" to the extent that it required, beyond the recognition of the father's positive role in history, also an act of remembering the father's murder. And yet there is for Freud an incontrovertibly regressive element to Christianity, dictated by the latter's inability to "maintain the high level of things of the mind" (88) that had previously been achieved by the Jewish religion. Ultimately, Christianity was unable to adhere to a strict monotheism; it returned to superstitions, magic, and the senses through the reinstatement of a great mother goddess. In a very fundamental sense, Christianity has never been Christian enough: it harkens back to an ancestry of "barbarous polytheism" (91) and is thus filled with a form of self-hatred that has expressed itself in history as hatred of the Other, and more specifically as anti-Semitism. Christianity has become a new way of acting out, insofar as it has refused to deal with murder as a form of commemoration. It has constituted itself solely in terms of this murder, now expressed as original sin, and it can do nothing but perpetually admit to this historic guilt. In that act it has participated in the destruction or killing-off of the possibility of a subjectivity afforded by the hypothesis of precisely this same subjectivity, a hypothesis articulated first by Moses and returned to thought by psychoanalysis.

Perhaps Freud sensed the *Unbehagen* of culture less in the fact that civilization enslaved human instincts than in his recognition that modern culture, in particular, bordered on the psychotic to the extent that is assailed the ego's boundaries and thus seemed to demand the abandonment of subjective interiority.[54] Modern culture produced, in other words, a thoroughly nonpsychological form of subjectivity, understood by Freud as the return of the senses and of the mother. Paradoxically enough, the modern individual was not moving from id to ego (a movement that must follow the laws of repression as self-mastery) but toward a situation where instinctual impulses were increasingly lending themselves to manipulation from the outside. The crisis of subjectivity (the very object of psychoanalysis) was simultaneously symptomatic of a crisis of the psychoanalytic project, the point, that is, that marked the very limits of Freudian analysis. "While psychology," Adorno remarks, "always denotes some bondage of the individual, it also presupposes freedom in the sense of a certain self-sufficiency and autonomy of the individual."[55] Freud's portrayal of the superego as persecuting law of enjoyment, a law unto itself not required to submit to the psychoanalytic laws of repression, marked both the end of classical bourgeois interiority and a reconfiguration of that interiority as radical and perpetual separation from the public sphere in the form of alienated mass movements. The nonpsychological nature of this new form of subjectivity had introduced a new form of bondage, one far worse than repression was ever to exact from the body, for now it no longer could posit freedom as its potential reward. Indeed, this appeared to be a form of servitude that was itself a form of enjoyment, a desire for guilt and punishment that Freud named moral masochism. Masochism, with its dependence on theatrical suspense and disavowal, radically externalized the subject's most intimate passions and did this precisely as theater: it constructed the symbolic order of law as a fiction, claiming it was this fiction we actually obeyed, and not what may lie behind or inside the individual's mask of pretense. For now it was this mask that had taken on the phantasmatic power of truth.

NOTES

Introduction

1. H. Heine, "Nachwort zu *Romanzero*," in *Sämtliche Schriften*, vol. 11, 1851–55 (Frankfurt: Ullstein Werkausgaben, 1976), p. 184.

2. Ibid., p. 180.

3. B. Ehrenreich, E. Hess, and G. Jacobs, *Re-making Love: The Feminization of Sex* (New York: Anchor-Doubleday, 1986), pp. 123–24.

4. G. Deleuze, "Coldness and Cruelty," in *Masochism* (Cambridge, Mass.: Zone Books, 1991).

5. Indeed, one may say that Deleuze performs a kind of rescue operation of Sacher-Masoch: it is by the latter's forced association with Sade that Sacher-Masoch has "suffered not only from unjust neglect" but also from unfair treatment.

6. As Pascal Bruckner has remarked, the pedagogical inversion—"the subordinate is our teacher"—is a distinctive mark of masochistic discourses within the context of colonialism. Thus, once pedagogy becomes a new form of theology, itself dependent on a conception of adulthood as a form of degeneracy, it becomes possible to put the child or the "native" into the position of the subject who knows all. This is tantamount to making the colonial subject or the child responsible for man's guilt (*The Tears of the White Man: Compassion as Contempt* [New York: The Free Press, 1986], pp. 122–23).

7. Deleuze, p. 99.

8. K. Silverman, *Male Subjectivity at the Margins* (New York: Routledge, 1992), p. 213.

9. Ibid., p. 2.

10. See J. Lacan, *Seminar Book VII: The Ethics of Psychoanalysis* (New York: Norton, 1992), p. 150.

11. S. Žižek, *Metastases of Enjoyment: Six Essays on Woman and Causality* (London: Verso Books, 1994), p. 92.

12. Ibid., p. 96.

13. Ibid., p. 95.

14. J. Lacan, "Desire and the Interpretation of Desire in *Hamlet*," *Yale French Studies* 55/56 (1977), p. 28.

15. S. Žižek, *Metastases of Enjoyment*, p. 108.

16. Ibid., pp. 108–9.

17. L. Bersani, *The Freudian Body: Psychoanalysis and Art* (New York: Columbia University Press, 1986), p. 39.

18. Ibid., p. 39.

19. Ibid., p. 41.

20. Ibid.

21. Linda Williams, in an essay on reading, essentially follows Bersani's line of argument, claiming that desire is not only a form of non-agency but also a prerequisite for any aesthetic practice. Masochism thus defines the act of reading, of submitting in ecstatic pain to a text. Nevertheless, in order to distinguish between such selflessness and enslavement to a text—this would define obedience, say, to the canon—Williams advocates an "active selflessness," a saying Yes that is not marked as a submission to an identity. The goal of all aesthetic practice should then be a form of active non-agency that undermines all forms of identity ("Submission and Reading: Feminine Masochism and Feminist Criticism," *new formations* 7, 1989).

22. L. Bersani, *The Freudian Body*, p. 45.

23. Ibid., p. 46.

24. Ibid., pp. 46–47. The replacement of the mother by a "loving father" has become a recurrent motif in popular culture. Films like *Nine Months* have the explicit theme of man's education by a woman to become a good father. Nevertheless, this generally happens at the expense of the woman in these films, inasmuch as the constitution of fatherhood is predicated on his replacement of the mother.

25. C. Siegel, *Male Masochism: Modern Revisions of the Story of Love* (Bloomington: Indiana University Press, 1995).

26. C. Dean, *The Self and Its Pleasures: Bataille, Lacan, and the History of the Decentered Subject* (Ithaca: Cornell University Press, 1992).

27. N. Lukacher, *Daemonic Figures: Shakespeare and the Question of Conscience* (Ithaca: Cornell University Press, 1994), pp. 6–7.

28. S. Žižek, "'There is No Sexual Relationship,'" in R. Salecl and S. Žižek, eds., *Gaze and Voice as Love Objects* (Durham: Duke University Press, 1996), p. 231.

29. D. W. Winnicott, *Playing and Reality* (New York: Routledge, 1971), p. 12.

30. Ibid., p. xii.

31. T. Modleski, *Feminism without Women: Culture and Criticism in a "Postfeminist" Age* (New York: Routledge, 1991). Modleski's analysis of the new "sensitive guy," who has come to be of such importance in modern American culture, is based on a critique of recent Hollywood films. She argues that despite their apparent weakness, men's newly acquired sensitivity to women's marginality is predicated on men usurping that marginality for themselves and thereby writing women completely out of the picture. One film—Jennifer Chamber Lynch's *Boxing Helena* (1993), made after the publication of Modleski's book—constitutes a powerful subversion of the new genre of the "feminist" man. Here, the marginalized man, the wimp, turns monstrous in his attempt to dominate the Cruel Woman, the femme fatale of the film, for he is able to put Helena quite literally on a pedestal only by gradually removing her arms and legs, by "boxing" her into her place of adored object.

Chapter 1. "A familiar smile of fascination": Masochism, Sublimation, and the Cruelty of Love

1. D. P. Schreber, *Memoirs of My Nervous Illness* (Cambridge, Mass.: Harvard University Press, 1988).

2. S. Freud, "Psychoanalytic Notes upon an Autobiographical Account of a Case of Paranoia (Dementia Paranoides)," in P. Rieff, ed., *Three Case Histories* (New York: Collier Books, 1963), p. 104.

3. Ibid., p. 181.

4. A. Warburg, *Images from the Region of the Pueblo Indians of North America*, translated, edited, and with an interpretive essay by M. P. Steinberg (Ithaca: Cornell University Press, 1995).

5. Quoted in A. Koschorke, *Leopold von Sacher-Masoch: Die Inszenierung einer Perversion* (Munich: Piper Verlag, 1988), p. 7.

6. B. Croce, *History of Europe in the Nineteenth Century* (London: George Allen & Unwin, 1934), p. 46.

7. Ibid., p. 51.

8. Ibid., p. 52.

9. R. von Krafft-Ebing, *Arbeiten aus dem Gesammtgebiet der Psychiatrie und Neuropathologie* (Leipzig: Johann Ambrosius Barth, 1899), pp. 127ff.

10. C. Dean, *The Self and Its Pleasures: Bataille, Lacan, and the History of the Decentered Subject* (Ithaca: Cornell University Press, 1992), p. 209.

11. E. Fuchs, *Das erotische Element in der Karikatur (Der Karikaturen der europäischen Völker dritter Band)* (Berlin, 1904), p. 263.

12. M. Salewski, "'Julian, begib dich in mein Boudoir': Weiberherrschaft und Fin-de-siècle," in M. Salewski and A. Bagel-Bohlan, eds., *Sexualmoral und Zeitgeist im 19. und 20. Jahrhundert* (Opladen: Leske + Budrich, 1990).

13. J. Le Conte, *Evolution: Its Nature, Its Evidence, and Its Relation to Religious Thought* (New York: D. Appleton, 1897), p. 280, 330.

14. Cited in B. Dijkstra, *Idols of Perversity: Fantasies of Feminine Evil in Fin-de-Siècle Culture* (New York: Oxford University Press, 1986), p. 365.

15. S. Freud, *Civilization and Its Discontents; Standard Edition*, vol. XXI.

16. Quoted in B. Dijkstra, *Idols of Perversity*, p. 224.

17. Quoted in E. Showalter, *Sexual Anarchy: Gender and Culture at the Fin de Siècle* (New York: Viking Press, 1990), p. 9.

18. Quoted in B. Dijkstra, *Idols of Perversity*, p. 367.

19. "The publication in the newspapers of the slate of candidates was a source of constant irritation for me. Beatrice was thereby also to gauge how I had voted—and I had to vote according to the wishes of my dominatrix" (Julian Robinson, *Die Weiberherrschaft*, quoted in M. Salewski, "'Julian, begib dich in mein Boudoir,'" p. 61).

20. Quoted in S. Freud, "'Civilized' Sexual Morality and Modern Nervousness," *Standard Edition*, vol. IX, pp. 183–84.

21. S. Freud, *Civilization and Its Discontents*, *Standard Edition*, vol. XXI, pp. 86, 96, 117, 125 n. 2.

22. F. Kittler, *Discourse Networks 1800/1900* (Stanford: Stanford University Press, 1990), p. 368.

23. Quoted in F. Kittler, *Discourse Networks*, p. 351.

24. F. Kittler, *Discourse Networks*, p. 355.

25. S. Freud, *Three Essays on the Theory of Sexuality*, *Standard Edition*, vol. VII.

26. S. Freud. "Instincts and Their Vicissitudes," *Standard Edition*, vol. XIV; "A Child is Being Beaten," *Standard Edition*, vol. XVII.

27. S. Freud, "The Economic Problem of Masochism," *Standard Edition*, vol. XIX, pp. 159, 160, 161.

28. Ibid., p. 161.

29. Theodor Reik's monumental study of masochism reflects a similar emphasis: for Reik, masochism is first and foremost moral masochism, or what he calls "social," indeed Christian, masochism (*Masochism in Sex and Society* [New York: Grove Press, 1962]).

30. S. Freud, "The Economic Problem of Masochism," *Standard Edition*, vol. XIX, pp. 167.

31. Ibid., p. 169.

32. Ibid., p. 170.

33. The specifically Freudian understanding of this articulation of sociology and egology is the focus of Chapter 4.

34. The blurring of distinctions between peace and war found expression in many contemporary political theorists, both on the left (Gramsci) and the right (Schmitt).

35. S. Freud, "Thoughts for the Times on War and Death," *Standard Edition*, vol. XIV.

36. S. Freud, "On the Grounds for Detaching a Particular Syndrome from Neurasthenia as 'Anxiety-Neurosis,'" *Standard Edition*, vol. III, p. 112.

37. For an excellent analysis of the Freudian theory of anxiety and the constitution of the ego, see S. Weber, *The Legend of Freud* (Minneapolis: University of Minnesota Press, 1982). Judith Butler makes a similar point with regard to Freud's concept of melancholia: melancholia is the introjection of the social into the psyche, an introjection that constitutes the very possibility of the psyche. See J. Butler, *The Psychic Life of Power: Theories in Subjection* (Stanford: Stanford University Press, 1997), p. xxx.

38. J. Laplanche and J.-B. Pontalis, "Fantasy and the Origins of Sexuality," in V. Burgin, J. Donald, and C. Kaplan, eds., *Formations of Fantasy* (New York: Routledge, 1986).

39. E. Jünger, "On Danger," *New German Critique* 59 (1993), pp. 27–32.

40. Ibid., pp. 29–30.

41. S. Žižek, *The Sublime Object of Ideology* (London: Verso Books, 1989), p. 30.

42. Ibid., pp. 33, 34.

43. Ibid., p. 43.

44. S. Žižek, *Metastases of Enjoyment: Six Essays on Woman and Causality* (London: Verso Books, 1994), pp. 16, 45.

45. Adorno made this point already, writing of "a growing tendency towards the abolition of psychological motivation in the old, liberalistic sense" that finds its most complete expression in the "post-psychological de-individualized social atoms which form the fascist collectivities" ("Freudian Theory and the Pattern of Fascist Propaganda," in *The Culture Industry: Selected Essays on Mass Culture* [London: Routledge, 1991], pp. 130–31).

46. Indeed, masochism may be understood as an aesthetic activity that has as one of its primary functions the rewriting of the past in the form of its staging. Wagner's reworking of the Nibelungen myths and their staging in Bayreuth are dramatic yet paradigmatic examples of such efforts.

47. G. Studlar, *In the Realm of Pleasure: Sternberg, Dietrich and the Masochistic Aesthetic* (New York: Columbia University Press, 1988), pp. 120, 20.

48. The masochist's gender has a history of its own. It is only in recent years that the term is applied more often to women. Nevertheless, the term was initially reserved for a specifically male malady. This is the case for Leopold von Sacher-Masoch and soon also with Krafft-Ebing's compilation of cases. Freud, by coining the term "feminine masochism," complicates the picture, though the term "perversion" is more stringently applied to men. Masochism in women rapidly becomes naturalized; indeed, women are understood to be constitutionally incapable of producing a full-fledged symptomatology of the perversion. In the words of Theodor Reik, "Compared with masculine masochism that of women shows a somewhat attenuated, one could almost say anemic character. It is more of a trespassing of the bourgeois border, of which one nevertheless remains aware, than an invasion into enemy territory. The woman's masochistic phantasy very seldom reaches the pitch of savage lust, of ecstasy, as does that of the man. . . . The masochistic phantasy of woman has the character of yielding and surrender rather than that of the rush ahead, of the orgiastic cumulation, of the self-abandonment of man" (*Masochism in Sex and Society*, p. 216).

49. G. Deleuze, "Coldness and Cruelty," in *Masochism* (Cambridge, Mass.: Zone Books, 1991), p. 95.

50. G. Studlar, *In the Realm of Pleasure*, p. 17.

51. Ibid., p. 16.

52. J. Kristeva, *Powers of Horror: An Essay on Abjection* (New York: Columbia University Press, 1982), 8, 9.

53. Freud claims in *Civilization and Its Discontents* that the peculiarity of the superego's power is founded in the fact that a good conscience is not produced by renunciation; instead, the act of renunciation generates more guilt.

54. Cited in G. Deleuze, "Coldness and Cruelty," in *Masochism*, p. 100.

55. As Kaja Silverman has correctly pointed out, Deleuze repeats the masochistic gesture of disavowing the role of the father in the masochistic fantasy. In other words, he takes the masochist, as it were, by his word. "The fact that both Deleuze and his male masochist are so busy disavowing the father's phallus and the mother's lack clearly indicates that both inhabit an Oedipal universe which only the force of a radically heterocosmic imagination can unmake, and not . . . a pre-Oedipal realm from which all masochism derives" (*Male Subjectivity at the Margins* [New York: Routledge, 1992], p. 212).

56. J. Lacan, *Seminar Book VII: The Ethics of Psychoanalysis* (New York: Norton, 1992), pp. 112ff. Slavoj Žižek has more recently made a similar connection between sublimation and masochism in *Metastases of Enjoyment*.

57. M. A. Doane, *Femme Fatale: Feminism, Film, Theory, Psychoanalysis* (New York: Routledge, 1991).

58. L. Bersani, "Sexuality and Aesthetics," *October* 28 (1984), p. 42.

59. Ibid., p. 38.

60. S. Freud, "Fragment of an Analysis of a Case of Hysteria," *Standard Edition*, vol. VII.

61. S. Freud, *Leonardo da Vinci and a Memory of His Childhood*, *Standard Edition*, vol. XI, pp. 134, 136.

62. Ibid., p. 63, 130.

63. S. Freud, *New Introductory Lectures on Psychoanalysis*, *Standard Edition*, vol. XXII, p. 97.

64. J. Lacan, *The Ethics of Psychoanalysis*.

65. S. Freud, "'Civilized' Sexual Morality," p. 188.

66. J. Laplanche, "To Situate Sublimation," *October* 28 (1984), p. 21.

67. S. Freud, *The Ego and the Id*, *Standard Edition*, vol. XIX, p. 45.

68. S. Freud, *Leonardo da Vinci and a Memory of His Childhood*, *Standard Edition*, vol. XI, p. 51; S. Freud, *Civilization and Its Discontents*. For an extended analysis of this passage, see Hubert Damisch, *The Judgment of Paris* (Chicago: Chicago University Press, 1996).

69. S. Freud, "Leonardo da Vinci," p. 76.

70. Ibid., p. 80.

71. Ibid., p. 79.

72. J. Laplanche, "To Situate Sublimation," p. 19.

73. Ibid., p. 16.

74. S. Freud, *Civilization and Its Discontents*, p. 97.

75. Ibid., p. 80 n. 1.

76. S. Freud, "'Civilized' Sexual Morality," p. 197.

77. S. Freud, *Civilization and Its Discontents*, p. 105.

78. S. Freud, "'Civilized' Sexual Morality," pp. 195, 199.

79. S. Freud, "Further Recommendations in the Technique of Psychoanalysis: Observations on Transference Love," in P. Rieff, ed., *Therapy and Technique* (New York: Collier Books, 1963), p. 175.

80. S. Freud, "'Civilized' Sexual Morality," pp. 195, 202.

81. S. Freud, *Civilization and Its Discontents*, pp. 128, 132.

82. S. Freud, "Leonardo da Vinci," pp. 117-18. All further page numbers are given in the text.

83. The bird in Leonardo's childhood memory is a kite, not a vulture, a mistranslation from the Italian that Freud misses but depends on for his analysis.

84. L. Bersani, *The Freudian Body: Psychoanalysis and Art* (New York: Columbia University Press, 1986), p. 44.

85. L. Bersani, "Sexuality and Aesthetics," p. 37.

86. L. Bersani, *The Freudian Body*, pp. 46–47.

87. J. Laplanche and J.-B. Pontalis, "Fantasy and the Origins of Sexuality," p. 15.

88. M. A. Doane, *Femme Fatale*.

89. In addition to Doane's analysis, see, for example, E. Showalter, *Sexual Anarchy*; B. Dijkstra, *Idols of Perversity*.

90. For an analysis of the consuming woman, see D. Silverman, *Art Noveau in Fin-de-Siècle France: Politics, Psychology and Style* (Berkeley: University of California Press, 1989), and R. Felski, *The Gender of Modernity* (Cambridge, Mass.: Harvard University Press, 1995).

91. M. A. Doane, *Femme Fatale*, p. 263.

92. Lacan has turned gaze and voice into drives that follow similar vicissitudes to the three enumerated by Freud: the oral, the anal, and the genital. Lacan sees the theoretical power of this "elevation" (itself, perhaps, an act of sublimation) as creating border-concepts that furnish conceptual tools capable of articulating the ways in which subjects are constituted within a wider cultural context. The drawback of Lacan's analysis is an absence of any interrogation of the ways in which such cultural constructions are themselves historically mediated, that is, of the ways in which these theoretical constructs arise as a consequence of historical redefinitions of subjectivity. Cf. J. Lacan, *The Four Fundamental Concepts of Psychoanalysis* (New York: Norton, 1977).

93. P. Bourdieu, *Language and Symbolic Power* (Cambridge, Mass.: Harvard University Press, 1991), pp. 121–22.

94. Ibid., p. 122.

Chapter 2. When Men Can No Longer Paint: Acts of Seeing in Leopold von Sacher-Masoch's *Venus in Furs*

1. D. P. Schreber, *Memoirs of My Nervous Illness* (Cambridge, Mass.: Harvard University Press, 1988), pp. 139, 229, 180.

2. Ibid., pp. 180–81.

3. Ibid., p. 63.

4. A. Warburg, *Images from the Region of the Pueblo Indians of North America*, translated, edited, and with an interpretive essay by M. P. Steinberg (Ithaca: Cornell University Press, 1995), pp. 53–54.

5. Ibid., p. 54.

6. R. von Krafft-Ebing, *Psychopathia Sexualis* (Munich: Matthes & Seitz Verlag, 1984), pp. 104–5; emphasis added.

7. Ibid., p. 105.

8. Ibid., p. 105.

9. Ibid., pp. 105–6.

10. L. von Sacher-Masoch, *Venus in Furs* (Cambridge, Mass.: Zone Books, 1991), p. 271. All further references are indicated in the text.

11. A. Koschorke, *Leopold von Sacher-Masoch: Die Inszenierung einer Perversion* (Munich: Piper Verlag, 1988).

12. Severin's supersensual (*übersinnlich*) being is precisely the individual as the subject of culture, that is, the man who has crossed the line and who has therefore left behind the domain of bodily drives and become a thoroughly cultural being. We find here Sacher-Masoch's theory of sublimation, articulated as the moment when the body is painfully submitted to the cultural process but nevertheless where this submission is perceived as *beyond* the body—to wit, *übersinnlich*—and hence beyond the pleasure principle. For Sacher-Masoch, as for Freud, modern culture is always the enactment or staging of a certain mechanical reproduction, that is, of the compulsion to repeat.

13. Franz Kafka's *Metamorphosis* (1915) tells the story of another vermin named Gregor. When he wakes up and finds himself changed, Gregor knows that he is not dreaming be-

cause he still sees the picture he has hung up in his room: a representation of a woman in furs. For a more extended analysis of Kafka's relationship to Sacher-Masoch, see M. Anderson, *Kafka's Clothes: Ornament and Aestheticism in the Habsburg Fin de Siècle* (Oxford: Oxford University Press, 1992), pp. 136ff.

14. When these limitations are overstepped, the consequences are catastrophic. One such transgression is marked, as noted above, by a too literal reading of role playing; another, when history enters the picture in the form of real relations of power. Thus in Sacher-Masoch's story "Nero in a Hoop Skirt," for example, telling of the love between Catherine the Great and the young officer Mirowitsch, the hero declares to the monarch, "Do with me what you will!" to which the Tsarina rightly answers, "Fool! Do I need your permission for that?" This story in fact ends with history the winner: Mirowitsch is decapitated.

15. Virginity is clearly an important aspect of the Cruel Woman. In his poem "Hérodiade," Mallarmé makes virginity a constituent sign of cruelty: "The horror of my virginity / Delights me, and I would envelop me / In the terror of my tresses, that, by night, / Inviolate reptile, I might feel the white / And glimmering radiance of thy frozen fire, / Thou art chaste and diest of desire, / White night of ice and of the cruel snow!"

16. The interlinking of art historical vision, the birth of Venuses, and the history of modern love as the history of coldness and cruelty appears in many contemporary commentators. Here is Walter Pater's gaze at Leonardo's Fatal Woman, the smiling head of the Gioconda: "The presence that arose so strangely beside the waters, is expressive of what in the ways of a thousand years men had come to desire. Hers is the head upon which all 'the ends of the world are come,' and the eyelids are a little weary. It is a beauty wrought out from within upon the flesh, the deposit, little cell by cell, of strange thoughts and fantastic reveries and exquisite passions. Set it for a moment beside one of those white Greek goddesses or beautiful women of antiquity, and how they would be troubled by this beauty, into which the soul with all its maladies has passed! All the thoughts and experiences of the world have etched and moulded there, in that which they have of power to refine and make expressive the outward form, the animalism of Greece, the lust of Rome, the mysticism of the Middle Age with its spiritual ambition and imaginative loves, the return of the pagan world, the sins of the Borgias. She is older than the rocks among which she sits; like the vampire, she has been dead many times, and learned the secrets of the grave; . . . and trafficked for strange webs with Eastern merchants. . . . The fancy of a perpetual life, sweeping together ten thousand experiences, is an old one; and modern philosophy has conceived the idea of humanity as wrought upon by, and summing up in itself, all modes of thought and life. Certainly Lady Lisa might stand as the embodiment of the old fancy, the symbol of the modern idea" (*The Renaissance* [New York: Oxford University Press, 1986], pp. 79–80).

17. When women alone are involved in sublimatory forms of representation, they must create fakes: "Woman's special form of neurosis would be to 'mimic' a work of art, to be *a bad (copy of a) work of art*. Her neurosis would be recognized as a counterfeit or parody of an artistic process. It is transformed into an aesthetic object, but one without value, which has to be condemned because it is *a forgery*" (L. Irigaray, *Speculum of the Other Woman* [Ithaca: Cornell University Press, 1985], p. 125). In the case of Sacher-Masoch's two paintings, the Titian is retroactively guaranteed its authenticity via a detour of looking at the painting of Severin's momentary transformation into a man.

18. The structure of the gaze here effects a gender reversal whereby, though woman is represented in the paintings, it is man who becomes the object of desire—though always the object of his own desire. Michael Salewski cites two pictures as exemplary of such a reversal: Jean-Léon Gérome's 1861 painting of "Phryne Before Her Judges," in which Phryne is released once her beauty is revealed to her judges, and Widhopff's 1899 caricature of the painting representing "Monsieur Phryne" in front of his female judges. Man turns in the caricature into woman's object of pleasure, and yet it is important to note that, like Sacher-Masoch, this takes place only insofar as the woman's "choice" as gaze depends on man turning into his own object of choice. It reassures man, in other words,

that he will be chosen. See "'Julian, begib dich in mein Boudoir': Weiberherrschaft und Fin-de-Siècle," in M. Salewski and A. Bagel-Bohlan, eds., *Sexualmoral und Zeitgeist im 19. und 20. Jahrhundert* (Opladen: Leske + Budrich, 1990), pp. 58–59.

19. M. Treut, *Die grausame Frau: zum Frauenbild bei de Sade und Sacher-Masoch* (Basel and Frankfurt: Stroemfeld/Roter Stern, 1984). Bram Dijkstra has noted that vacant eyes and mirrors are the most favoured tropes for representing women's gazes in the latter half of the nineteenth century, a fact of which Sacher-Masoch must have been aware. See *Idols of Perversity: Fantasies of Feminine Evil in Fin-de-Siècle Culture* (New York: Oxford University Press, 1986). One might also mention here the proliferation of the so-called "Anatomical Venuses" that made their appearance during the eighteenth century and that by the nineteenth had become so popular that they were bought by private individuals for display in their living rooms. These anatomical Venuses had been designed for medical research, and featured life-size wax figures of women in erotic positions, often adorned with jewelry and with their stomachs wide open in order to reveal the female reproductive system. Some apparently even had embryos at various stages of development. They were in any case the object of a male medical gaze. A rather colorful specimen of one such Venus may be viewed on the cover of Slavoj Žižek's *Metastases of Enjoyment: Six Essays on Woman and Causality* (New York: Verso Books, 1994).

20. A. Koschorke, *Leopold von Sacher-Masoch.*

21. Thus, for example, Jean-Jacques Rousseau, in his *Essay on the Origin of Languages* (New York: Frederick Ungar Publishing Company, 1966), describes the move to the North in these terms: "To the degree that needs multiply, that affairs become complicated, that light is shed, language changes character. It becomes more regular and less passionate. It substitutes ideas for feelings. It no longer speaks to the heart but to reason. Similarly, accent diminishes, articulation increases. Language becomes more exact and clearer, but more prolix, duller and colder" (p. 16).

22. G. Deleuze, "Coldness and Cruelty," in *Masochism*, p. 52.

23. M. Treut, *Die grausame Frau.*

24. J. Noyes, "Der Blick des Begehrens," *Acta Germanica* 19 (1988), p. 13.

25. S. Freud, "Instincts and Their Vicissitudes," *Standard Edition*, vol. XIV, p. 130.

26. J. Laplanche, *Life and Death in Psychoanalysis* (Baltimore: Johns Hopkins University Press, 1976).

27. Ibid., p. 102.

28. J. Laplanche and J.-B. Pontalis, "Fantasy and the Origins of Sexuality," in V. Burgin, J. Donald, and C. Kaplan, eds., *Formations of Fantasy* (New York: Routledge, 1986), p. 26.

29. J. Noyes, "Der Blick des Begehrens," p. 17.

30. Such scenes are no doubt favorites for Sacher-Masoch. Thus he writes in *Die geschiedene Frau* (The Divorced Woman): "And what wonderful condition of my senses, of my entire being, which, completely satisfied by my gaze, appeared to feel no more desire and in the face of the power of nature experienced a liberation from all earthly lust, sensed a devotion such had never sunk upon me from the dignified old dome of a consecrated cathedral. It was as if light streamed from her over me, as well as a fragrance—the sweet fragrance of flowers—purer and holier than incense. There was nothing lustful in my soul, no shadows, no darkness. When she stretched out her hand to me, shining in well-disposed mercy, I sank to my knees in silent awe and my lips touched her foot. She understood me. With chaste majesty she pulled up her ermine furs and signaled for me to leave" (quoted in A. Koschorke, *Leopold von Sacher-Masoch*, p. 82).

31. A. Koschorke, *Leopold von Sacher-Masoch*, pp. 82–83.

32. M. Treut, *Die grausame Frau*, p. 142.

33. J. Noyes, "Der Blick des Begehrens," p. 20.

34. M. Treut, *Die grausame Frau.*

35. And yet, like Kafka's door that leads to the Law, the contract is always already written, and only for him.

36. A. Koschorke, *Leopold von Sacher-Masoch*, p. 12.

Chapter 3. The Theft of the Operatic Voice: Masochistic Seduction
in Richard Wagner's *Parsifal*

1. R. Wagner, "'Parsifal' at Bayreuth," in *Religion and Art* (Lincoln: University of Nebraska Press, 1994), pp. 303, 306.
2. Quoted in L. Beckett, *Richard Wagner: Parsifal* (New York: Cambridge University Press, 1981), pp. 104–5.
3. Quoted in C. Floros, "Studien zur 'Parsifal'-Rezeption," *Musik-Konzepte* 25 (1982), p. 15.
4. R. Gutman, *Richard Wagner: The Man, His Mind and His Music* (New York: Harcourt, Brace and Jovanovich, 1990), p. 439.
5. J. Derrida, *The Ear of the Other* (New York: Schocken Books, 1985), p. 24.
6. F. Nietzsche, *The Case of Wagner* (New York: Vintage Books, 1967), pp. 160–61.
7. Ibid., p. 177.
8. T. Mann, "Sufferings and Greatness of Richard Wagner," in *Essays* (New York: Vintage Books, 1957).
9. F. Nietzsche, *The Case of Wagner*, p. 180.
10. S. Žižek, *Metastases of Enjoyment: Six Essays on Woman and Causality* (London: Verso Books, 1994), p. 21.
11. F. Kittler, "World-Breath: On Wagner's Media Technology," in D. J. Levin, ed., *Opera Through Other Eyes* (Stanford: Stanford University Press, 1993).
12. *Entrücken* itself has the additional meaning in German of "displacing" or "removing."
13. R. Wagner, "Public and Popularity," in *Religion and Art*, p. 81.
14. R. Wagner, "The Public in Time and Space," in *Religion and Art*, p. 86.
15. R. Wagner, "What Boots This Knowledge?" in *Religion and Art*, pp. 258, 260.
16. R. Wagner, "Religion and Art," in *Religion and Art*, pp. 217, 231.
17. Ibid., p. 249.
18. R. Wagner, *Richard Wagner to Mathilde Wesendonck* (Boston: Milford House, 1971), pp. 140–41.
19. M. Poizat, *The Angel's Cry: Beyond the Pleasure Principle in Opera* (Ithaca: Cornell University Press, 1992), p. 5.
20. I use the term "interpellation" here in Louis Althusser's sense, as the "hailing function" of ideology, that is, the notion that "all ideology hails or interpellates concrete individuals as concrete subjects" (*"Lenin and Philosophy" and Other Essays* [New York: Monthly Review Press, 1971], p. 173). Ideology is understood here as the constitution of subjects through a calling or address by the symbolic order, a call to which the always already existing subject must respond or risk psychosis.
21. S. Žižek, "'The Wound is Healed Only by the Spear That Smote You,'" in D. J. Levin, *Opera through Other Eyes*, pp. 192–93. Kafka's parable "Leopards in the Temple" comes to mind: "Leopards break into the temple and drink to the dregs what is in the sacrificial pitchers; this is repeated over and over again; finally it can be calculated in advance, and it becomes a part of the ceremony" (F. Kafka, *Parables and Paradoxes* [New York: Schocken Books, 1958]).
22. F. Kittler, "World-Breath: On Wagner's Media Technology."
23. Ibid., p. 222.
24. T. Adorno, *In Search of Wagner* (London: Verso Books, 1981), pp. 101, 150.
25. Identification is a form of mastery when one is confronted with an authority figure; it can take on, according to William Grossman, either normal forms (such as with the formation of the superego, that is, the child's interiorization of parental authority) or pathological forms (when, for instance, the child is faced with the need to master serious trauma). See "Notes on Masochism: A Discussion of the History and Development of a Psychoanalytic Concept," *Psychoanalytic Quarterly* 55, no. 3 (1986). For a more extended analysis of the Freudian understanding of identification, see Chapter 4 below.

26. C. Dahlhaus, *Richard Wagner's Music Dramas* (New York: Cambridge University Press, 1979).

27. Wieland Wagner developed what he called the "Parsifal-Kreuz," in his program notes for his 1951 Bayreuth production of Parsifal. While his cross represents the specular structure of the opera, Wieland misses the instability and vacillating nature of the oppositions and articulations. Wieland positions the central characters along the cross's horizontal axis and their development along the vertical axis. He thereby highlights the paradox of a narrative development that is synchronically ordered, in other words, that is essentially timeless. He thus lines up the characters in the following positions: Klingsor—Kundry—Parsifal—Amfortas—Titurel. With Parsifal constituting the dramatic and pivotal center of the opera, Klingsor and Titurel—the two old masters who must die—are both opposed to each other and also identical (they both mismanage power and sexuality). Kundry and Amfortas are viewed as occupying an essentially feminine position; they are both traumatized subjects (they carry the wound) and are thus in search of redemption. Parsifal himself is the one who will bring this redemption by resolving the specular structure through the elimination of all difference. The specular structure of the opera is therefore a representation of both the crisis itself and its resolution.

28. R. Gutman, *Richard Wagner*; S. Žižek, *The Sublime Object of Ideology* (London: Verso Books, 1989). It is noteworthy how these two analyses repeat the objects of their analysis, Gutman in his overcontextualization of the opera, and Žižek in his purely internal reading of symbolic structures. Dominick LaCapra has stated in a different context, but one that is nevertheless pertinent here: "Extreme contextualization of the past in its own terms and for its own sake may lead to the denial of transference through total objectification of the other and the constitution of the self either as a cipher for empathetic self-effacement or as a transcendental spectator of a scene fixed in amber. By contrast, unmitigated 'presentist' immersion in contemporary discourses, reading strategies, and performative free play may at the limit induce narcissistic obliteration of the other as other and the tendency to act out one's own obsession or narrow preoccupations" (*Representing the Holocaust: History, Theory, Trauma* [Ithaca: Cornell University Press, 1991], p. 34).

29. This distinction between identification with the other and the incorporation of that other is reflected in Freud's dual use of the term "identification": identification is either heteropathic (the subject identifies with the other) or idiopathic (the subject incorporates the other). Freud analyzes the first form in terms of fantasy, hysteria, hypnosis, being in love, and the psychology of groups, insofar as it allows for the cathexis of a leader; the second appears in his discussion of oral incorporation or cannibalism, particularly in his analysis of the totem and of melancholia.

30. R. Gutman, *Richard Wagner*, p. 432.

31. T. Adorno, *In Search of Wagner*, p. 94.

32. P. Lacoue-Labarthe, *Musica Ficta (Figures of Wagner)* (Stanford: Stanford University Press, 1994), p. 48.

33. I use the term "rendering" in Michel Chion's sense: Chion perceives a shift in cinema from the establishing shot of the camera to the soundtrack, whereby content is not represented in symbolic codes but instead rendered in sound; this sound "seizes" the spectator (*La toile trouée* [Paris: Cahiers du Cinema, Editions de l'Etoile, 1988]).

34. F. Kittler, "World-Breath: On Wagner's Media Technology."

35. S. Žižek, *Enjoy Your Symptom: Jacques Lacan in Hollywood and Out* (New York: Routledge, 1992), p. 22. Žižek continues: "The Freudian duality of life and death drives is *not* a symbolic opposition but a tension, and antagonism, inherent to the presymbolic Real. . . . And the name of this life substance that proves a traumatic shock for the symbolic universe is of course *enjoyment*. . . . the very gesture of renouncing enjoyment produces inevitably a surplus enjoyment that Lacan writes down as the 'object small a.' . . . This dialectic of enjoyment and surplus enjoyment—i.e., the fact that there is no "substantial" enjoyment preceding the excess of surplus enjoyment, that enjoyment itself is a

kind of surplus enjoyment produced by renunciation—is perhaps what gives a clue to so-called "primal masochism."

36. Hans-Jürgen Syberberg's film version of *Parsifal* emphasizes this simultaneous inside/outside quality, in that Syberberg has Amfortas carry his wound on a platter.

37. Titurel is, one could argue, the allegory of musical composition, the embodiment of musical law to which the composer must submit: "*Dramatic* composers of my 'manner,' . . . I would recommend to never think of adopting a text before they see in it a plot and characters to carry out this plot, that inspire the musician with a lively interest on some account or other. Then let him take a good look at the one character, for instance, which appeals to him the most this very day: bears it a mask—away with it. . . . Let him set it in a twilight spot, where he can merely see the gleaming of its eye; if that speaks to him, the shape itself will now most likely fall a-moving, which perhaps will even terrify him—but he must be put with that; at last its lips will part, it opens its mouth, and a ghostly voice breathes something quite distinct, intensely seizable, but so unheard-of . . . that—he wakes from out his dream. All has vanished; but in the spiritual ear it still rings on: he has had an 'idea' (*Einfall*), a so-called musical 'Motiv'; God knows if other men have heard the same, or something similar, before? . . . It is *his* motiv, legally delivered to and settled on him by that marvelous shape in that wonderful fit of absorption" (R. Wagner, "Opera Poetry and Composition," in *Religion and Art*, p. 170).

38. R. Wagner, "Shall We Hope?" in *Religion and Art*, p. 124.

39. R. Wagner, "Introduction to Gobineau," in *Religion and Art*, pp. 39–40.

40. S. Žižek, *Metastases of Enjoyment*, p. 94.

41. J. Lacan, *Seminar Book VII: The Ethics of Psychoanalysis* (New York: Norton, 1992), p. 152.

42. S. Žižek, *Metastases of Enjoyment*, p. 95.

43. S. Weber, "Taking Place: Towards a Theater of Dislocation," in D. J. Levin, ed., *Opera Through Other Eyes*, p. 132.

44. R. Gutman, *Richard Wagner*, p. 436.

45. L. Beckett, *Parsifal*, p. 21.

46. According to Michel Poizat, the history of this embodiment moves from the angel (the voice of heaven), to the child, the castrato, and through to the soprano. Whereas the soprano's predecessors were marked by sexual indeterminacy, this changes with the domination in opera of the soprano voice, who now is not only angel but also demon. See *The Angel's Cry*.

47. Kundry's sisters, among many others, are Turandot and of course Salome, who wanted to know of Jokanaan, why "does he not cry out, this man?" thus seducing the man into the domain of their own crazed voice.

48. M. Poizat, *The Angel's Cry*, p. 180. See here also the analysis of Catherine Clément, *Opera, or the Undoing of Woman* (Minneapolis: University of Minnesota Press, 1988).

49. B. Emslie, "Woman as Image and Narrative in Wagner's *Parsifal*: A Case Study," *Cambridge Opera Journal* 3, no. 2 (1991), p. 112.

50. Ibid., p. 119.

51. The drive of making the voice present in a perpetual Now also lies behind Edison's discovery of the phonograph. The human voice was recorded for the first time in 1877, and by 1888 the gramophone had entered into mass production, at the same time when Edison had begun, significantly, the marketing of speaking dolls. Not insignificantly, the first records had a writing angel as their trademark. In this sense, it is possible to view the theft of Kundry's voice as a recording studio session. The theme of stealing the voice and the gaze through their reproduction in the newly invented media is a ubiquitous theme that begins in the late nineteenth century and extends well into our own. E. T. A. Hoffmann's tales and their operatic staging by Offenbach come to mind, as well as Jules Verne's novel *The Carpathian Castle*; Philippe Villiers de l'Isle-Adam's novel about Edison's construction of the perfect doll/woman, *Tomorrow's Eve*; Bram Stoker's *Dracula*; and most re-

cently Jean-Jacques Beineix's film *Diva*, which makes explicit both the theft or pirating of the woman's voice as well as the doubling of woman into goddess (diva) and whore.

52. I owe this observation to Judith Surkis.

53. C. Dahlhaus, *Richard Wagner's Music Dramas*.

54. S. Žižek, *Metastases of Enjoyment*, p. 97.

55. S. Žižek, "'The Wound Is Healed Only by the Spear That Smote You': The Operatic Subject and Its Vicissitudes," p. 206.

56. Lacan, like Freud, distinguishes between two forms of identification: with imaginary identification, the subject identifies with an image in which he appears likable to himself; with symbolic identification, the subject identifies with the place from which he is being observed and judged.

57. J. Kristeva, *Powers of Horror: An Essay on Abjection* (New York: Columbia University Press, 1982), pp. 63–64.

58. Love as torture, claims Adorno, "means also to discover that the claims of pleasure, where they were followed through, would burst asunder that concept of the person as autonomous, self-possessed being that degrades its own life to that of a thing, and which deludes itself into believing that it will find pleasure in the full possession of itself, whereas in reality that pleasure is frustrated by the fact of self-possession" (*In Search of Wagner*, p. 154).

59. According to Poizat, the history of opera shows the traces of a battle between self-annihilation through pure or absolute music and the reassertion of meaning through the power of the word. Thus, the old debate of "prima la musica/prima le parole" must be understood in these terms, a debate that shows itself symptomatically in the distinction between aria and recitative.

60. R. Wagner, "The Modern," in *Religion and Art*, pp. 46–47. Ornamentation and its relationship to images of masculinity occupied many a critic during the first decades of the twentieth century. In "Ornament and Crime," Adolf Loos considered ornamentation on the part of men a sign of degeneracy; proper masculinity required the renunciation of a male display of sexuality (in L. Munz and G. Kunstler, eds., *Adolf Loos, Pioneer of Modern Architecture* [New York: Praeger, 1966]). Similar themes were taken up by the British psychologist C. J. Flugel in 1930 in *The Psychology of Clothes* (New York: International Universities Press, 1930). Flugel claimed that male sartorial displays were curbed in the late eighteenth century: the "Great Masculine Renunciation" required that men's dress represented masculine sexuality as dedicated to equality, self-control and a sense of civic duty. For an extended analysis of masculinity, ornamentation and self-loss, see also M. Boscagli, *Eye on the Flesh: Fashions of Masculinity in the Early Twentieth Century* (Boulder, Colo.: Westview Press, 1996).

61. R. Wagner, "Shall We Hope?" p. 122.

62. R. Wagner, "Opera Poetry and Composition," p. 165.

63. German women were not granted the right to vote until 1918. Indeed, the first major women's organization (the Allgemeiner Deutscher Frauenverein, founded in 1865) did not even have female suffrage on its platform of demands. Yet the question of women's voice was the source of much anxiety during the second half of the century; this issue was much discussed in the German press, compelling even the editors of the 1898 Brockhaus encyclopedia to include an entry on what to do with Germany's women. See Ute Frevert, *Women in German History: From Bourgeois Emancipation to Sexual Liberation* (New York: Berg/St. Martin's Press, 1988), pp. 113ff.

64. R. Wagner, "The Human Womanly," in *Religion and Art*, p. 337.

65. S. Žižek, "'There is No Sexual Relationship,'" in R. Salecl and S. Žižek, eds., *Gaze and Voice as Love Objects* (Durham: Duke University Press, 1996), p. 220.

66. Klingsor represents the obscene, ludic father of pure jouissance who stands for the return of the Freudian narcissistic father of the primal horde. For an analysis of this new father figure, see S. Žižek, *Enjoy Your Symptom*, and E. Santner, *My Own Private Germany:*

Daniel Paul Schreber's Secret History of Modernity (Princeton: Princeton University Press, 1996).

67. R. Wagner, "The Human Womanly," p. 336. Wagner writes in a letter to Liszt regarding his love affair with Mathilde Wesendonck, "The love of a tender woman has made me happy; she dared to throw herself into a sea of suffering and agony so that she should be able to say to me 'I love you!' No one who does not know all her tenderness can judge how much she had to suffer. We were spared nothing—but as a consequence I am redeemed and she is blessedly happy because she is aware of it." Quoted in S. Žižek, "'The Wound is Healed." To Wesendonck herself (whom he consistently addresses as "mein Kind"), Wagner in 1860 describes the composition of *Parsifal* as a long and difficult, but nonetheless pleasurable, pregnancy: "the bringing of this poem into the world will be for me an extreme pleasure. But between now and then a good few years may have to pass. . . . I shall put it off as long as I can, and concern myself with it only when it forces me to. But then this extraordinary process of generation does let me forget all my troubles." Cosima, too, appears to have been possessed by her assigned role as servant to the Cause: her diaries obsessively repeat her need to serve (*dienen*), like Kundry, her new master.

68. Tannhäuser tells Venus, "At your side, I can only become a slave; but I desire freedom." Parsifal, on the other hand, has transcended this desire for freedom in the name of redemption, for it is a redemption that takes place as the pure caprice of power.

Chapter 4. Saving Love: Is Sigmund Freud's Leader a Man?

1. William McGrath has traced Freud's stay in Trieste through the latter's correspondence with Eduard Silberstein. McGrath remarks that Freud's scientific pursuits of dissecting the descendants of ichthyosauri are closely intertwined with his parallel interests in the women of Trieste (of whom there are many descriptions in his letters), as well as with his relinquished love for Gisela Fluss, whom he called, to his friend Silberstein, Ichthysaura (*Freud's Discovery of Psychoanalysis: The Politics of Hysteria* [Ithaca: Cornell University Press, 1986]).

2. S. Freud, *Group Psychology and the Analysis of the Ego, Standard Edition*, vol. XXIII, p. 124.

3. Cited in P. Grosskurth, *The Secret Ring: Freud's Inner Circle and the Politics of Psychoanalysis* (New York: Addison-Wesley Publishing Company, 1991), p. 113.

4. S. Freud, "On Narcissism: An Introduction," *Standard Edition*, vol. XIV, pp. 73, 75.

5. Ibid., p. 76.

6. Ibid., p. 89.

7. D. de Rougemont, *Love in the Western World* (New York: Fawcett Premier Books, 1956).

8. S. Freud, "On Narcissism," pp. 89, 90.

9. M. Borch-Jacobsen, *The Freudian Subject* (Stanford: Stanford University Press, 1988), pp. 111–12.

10. S. Freud, "A Child is Being Beaten," *Standard Edition*, vol. XVII.

11. Ibid., p. 199.

12. K. Silverman, *Male Subjectivity at the Margins* (New York: Routledge, 1992), p. 210.

13. S. Freud, *Group Psychology*. James Strachey translates the German *Masse* as "group," thereby losing all connotations attached to "mass" or "masses."

14. S. Freud, *Introductory Lectures on Psychoanalysis, Standard Edition*, vol. XVI, p. 345.

15. S. Freud, *The Interpretation of Dreams* (New York: Avon Books, 1965), p. 183. For an extended analysis of this "*starke Gemeinsamkeit*," see also Mikkel Borch-Jacobsen, *The Freudian Subject*, pp. 14ff.

16. S. Freud, *Group Psychology*, p. 70. All further references will appear in the text.

17. M. Borch-Jacobsen, *The Freudian Subject*, pp. 130ff.

18. According to Borch-Jacobsen, this reduction makes a thinking of the Other an impossibility: "What intervenes here to block or inhibit the 'reduction' begun by Freud is the 'narcissistic evidence,' the (self-) evidence of the subject. It is because Freud continues to operate in full view of that evidence, without confronting it, that the problem of the social bond remains a problem, and a problem of the 'other'" (*The Freudian Subject*, pp. 132–33).

19. "The beast must have its head. . . . Even liberty must have its master," says one of the characters in Schiller's *The Robbers*. William McGrath has argued that Schiller's play was extremely important for the formation of Freud's political ideas. See *Freud's Discovery of Psychoanalysis*, pp. 66–67.

20. The word Freud uses is "*künstlich*" (artificial), which in itself constitutes a radical departure from Le Bon's *foule*. Nevertheless, we are still in *Massenpsychology*, according to Freud.

21. M. Borch-Jacobsen, *The Freudian Subject*, p. 147.

22. For Borch-Jacobsen, the matter is clear: if underneath suggestion there really is love, then this must mean that the subject lets himself be hypnotized not because he is a victim of violence but because in actuality he really desires it. The subject's servitude, in the Freudian schema, must therefore be voluntary. This voluntary servitude must, according to Borch-Jacobsen, head into direct conflict with Freud's other assertion of free subjectivity. My own sense is that the matter is less clear. The greater complexity of Freud's position lies, I believe, in the space of his "refusal," that is, in the space where the subject can, perhaps must (in the Freudian structure of ethics) say no.

23. There are, furthermore, more immediate, historical reasons for this choice: Freud published "Group Psychology" three years after the end of World War I, at a time when the problem of war neuroses was an immediate concern for psychoanalysis and for the states of Europe, when in fact psychoanalysis may have enjoyed its period of greatest legitimacy and cooperation with those states in the treatment of that problem. As to the Catholic Church, whose analysis Freud would take even further in *Civilization and Its Discontents* (1930), Freud could not help but be aware of the conflict between rising anti-Semitism and the "religion of love" professed by the Church.

24. Freud's modern leader, according to Juliet Flower McCannell, is just like any other member of the group, only greater. Unlike the Oedipal father, who functions as ego ideal, the leader of today provides a model and aspiration for the group as a whole. He is thus an ideal ego. The modern leader, who is a *son*, acts like the father without actually being one; he acts as if he were the father without taking responsibility. The son occupies the father's empty place in the form of a simulation of the symbolic order. See *The Regime of the Brother: After the Patriarchy* (New York: Routledge, 1991), pp. 12ff.

25. M. Borch-Jacobsen, *The Freudian Subject*, p. 218.

26. Carl Schorske and William McGrath have argued that Freud, faced with the disappointment of political and professional exclusion in Austria after the collapse of the *Bürgermimisterium*, converted his youthful political radicalism into scientific radicalism, his frustrated political freedom into the freedom of psychoanalytic insight (C. Schorske, *Fin-de-Siècle Vienna: Politics and Culture* [New York: Vintage Books, 1961]; W. McGrath, *Freud's Discovery of Psychoanalysis*). I agree with this shift, though interpret it not as a move toward depoliticization but as an attempt on Freud's part to reformulate the political domain in light of his psychoanalytic discoveries.

27. S. Freud, "Thoughts for the Times on War and Death," *Standard Edition*, vol. XIV, pp. 281, 282.

28. In the essay "Thoughts for the Times on War and Death," it appears that it is the egoistic instincts which must be renounced. But plenty of other texts insist it is the erotic impulses that succumb to the demands of civilization. For example, in "On the Universal Tendency to Degradation in the Sphere of Love" (*Standard Edition*, vol. XI), Freud states that it is the renunciation of erotic instincts that causes psychic impotence in men and

frigidity in women. Such impotence results from a split between feelings of love and affection and those of desire or sensuality and is the direct product of the demands of civilization.

29. S. Freud, "Thoughts for the Times on War and Death," p. 282.

30. E. Santner, *My Own Private Germany: Daniel Paul Schreber's Secret History of Modernity* (Princeton: Princeton University Press, 1996), p. 89.

31. S. Freud, "Thoughts for the Times on War and Death," pp. 284, 293.

32. S. Freud, "On the Universal Tendency."

33. "Those sexual instincts which are inhibited in their aims [i.e., sublimated] have a great functional advantage over those which are uninhibited. Since they are not capable of really complete satisfaction, they are especially adapted to create permanent ties; while those instincts which are directly sexual incur a loss of energy each time they are satisfied, and must wait to be renewed by a fresh accumulation of sexual libido, so that meanwhile the object may have changed" (*Group Psychology*, p. 139). Permanent ties have the structure of capitalist investment, in other words; the immediate expenditure of value undermines the possibility for investment in the economy's continuity, in the production of capitalist goods.

34. "On the Universal Tendency," p. 189.

35. S. Freud, "The Taboo of Virginity," *Standard Edition*, vol. XI, p. 199.

36. Freud provides a list of examples of such a narcissism of small differences: families that come together by marriage, neighboring towns, closely related races, Southern Germany and Northern Germany, Englishmen and Scots, the Spaniards and the Portuguese. Even greater differences lead to "insuperable repugnance," felt, for example, by the French for the German, the Aryan for the Semite, the white races for the colored (*Group Psychology*, p. 101). Freud appears here to be articulating a kind of continuum along which small differences suddenly turn into a repugnance that gives birth to radical otherness. In *Civilization and Its Discontents*—which gives a very similar list of the narcissism of small differences—this continuum is abolished, for here the moment of radical otherness is thought to occur at the moment of greatest intimacy: in the commandment to love one's neighbor as oneself.

37. Directly sexual impulses are never favorable to the group: there is no space for women in the army and the Church because the group would disintegrate as soon as love breaks into these organizations. Interestingly, homosexual ties between members would be considerably less threatening to the group, indeed they would provide the basis for strong bonds. Homosexuality is inherently more social than heterosexual love (*Group Psychology*, pp. 140–42). See also M. Borch-Jacobsen, *The Freudian Subject*, pp. 81ff.

38. The difficulty of articulating a new political fraternal order after the killing of the father constitutes the crux of Lynn Hunt's analysis of contract theory immediately before and after the French Revolution (*The Family Romance of the French Revolution* [Berkeley: University of California Press, 1992]). Once the king had been executed, Hunt asks, "what was to be the model that ensured the citizens' obedience?" (p. 3). She suggests that several themes dominated contemporary discussions and indeed continued to preoccupy Freud as well: "the killing of the father, the nature of fraternity, the assignation of guilt, the fate of the 'liberated women,' the choice of new totems to replace the dead father, and the enforcement of the incest taboo" (p. 9). Hunt claims that ultimately the new order required the domestication of the idea of fraternity and the exclusion of woman from the social contract.

39. The origin of identification in the nursery provides Freud with his argument against an inborn herd instinct. The demand for justice is a reaction-formation stemming from sibling rivalry. If, that is, one cannot be the father's favorite, then no one else can either: *Gemeingeist* had its birth in envy. Thus, "social feeling is based upon the reversal of what was first a hostile feeling into a positively-toned tie in the nature of identification" (*Group Psychology*, p. 121).

40. William McGrath has noted the frequency of the confusion between father and brother in Freud's work, and he explains this by the peculiar family constellation in Freud's family, the presence, that is, of brothers by the senior Freud's first marriage. These brothers were old enough to be Freud's father. McGrath connects the Freudian family structure to Freud's early interest in politics: "The strong interest in politics that Freud developed during his adolescence drew much of its psychic energy from unresolved emotional problems involving brothers and fathers. He translated his family drama into a larger political drama" (*Freud's Discovery of Psychoanalysis*, p. 66).

41. This is ultimately the conclusion reached by René Girard and shared by Mikkel Borch-Jacobsen, for whom the social bond is constituted solely on the basis of mimetic desire, a desire founded in an act of violence and always threatened by a crisis of exclusion, a sacrifice or scapegoating (R. Girard, *Violence and the Sacred* [Baltimore: Johns Hopkins University Press, 1977]).

42. J. Lacan, *Seminar Book VII: The Ethics of Psychoanalysis* (New York: Norton), pp. 181, 143, 145.

43. A very similar story may be found in *The Interpretation of Dreams*, in the context of Freud's first published discussion of identification: "Supposing a physician is treating a woman patient, who is subject to a particular kind of spasm, in a hospital ward among a number of another patients. He will show no surprise if he finds one morning that this particular kind of hysterical attack has found imitators. He will merely say: 'The other patients have seen it and copied it; it's a case of psychical infection.' That is true; but the psychical infection has occurred along the same lines as these. As a rule, the patients know more about one another than the doctor does about any of them; and after the doctor's visit is over they turn their attention to one another. Let us imagine that this patient had her attack on a particular day; then the others will quickly discover that it was caused from a letter from home, the revival of some unhappy love-affair, or some such thing. Their sympathy is aroused and they draw the following inference, though it fails to penetrate their consciousness: 'If a cause like this can produce an attack like this, I may have the same kind of attack since I have the same grounds for having it.' If this inference were capable of entering consciousness, it might possibly give rise to a *fear* of having the same attack. But in fact the inference is made in a different psychical region. . . . Thus identification is not simple imitation but *assimilation* on the basis of a similar aetiological pretension; it expresses a resemblance and is derived from a common element [*eine starke Gemeinsamkeit*] which remains in the unconscious" (p. 183). Significantly, Freud continues by insisting that this common element is always sexual in nature.

44. Leontine Sagan's 1931 film *Mädchen in Uniform* uses a girls' boarding school as an allegory of the Weimar republic. Both Freud's and Sagan's stagings of power in crisis interrogate the fundamental question of political power as the absence of love. In the Sagan's film, however, the articulation of love and power is explicitly homosexual; thus, the leader is a woman—the bad, unloving mother/leader initially who abdicates to the good, loving mother/leader at the end of the film.

45. Quoted in P. Grosskurth, *The Secret Ring*, p. 129.

46. S. Freud, *Civilization and Its Discontents, Standard Edition*, vol. XXI, p. 64. All further references will appear in the text.

47. There is, however, one significant exception to this love: the mother's love for her male child. In other words, Freud continues to keep the relationship between mother and son completely out of the social domain, while at the same time making this love the foundation of all object-love and thus of the social bond itself. The founding moment of society is not itself part of society.

48. Jürgen Habermas describes the collapse of liberal subjectivity in terms of the destruction of the public sphere and the deprivatization of interiority. From approximately the mid-nineteenth century onward, "there was no longer institutional support for an individuation of the person on the model of the 'Protestant Ethic'; nor . . . were there social conditions within sight that could replace the classical path of internalization via the

educational route of 'a political ethics' and in this fashion supply a new foundation for the process of individuation." Eventually, "the deprivatized province of interiority was hollowed out by the mass media; a pseudo-public sphere of a no longer literary public was patched together to create a sort of superfamilial zone of familarity" (*The Structural Transformation of the Public Sphere: An Inquiry into a Category of Bourgeois Society* [Cambridge, Mass.: MIT Press, 1989], pp. 161–62).

49. Freud ends the chapter with, in my view, a completely incomprehensible statement: "But I shall avoid the temptation of entering upon a critique of American civilization; I do not wish to give an impression of wanting myself to employ American methods" (116). Freud is in my view very close to Foucault's perception that modern sovereign power has been supported if not supplanted by disciplinary power. Foucault has insisted that it is disciplinary power that has done away with repression, that what characterizes modern power is not "the domination of the King in his central position, therefore, but that of his subjects in their mutual relations: not the uniform edifice of sovereignty, but the multiple forms of subjugation that have a place and function within the social organism" (*Power/Knowledge* [New York: Harvester Press, 1980], pp. 95–96).

50. M. Foucault, *The History of Sexuality* (New York: Pantheon Books, 1978), p. 44.

51. In the words of Leo Bersani, "The renunciation of aggressiveness is inherent in its constitution. But it is a renunciation which multiplies the force of aggression. . . . Given the limitations of our effective power over the external world, it could be said that the curbing of aggressiveness offers the only realistic strategy for satisfying aggressiveness. . . . From this perspective, civilization is not the tireless if generally defeated opponent of individual aggressiveness; rather, it is the *cause* of the very antagonism which *Civilization and Its Discontents* sets out to examine. The regulator of aggressiveness is identical to the very problem of aggressiveness" (*The Freudian Body: Psychoanalysis and Art* [New York: Columbia University Press, 1986], p. 23).

52. In *The Ego and the Id*, Freud claims that the constitution of the superego involves identification with the father, but he adds in a footnote, "Perhaps it would be safer to say 'with the parents'; for before a child has arrived at a definite knowledge of the difference between the sexes, the lack of a penis, it does not distinguish in value between its father and its mother." He ends the footnote by adding, "In order to simplify my presentation I shall discuss only identification with the father" (*Standard Edition*, vol. XIX, p. 31 n. 1). And a few pages later, another shift occurs: the superego is now equated not with the father per se but with love for the father: the superego represents a "substitute for a longing for the father" (p. 27), in other words, *Vatersehnsucht* (p. 37).

53. A. Yaeger Kaplan, *Reproductions of Banality: Fascism, Literature, and French Intellectual Life* (Minneapolis: University of Minnesota Press, 1986), p. 12. The problem of keeping in focus both the mother and father at the same time is a recurring one in Freud's work. I have addressed this problem in relation to the theory of sublimation. It also occurs in his earliest work around the question of the seduction theory. According to the latter, it is the father who seduces; once the seduction theory is abandoned, however, it is the mother who becomes the source of infantile sexuality insofar as it is her to whom the son attaches all his libidinal energy. Thus is born the Oedipus complex.

54. H. D., *Tribute to Freud* (Boston: David Godine, 1974), pp. 146–47.

55. Not coincidentally, Freud rethought his theory of anxiety in response to Otto Rank's theory of the birth trauma. Cf. S. Freud, *Inhibition, Symptoms and Anxiety, Standard Edition*, vol. XX.

56. S. Freud, *Moses and Monotheism, Standard Edition*, vol. XXIII, p. 114.

57. S. Freud, "Family Romances," *Standard Edition*, vol. IX, p. 239.

58. In his essay on the uncanny, Freud makes these connections explicit. Freud insists that intellectual uncertainty has nothing to do with the production of uncanny effects. Speaking of the uncanny quality of Hoffmann's "The Sand-Man," he states, "There is no question, therefore, of any intellectual uncertainty here: we know now that we are not supposed to be looking on at the products of a madman's imagination behind which we,

with the superiority of rational minds, are able to detect the sober truth; and yet this knowledge does not lessen the impression of uncanniness in the least degree. The theory of intellectual uncertainty is thus incapable of explaining that impression" (pp. 230–31). Uncanniness is produced instead by a doubling, significantly between the good and the castrating fathers: "the figures of [Nathaniel's] father and Coppelius represent the two opposites into which the father-imago is split by [the child's] ambivalence; whereas the one threatens to blind him—that is, to castrate him—the other, the 'good' father, intercedes for his sight. That part of the complex which is most strongly repressed, the death-wish against the father, finds expression in the death of the 'good' father, and Coppelius is made answerable for it" (p. 232 n. 1). The question remains, however, whether this doubling does not in fact lead to intellectual uncertainty, that is, to the problem of being able to distinguish between the good and the bad father. Indeed, Freud ends the essay with a discussion of the differential effects the uncanny has in real life and in fiction, leading him to state that uncanny effects can only be produced by a *"conflict of judgment"* (p. 250), that is, from the very inability of the subject to distinguish between fantasy and reality ("The Uncanny," *Standard Edition*, vol. XVII).

Chapter 5. The Rhetoric of Powerlessness

1. B. Johnson, "Charles Baudelaire and Marceline Desbordes-Valmore," in J. Dejean and N. K. Miller, eds., *Displacements: Women, Tradition, Literatures in French* (Baltimore: Johns Hopkins University Press, 1991).
2. J. Bachofen, "Mother Right," in *Myth, Religion and Mother Right: Selected Writings* (Princeton: Princeton University Press, 1967).
3. "With the hypnotic stare of a snake, the paws of a cat, lethally protuberant breasts, and the overblown musculature of a late twentieth-century body-builder, this sphinx represented a masochistic male fantasy of the ultimate dominatrix, the goddess of stony bestiality" (B. Dijkstra, *Idols of Perversity: Fantasies of Feminine Evil in Fin-de-Siècle Culture* [New York: Oxford University Press, 1986], p. 327).
4. Ibid., p. 240.
5. Quoted in B. Dijkstra, *Idols of Perversity*, p. 358.
6. B. Dijkstra, *Idols of Perversity*, pp. 363–64.
7. R. Felski, *The Gender of Modernity* (Cambridge, Mass.: Harvard University Press, 1995), p. 71.
8. In "Don Juan von Kolomea," Sacher-Masoch has his hero say the following about the problems involved in creating domestic peace: "Man has his work, his plans, his enterprises, his ideas! They hover about him like wings of doves, they lift him up with the pinions of eagles. They don't let him drown. But the wife [*Weib*]? She calls for help. Her 'I don't want to die,' she does not want it! and no help! And then she carries his image under her heart, feels how it grows and moves—lives!—There—there she finally holds it in her arms. She lifts it up—How does she feel now? Is she dreaming? Then the child speaks to her: 'I am you, and you live in me. Just look at me, I will save you.' She holds the child to her breast and is saved.... Do you know how one shoots the woodcock [*Schnepfen*, which in German also means of hussy or tart]?—No?—One must know, how does the woodcock fly? It flies up, thrusts three times, just like a will-o'-the-wisp, zick! zack! and then forwards. That is the moment. Then I aim straight and the woodcock is mine. The same goes for women. If one shoots right away—it's all over. But once one has the right timing, one gets them all—And at home there was peace" ("Don Juan von Kolomea," in M. Farin, ed., *Don Juan von Kolomea: Galizische Geschichten* [Bonn: Bouvier Verlag Herbert Grundmann, 1985], pp. 43–44, 57).
Compare this to Freud's statements about modern marriage: "Fear of the consequences of sexual intercourse first brings the married couple's physical affection to an end; and then, as a remoter result, it usually puts a stop as well to the mental sympathy be-

tween them, which should have been the successor to their original passionate love. The spiritual disillusionment and bodily deprivation to which most marriages are thus doomed puts both partners back in the state they were in before their marriage, except for being the poorer by the loss of an illusion, and they must once more have recourse to their fortitude in mastering and deflecting their sexual instinct. . . . experience shows as well that women, who, as being the actual vehicle of the sexual interests of mankind, are only endowed in a small measure with the gift of sublimating their instincts, and who, though they may find a sufficient substitute for the sexual object in an infant at the breast, do not find one in a growing child—experience shows, I repeat, that women, when they are subjected to the disillusionments of marriage, fall ill of severe neuroses which permanently darken their lives. . . . A neurotic wife who is unsatisfied by her husband is, as a mother, over-tender and over-anxious towards her child, on to whom she transfers her need for love; and she awakens it to sexual precocity" ("'Civilized' Sexual Morality and Modern Nervousness," *Standard Edition*, vol. IX, pp. 194–95, 202).

9. Either of these readings predominate in the literature on masochism: either the woman is seen to "really" represent the father (cf., for example, G. Lenzer, "On Masochism: A Contribution to the History of a Phantasy and Its Theory," *Signs* 1, no. 2 [1975]; S. Marcus, *The Other Victorians: A Study of Sexuality and Pornography in Mid-Nineteenth Century England* [New York: Basic Books, 1964]), in which case masochistic desire is simply disavowed homosexual desire; or she is read as a "phallic mother," the usurper of power and cause of the decline of the patriarchal ego (G. Deleuze, "Coldness and Cruelty," in *Masochism*; S. Žižek, *Looking Awry: An Introduction to Jacques Lacan through Popular Culture* [Cambridge, Mass.: MIT Press, 1991]; C. Siegel, *Male Masochism: Modern Revisions of the Story of Love* [Bloomington: Indiana University Press, 1995]), a reading that uncritically reproduces the masochistic fantasy of the Cruel Woman.

10. The proliferation of male fantasies of self-creation at the end of the nineteenth century finds its expression, above all, in the genre of male quest romances that articulate the need for female exclusion and male bonding in terms of the various processes of splitting, cloning, reincarnation, transfusion, aesthetic duplication, or vivisection. These are frequently, as Elaine Showalter points out, stories by men for other men (*Sexual Anarchy: Gender and Culture at the Fin de Siècle* [New York: Viking Books, 1990]). *Venus in Furs* follows the model: the story is told by Severin to a male narrator, who in turn retells it to a presumably male reader. *Parsifal*, too, replicates this structure insofar as the action of the drama is narrated by Gurnemanz to a group of young knights at the beginning of the first act. In Freud's description of the birth of the individual out of group psychology in *Group Psychology and the Analysis of the Ego*, we also find a male audience that hears the poet and identifies with him, thus allowing them too to emerge out of the group and constitute themselves as subjects. In all three cases, this constitutes a specifically male *Bildung*, a moment of transmission and induction into male sexuality.

11. C. Schorske, *Fin-de-Siècle Vienna: Politics and Culture* (New York: Vintage Books, 1961), p. 183.

12. J. Crary, *Techniques of the Observer: On Vision and Modernity in the Nineteenth Century* (Cambridge, Mass.: MIT Press, 1990), p. 75.

13. Ibid., p. 76.

14. S. Freud, "Creative Writers and Day Dreaming," *Standard Edition*, vol. IX, p. 147.

15. S. Freud, "The Taboo of Virginity," *Standard Edition*, vol. XI, p. 193.

16. Woman's mysterious nature is, however, a problem. Women do not show their love; they have, as Freud tells us in "On the Universal Tendency to Degradation in the Sphere of Love" (*Standard Edition*, vol. XI), no desire to overvalue their men. They prefer to keep their desire a secret. Indeed, this is their greatest desire.

17. Compare this to Mario Praz, in his analysis of masochistic literature: "This chapter must begin, like an article in an encyclopedia, with an extremely obvious and bald statement. There have always existed Fatal Women both in mythology and in literature, since mythology and literature are imaginative reflections of the various aspects of real life, and

real life has always provided more or less complete examples of arrogant and cruel female characters" (*The Romantic Agony* [New York: Oxford University Press, 1970], p. 199). Praz had obviously found *his* dream woman.

18. "Your love has a terrible logic," Mirowitsch tells Catherine the Great in Sacher-Masoch's short story "Nero in Reifrock."

19. L. von Sacher-Masoch, *Graf Donski*, quoted in A. Koschorke, *Leopold von Sacher-Masoch: Die Inszenierung einer Perversion* (Munich: Piper Verlag, 1988), p. 41.

20. A. Koschorke, *Leopold von Sacher-Masoch*, p. 41.

21. Quoted in L. von Sacher-Masoch, *Das schwarze Kabinett and Soziale Schattenbilder*, with an afterword by Karl Emmerich (Berlin: Verlag Das Neue Berlin, n.d., p. 235).

22. L. von Sacher-Masoch, "Der wahnsinnige Graf," in *Das schwarze Kabinett and Soziale Schattenbilder*, pp. 219, 220, 226.

23. C. Dean, *The Pleasures of the Self: Bataille, Lacan and the History of the Decentered Subject* (Ithaca: Cornell University Press, 1992).

24. Ibid., p. 196.

25. P. Bruckner, *The Tears of the White Man: Compassion as Contempt* (New York: The Free Press, 1986).

26. G. Deleuze, "Coldness and Cruelty," in *Masochism* (Cambridge, Mass.: Zone Books, 1991).

27. V. Smirnoff, "The Masochistic Contract," in M. A. F. Hanly, ed., *Essential Papers on Masochism* (New York: New York University Press, 1995), p. 69.

28. S. Žižek, "The Wound is Healed Only by the Spear That Smote You," in D. J. Levin, ed., *Opera Through Other Eyes* (Stanford: Stanford University Press, 1993), p. 211.

29. J. Flower McCannell, *The Regime of the Brother: After the Patriarchy* (New York: Routledge, 1991), p. 54.

30. F. Kittler, "World-Breath: On Wagner's Media Technology," in D. J. Levin, ed., *Opera through Other Eyes*, p. 231.

31. T. Adorno, *In Search of Wagner* (London: Verso Books, 1981), p. 62.

32. Ibid., p. 51.

33. P. Lacoue-Labarthe, *Musica Ficta (Figures of Wagner)* (Stanford: Stanford University Press, 1994).

34. This is true not only in Germany. One may simply recall Verdi's close connection to the Italian risorgimento, though here with very different political effects.

35. R. Wagner, "The Role of the Bayreuther Blätter," in *Religion and Art* (Lincoln: University of Nebraska Press, 1994).

36. P. Lacoue-Labarthe, *Musica Ficta*, p. 10.

37. T. Adorno, *In Search of Wagner*.

38. G. Bataille, *The Accursed Share*, vol. I (Cambridge, Mass.: Zone Books, 1991).

39. B. Dijkstra, *Idols of Perversity*, p. 352.

40. J. Kristeva, *Powers of Horror: An Essay on Abjection* (New York: Columbia University Press, 1982), p. 169.

41. I. Nagel, *Autonomy and Mercy* (Cambridge, Mass.: Harvard University Press, 1991), pp. 147–48.

42. T. Adorno, *In Search of Wagner*, p. 119.

43. A. Whittall, "The Music," in L. Beckett, *Richard Wagner: Parsifal* (New York: Cambridge University Press, 1981), pp. 85–86.

44. A. Koschorke, *Leopold von Sacher-Masoch*, p. 25.

45. The Orientalism of masochistic literature and art is pronounced, reflected in the frequent representation of biblical and Eastern themes in late-nineteenth-century painting (Salome and Judith "head" the list), and in the many literary expressions where the hero must go to exotic places in order to play out his fantasies. See, for example, P. Loti, *Aziyade* (New York: Routledge, 1989); T. E. Lawrence, *Seven Pillars of Wisdom* (London: Cape, 1973); R. Haggard, *She* (New York: Caxton House, 1960).

46. B. Dijkstra, *Idols of Perversity*, p. 352.

47. Ibid., p. 352.

48. M. Foucault, *The History of Sexuality* (New York: Vintage Books, 1990). For an analysis of Daniel Paul Schreber's experience of the "rottenness" of modern man's relation to the Law, see Eric Santner, *My Own Private Germany: Daniel Paul Schreber's Secret History of Modernity* (Princeton: Princeton University Press, 1996). Schreber experiences this rottenness as his own abjection, or what he calls his "*Ludertum*," another variation on the kind of lumpen existence implied by Bram Dijkstra.

49. The crisis of liberalism that this capriciousness reflects runs as a continuous thread throughout much of the political and legal writing of the period: Carl Schmitt viewed law as founded not in rule but in the exceptional moment of its transgression; Benjamin posited law making violence at the basis of all states; Weber could only make sense of the iron cage of bureaucracy as ultimately founded in a charismatic vocation or calling from within the inner recesses of private guilt; and Schreber, most explicit of all, was willing to occupy this power that nevertheless resides beyond power *as* a woman.

50. Slavoj Žižek is in all probability the latest and most accomplished theorist of the masochistic universe. The subject in capitalist society has passed, according to Žižek, through three stages during the last century: the autonomous subject of Max Weber's Protestant ethic, the heteronomous organization man, and finally, the pathological narcissist. It is in this final incarnation of male subjectivity that the law loses its consistency: the integration of a symbolic law is replaced by a multiplicity of rules that must be followed. The disintegration of both law and autonomous ego "entails the installation of a 'maternal' superego that does not prohibit enjoyment but, on the contrary, imposes it and punishes 'social failure' in a far more cruel and severe way, through an unbearable and self-destructive anxiety" (*Looking Awry*, p. 103). According to Žižek, this maternal superego relies for its operative power and enjoyment on a reorganization of the gaze and the voice in the subject's libidinal economy. Gaze and voice become "stains": "The gaze as object is a stain preventing me from looking at the picture from a safe, 'objective' distance, from enframing it as something that is at my grasping view's disposal. The gaze is, so to speak, a point at which the very frame (of my view) is already inscribed in the 'content' of the picture viewed" (p. 125). The parallel to Freud's analogy of ambition and love is striking here. And apropos the voice: "it is, of course, the same with the voice as object: this voice—the superegoic voice, for example, addressing me without being attached to any particular bearer—functions again as stain, whose inert presence interferes like a strange body and prevents me from achieving my self-identity" (pp. 125–26).

51. S. Freud, *Moses and Monotheism*, *Standard Edition*, vol. XXIII, p. 54. All further page numbers appear in the text.

52. Freud quite curiously omits to state that Jewishness by birth is matrilineally determined.

53. T. Laqueur, *Making Sex: Body and Gender from the Greeks to Freud* (Cambridge, Mass.: Harvard University Press, 1990), p. 243.

54. This is undoubtedly Michel Foucault's strongest claim as well: juridical relations collapsed in the nineteenth century; the "repressive hypothesis" was replaced by panoptic procedures, thereby obliterating the bourgeois individual who at least still had some degree of privacy.

55. T. Adorno, "Freudian Theory and the Pattern of Fascist Propaganda," in *The Culture Industry: Selected Essays on Mass Culture* (London: Routledge, 1991), p. 130.

SELECTED WORKS CITED

Adorno, Theodor. "Freudian Theory and the Pattern of Fascist Propaganda." In *The Culture Industry: Selected Essays on Mass Culture*. Edited and with an introduction by J. M. Bernstein. London: Routledge, 1991.
————. *In Search of Wagner*. Translated by R. Livingstone. London: Verso Books, 1981.
Althusser, Louis. *"Lenin and Philosophy" and Other Essays*. Translated by B. Brewster. New York: Monthly Review Press, 1971.
Anderson, Mark. *Kafka's Clothes: Ornament and Aestheticism in the Habsburg Fin de Siècle*. Oxford: Oxford University Press, 1992.
Bachofen, Johann Jakob. *Myth, Religion and Mother Right: Selected Writings*. Translated by R. Mannheim, with a preface by G. Boas and an introduction by J. Campbell. Princeton: Princeton University Press, 1967.
Bataille, Georges. *The Accursed Share*, vol. 1. Translated by R. Hurley. Cambridge, Mass.: Zone Books, 1991.
Beckett, Lucy. *Richard Wagner: Parsifal*. New York: Cambridge University Press, 1981.
Bersani, Leo. *The Freudian Body: Psychoanalysis and Art*. New York: Columbia University Press, 1986.
————. "Sexuality and Aesthetics." *October*, no. 28 (1984).
Borch-Jacobsen, Mikkel. *The Freudian Subject*. Translated by C. Porter, with a foreword by F. Roustang. Stanford: Stanford University Press, 1988.
Boscagli, Maurizia. *Eye on the Flesh: Fashions of Masculinity in the Early Twentieth Century*. Boulder, Colo.: Westview Press, 1996.
Bourdieu, Pierre. *Language and Symbolic Power*. Translated by G. Raymond and A. Adamson; edited and with an introduction by J. B. Thompson. Cambridge, Mass.: Harvard University Press, 1991.
Bruckner, Pascal. *The Tears of the White Man: Compassion as Contempt*. Translated and with an introduction by W. R. Beer. New York: The Free Press, 1986.

Butler, Judith. *The Psychic Life of Power: Theories in Subjection.* Stanford, Calif.: Stanford University Press, 1997.

Chion, Michel. *La toile trouée.* Paris: Cahiers du Cinema, Editions de l'Etoile, 1988.

Clément, Catherine. *Opera, Or the Undoing of Woman.* Translated by B. Wing, with a foreword by S. McClary. Minneapolis: University of Minnesota Press, 1988.

Crary, Jonathan. *Techniques of the Observer: On Vision and Modernity in the Nineteenth Century.* Cambridge, Mass.: MIT Press, 1990.

Croce, Benedetto. *History of Europe in the Nineteenth Century.* Translated by H. Furst. London: George Allen & Unwin, 1934.

Dahlhaus, Carl. *Richard Wagner's Music Dramas.* Translated by M. Whittal. Cambridge: Cambridge University Press, 1979.

Damisch, Hubert. *The Judgment of Paris.* Translated by J. Goodman. Chicago: Chicago University Press, 1996.

Dean, Carolyn. *The Self and Its Pleasures: Bataille, Lacan, and the History of the Decentered Subject.* Ithaca: Cornell University Press, 1992.

Deleuze, Gilles. "Coldness and Cruelty." In *Masochism.* Translated by J. McNeil. Cambridge, Mass.: Zone Books, 1991.

de Rougemont, Denis. *Love in the Western World.* Translated by M. Belgion. New York: Fawcett Premier Books, 1956.

Derrida, Jacques. *The Ear of the Other.* Edited by C. McDonald; translated by P. Kamuf. New York: Schocken Books, 1985.

Dijkstra, Bram. *Idols of Perversity: Fantasies of Feminine Evil in Fin-de-Siècle Culture.* New York: Oxford University Press, 1986.

Doane, Mary Ann. *Femme Fatale: Feminism, Film, Theory, Psychoanalysis.* New York: Routledge, 1991.

Ehrenreich, Barbara, Elizabeth Hess, and Gloria Jacobs, *Re-making Love: The Feminization of Sex.* New York: Anchor-Doubleday, 1986.

Emslie, Barry. "Woman as Image and Narrative in Wagner's Parsifal: A Case Study." *Cambridge Opera Journal* 3, no. 2 (1991).

Felski, Rita. *The Gender of Modernity.* Cambridge, Mass.: Harvard University Press, 1995.

Floros, Constantin. "Studien zur 'Parsifal'-Rezeption." *Musik-Konzepte*, no. 25 (1982).

Flower McCannell, Juliet. *The Regime of the Brother: After the Patriarchy.* New York: Routledge, 1991.

Flugel, J. C. *The Psychology of Clothes.* New York: International Universities Press, 1930.

Foucault, Michel. *The History of Sexuality.* Translated by R. Hurley. New York: Pantheon Books, 1978.

———. *Power/Knowledge.* Translated and edited by C. Gordon. New York: Harvester Press, 1980.

Freud, Sigmund. *The Standard Edition: The Complete Psychological Works.* Translated by and under the general editorship of J. Strachey, in collaboration with A. Freud, assisted by A. Strachey and A. Tyson. London: Hogarth Press, 1953–1974.

Frevert, Ute. *Women in German History: From Bourgeois Emancipation to Sexual Liberation.* Translated by S. McKinnon-Evans. New York: Berg/St. Martin's Press, 1988.

Fuchs, Eduard. *Das erotische Element in der Karikatur (Der Karikaturen der europäischen Völker dritter Band).* Berlin, 1904.

Girard, René. *Violence and the Sacred.* Translated by P. Gregory. Baltimore: Johns Hopkins University Press, 1977.

Grosskurth, Phyllis. *The Secret Ring: Freud's Inner Circle and the Politics of Psychoanalysis.* New York: Addison-Wesley Publishing Company, 1991.

Grossman, William. "Notes on Masochism: A Discussion of the History and Development of a Psychoanalytic Concept." *Psychoanalytic Quarterly* 55, no. 3 (1986).

Gutman, Robert. *Richard Wagner: The Man, His Mind and His Music.* New York: Harcourt, Brace and Jovanovich, 1990.

Habermas, Jürgen. *The Structural Transformation of the Public Sphere: An Inquiry into a Category of Bourgeois Society*. Translated by T. Burger with the assistance of F. Lawrence. Cambridge, Mass.: MIT Press, 1989.

Haggard, Henry Rider. *She*. New York: Caxton House, 1940.

Heine, Heinrich. "Nachwort zu *Romanzero*." In *Sämtliche Schriften*, vol. 11: 1851–1855. Frankfurt: Ullstein Werkausgaben, 1976.

Hunt, Lynn. *The Family Romance of the French Revolution*. Berkeley: University of California Press, 1992.

Irigaray, Luce. *Speculum of the Other Woman*. Translated by G. C. Gill. Ithaca: Cornell University Press, 1985.

Johnson, Barbara. "Charles Baudelaire and Marceline Desbordes-Valmore." In J. Dejean and N. K. Miller, eds., *Displacements: Women, Tradition, Literatures in French*. Baltimore: Johns Hopkins University Press, 1991.

Jünger, Ernst. "On Danger." Translated by D. Reneau. *New German Critique*, no. 59 (1993).

Kaes, Anton. "The Cold Gaze: Notes on Mobilization and Modernity." *New German Critique*, no. 59 (1993).

Kafka, Franz. *Parables and Paradoxes*. Bilingual edition. New York: Schocken Books, 1958.

Kaplan, Alice Yaeger. *Reproductions of Banality: Fascism, Literature, and French Intellectual Life*. Minneapolis: University of Minnesota Press, 1986.

Kittler, Friedrich. *Discourse Networks 1800/1900*. Translated by M. Metteer with C. Cullens; foreword by D. E. Wellbery. Stanford: Stanford University Press, 1990.

———. "World-Breath: On Wagner's Media Technology." In D. J. Levin, ed., *Opera Through Other Eyes*. Translated by F. Kittler and D. J. Levin. Stanford: Stanford University Press, 1993.

Koschorke, Albrecht. *Leopold von Sacher-Masoch: Die Inszenierung einer Perversion*. Munich: Piper Verlag, 1988.

Krafft-Ebing, Richard von. *Arbeiten aus dem Gesammtgebiet der Psychatrie und Neuropathologie*. Leipzig: Johann Ambrosius Barth, 1899.

———. *Psychopathia Sexualis*. Munich: Matthes & Seitz Verlag, 1984.

Kristeva, Julia. *Powers of Horror: An Essay on Abjection*. Translated by L. S. Roudiez. New York: Columbia University Press, 1982.

Lacan, Jacques. "Desire and Interpretation of Desire in *Hamlet*." Translated by J. Hulbert. *Yale French Studies*, no. 55/56 (1977).

———. *The Four Fundamental Concepts of Psychoanalysis*. Edited by J.-A. Miller; translated by A. Sheridan. New York: Norton, 1977.

———. *Seminar Book VII: The Ethics of Psychoanalysis*. Translated by D. Porter. New York: Norton, 1992.

LaCapra, Dominick. *Representing the Holocaust: History, Theory, Trauma*. Ithaca: Cornell University Press, 1991.

Lacoue-Labarthe, Philippe. *Musica Ficta (Figures of Wagner)*. Translated by F. McCarren. Stanford: Stanford University Press, 1994.

Laplanche, Jean. *Life and Death in Psychoanalysis*. Translated and with an introduction by J. Mehlman. Baltimore: Johns Hopkins University Press, 1976.

———. "To Situate Sublimation." *October*, no. 28 (1984).

Laplanche, Jean., and J.-B. Pontalis. "Fantasy and the Origins of Sexuality." In V. Burgin, J. Donald, and C. Kaplan, eds., *Formations of Fantasy*. New York: Routledge, 1986.

Laqueur, Thomas. *Making Sex: Body and Gender from the Greeks to Freud*. Cambridge, Mass.: Harvard University Press, 1990.

Lawrence, Thomas Edward. *Seven Pillars of Wisdom: A Triumph*. London: Cape, 1973.

Le Conte, Joseph. *Evolution: Its Nature, Its Evidence, and Its Relation to Religious Thought*. New York: D. Appleton, 1897.

Lenzer, Gertrude. "On Masochism: A Contribution to the History of a Phantasy and Its Theory." *Signs* 1, no. 2 (1975).

Loos, Adolf. "Ornament and Crime." In L. Munz and G. Kunstler, eds., *Adolf Loos, Pioneer of Modern Architecture*. With an introduction by N. Pevsner and an Appreciation by O. Kokoschka; translated by H. Meek. New York: Praeger Press, 1966.

Loti, Pierre. *Aziyade*. Translated by Marjorie Laurie. New York: Routledge, 1989.

Lukacher, Ned. *Daemonic Figures: Shakespeare and the Question of Conscience*. Ithaca: Cornell University Press, 1994.

Mann, Thomas. "Sufferings and Greatness of Richard Wagner." In *Essays*. New York: Vintage Books, 1957.

Marcus, Steven. *The Other Victorians: A Study of Sexuality and Pornography in Mid-Nineteenth Century England*. New York: Basic Books, 1964.

McGrath, William. *Freud's Discovery of Psychoanalysis: The Politics of Hysteria*. Ithaca: Cornell University Press, 1986.

Modleski, Tania. *Feminism Without Women: Culture and Criticism in a "Postfeminist" Age*. New York: Routledge, 1991.

Nagel, Ivan. *Autonomy and Mercy*. Translated by M. Faber and I. Nagel. Cambridge, Mass.: Harvard University Press, 1991.

Nietzsche, Friedrich. *The Case of Wagner*. Translated by W. Kaufmann. New York: Vintage Books, 1967.

Noyes, John. "Der Blick des Begehrens." *Acta Germanica* 19 (1988).

Pater, Walter. *The Renaissance*. New York: Oxford University Press, 1986.

Poizat, Michel. *The Angel's Cry: Beyond the Pleasure Principle in Opera*. Translated by A. Denner. Ithaca: Cornell University Press, 1992.

Praz, Mario. *The Romantic Agony*. Translated by A. Davidson. New York: Oxford University Press, 1970.

Reik, Theodor. *Masochism in Sex and Society*. Translated by H. Beigel and G. M. Kurth. New York: Grove Press, 1962.

Rousseau, Jean-Jacques. *Essay on the Origin of Languages*. Translated and with an afterword by J. H. Moran and A. Gode and an introduction by A. Gode. New York: Frederick Ungar Publishing Company, 1966.

Sacher-Masoch, Leopold von. *Das schwarze Kabinett and Soziale Schattenbilder: Aus den Memoiren eines österreichischen Polizeibeamten*. Berlin: Verlag Das Neue Berlin, n.d.

———. "Don Juan von Kolomea." In M. Farin, ed., *Don Juan von Kolomea: Galizische Geschichten*. Bonn: Bouvier Verlag Herbert Grundmann, 1985.

———. "Nero im Reifrock." In *Katharina II., Zarin der Lust*. Munich, 1982.

———. *Venus im Pelz*. Frankfurt: Insel Verlag, 1968.

———. *Venus in Furs*. In *Masochism*. Translated by J. McNeil. Cambridge, Mass.: Zone Books, 1991.

von Sacher-Masoch, Wanda. *Confessions*. Translated by M. Phillips, C. Hébert, and V. Vale. San Francisco: Re/Search Publications, 1990.

Salewski, Michael. "'Julian, begib dich in mein Boudoir': Weiberherrschaft und Fin-de-Siècle." In M. Salewski and A. Bagel-Bohlan, eds., *Sexualmoral und Zeitgeist im 19. und 20. Jahrhundert*. Opladen: Leske + Budrich, 1990.

Santner, Eric. *My Own Private Germany: Daniel Paul Schreber's Secret History of Modernity*. Princeton: Princeton University Press, 1996.

Schorske, Carl. *Fin-de-Siècle Vienna: Politics and Culture*. New York: Vintage Books, 1961.

Schreber, Daniel Paul. *Memoirs of My Nervous Illness*. Translated by I. Macalpine and R. A. Hunter. Cambridge, Mass.: Harvard University Press, 1988.

Showalter, Elaine. *Sexual Anarchy: Gender and Culture at the Fin de Siècle*. New York: Viking Books, 1990.

Siegel, Carol. *Male Masochism: Modern Revisions of the Story of Love*. Bloomington: Indiana University Press, 1995.

Silverman, Debora. *Art Nouveau in Fin-de-Siècle France: Politics, Psychology and Style*. Berkeley: University of California Press, 1989.

Silverman, Kaja. *Male Subjectivity at the Margins*. New York: Routledge, 1992.

Smirnoff, Victor. "The Masochistic Contract." In M. A. F. Hanly, ed., *Essential Papers on Masochism*. New York: New York University Press, 1995.

Studlar, Gaylin. *In the Realm of Pleasure: Sternberg, Dietrich and the Masochistic Aesthetic*. New York: Columbia University Press, 1988.

Treut, Monika. *Die grausame Frau: Zum Frauenbild bei de Sade und Sacher-Masoch*. Basel: Stroemfeld/Roter Stern, 1984.

Wagner, Richard. *Religion and Art*. Translated by W. A. Ellis. Lincoln: University of Nebraska Press, 1994.

———. *Richard Wagner to Mathilde Wesendonck*. Translated and with a preface by W. A. Ellis. Boston: Milford House, 1971.

Warburg, Aby. *Images from the Region of the Pueblo Indians of North America*. Translated, edited, and with an interpretive essay by M. P. Steinberg. Ithaca: Cornell University Press, 1995.

Weber, Sam. *The Legend of Freud*. Minneapolis: Minnesota University Press, 1982.

———. "Taking Place: Towards a Theater of Dislocation." In D. J. Levin, ed., *Opera Through Other Eyes*. Stanford: Stanford University Press, 1993.

Williams, Linda R. "Submission and Reading: Feminine Masochism and Feminist Criticism." *new formations*, no. 7 (1989).

Winnicott, Donald W. *Playing and Reality*. New York: Routledge, 1971.

Žižek, Slavoj. *Enjoy Your Symptom: Jacques Lacan in Hollywood and Out*. New York: Routledge, 1992.

———. *Looking Awry: An Introduction to Jacques Lacan Through Popular Culture*. Cambridge, Mass.: MIT Press, 1991.

———. *Metastases of Enjoyment: Six Essays on Woman and Causality*. London: Verso Books, 1994.

———. *The Sublime Object of Ideology*. London: Verso Books, 1989.

———. "'There is No Sexual Relationship.'" In R. Salecl and Žižek, eds., *Gaze and Voice as Love Objects*. Durham: Duke University Press, 1996.

———. "'The Wound is Healed Only by the Spear That Smote You.'" In D. J. Levin, ed., *Opera Through Other Eyes*. Stanford: Stanford University Press, 1993.

INDEX

Abject, 38, 104, 212
Adorno, Theodor, 98, 101, 180, 181, 183, 193, 198
Against Nature (Huysmans), 165
Althusser, Louis, 203
Anaclisis, 45, 118, 119, 122, 141
Anamorphosis, 103–104, 110–111
Anxiety, 24, 27, 31–32, 45, 53, 59, 136, 158, 162, 166, 177, 211, 215
Autoerotism, 118

Bachofen, Johann, 164–165
Bataille, George, 10, 182
Baudelaire, Charles, 165
Bayreuth, 89, 90, 198, 204
Benjamin, Walter, 55, 215
Bersani, Leo, 7, 8, 10, 41, 53–54, 196, 211
Borch-Jacobsen, Mikkel, 120–121, 123, 125, 128, 130–131, 208, 210
Bourdieu, Pierre, 56–57
Bourgeois subject, 2, 14, 33, 40, 98, 115, 176–178, 210
Boxing Helena (J. Chambers Lynch), 196
Brother, 39, 123, 129–130, 137, 144, 167, 209, 210

Castration, 6, 14, 39, 53, 105, 112–115, 131, 139, 156–157, 162–163, 166, 171–172

Charcot, J. M., 90, 128, 129
Christianity, 69, 70, 89, 91, 95–96, 101, 103, 109, 153, 192, 197
Civilization and Its Discontents (Freud), 24, 117, 144–163, 199, 208, 209
Colonialism, 5, 195
Conscience, 25, 29, 39, 49, 102, 155–157, 180, 192
Consensus, 139–140
Courtly love, 5–7, 40, 43, 170
Crary, Jonathan, 169
Creative Writers and Day-Dreaming (Freud), 170–172
Croce, Benedetto, 19–20
Cruel Woman, 3, 13–15, 37, 39–40, 54, 67, 70–73, 76–77, 83, 85, 87, 107, 121, 164, 167, 170, 173, 175–176, 185–186, 196, 201, 213–214
Cynical reason, 34

Dahlhaus, Carl, 99
Danger, 32–33, 46, 131, 172
Dean, Carolyn, 10, 20
Death drive, 27, 30, 49, 118, 135, 154
Debussy, Claude, 91
Deleuze, Gilles, 3–5, 8–10, 37–39, 76, 195, 199, 213
Democracy, 33, 117, 123, 129, 163

deRougemont, Denis, 120
Derrida, Jacques, 92
Dijkstra, Bram, 22, 55, 182, 202, 215
Disavowal, 3, 5, 9, 14, 36–37, 39, 44, 54,
    56, 76, 88, 95, 102, 104, 108–110, 161,
    167–168, 192–193
Diva, 107
Diva (Beineix), 206
Doane, Mary Ann, 41, 54
H.D. (Doolittle, Henrietta), 162

The Economic Problem of Masochism (Freud),
    26, 27–30, 79
Edison, Thomas, 16, 205
Ego, 29, 31, 33–35, 44, 98–99, 118, 124,
    135, 140–141, 145–149, 154–155, 157,
    190, 193, 213, 215
Ellis, Havelock, 23
Enjoyment, 6, 8, 34–38, 49, 97, 102–103,
    112, 115, 177, 193, 204, 206, 215

Family, 23, 26, 166–167
Father: banished, 3, 109; dead or murdered,
    40, 49, 111, 117, 121, 123, 131, 137, 138,
    140, 153, 190, 209 (*see also* Freud: scien-
    tific myth of the primal horde); humili-
    ated, 37, 183; narcissistic, *see* father, pri-
    mal; Oedipal, 8, 54, 157, 160, 165–166,
    208; primal, 117, 123, 137–138, 153–154,
    156, 158, 163, 186–188, 206; weak, 23
Feminine masochism, 5, 28, 29, 198
Foucault, Michel, 211, 215; on sovereign vs.
    disciplinary power, 211
Freud, Sigmund, 9–11, 13, 17, 22, 26–31,
    61–62, 68–69, 75, 78–79, 116–163, 165,
    169, 170–172, 183, 186–193, 198–199,
    204, 206, 208–209, 211, 212, 213; on
    aggression, 31, 128, 135, 143, 152–155,
    159; on ambition, 170–172; on ambiva-
    lence, 133, 135, 212; on anti-Semitism,
    153, 192–193, 208; on anxiety, 31–33;
    on the army, 129–132, 136, 143; on the
    Catholic Church, 129–132, 136, 143, 151,
    186, 192, 208, 209; critique of LeBon,
    126–129; critique of suggestion, 126–
    128, 131, 208; on crowds, 126, 128; on
    daydreaming, 170–172; on the ego-ideal,
    117, 125, 130, 132, 136–137, 140, 158,
    208; on great men, 41–42, 144–145,
    186–193; on group psychology, 116–117,
    124–127, 136–139, 148, 159–160, 188,
    190; on hypnosis, 128–129; on individual
    psychology, 116–117, 125–127, 136–139,
    159, 188; on Judaism, 186–192; on judg-
    ment, 144–146; on longing for the father
    (*Vatersehnsucht*), 146–148, 160, 187, 211;

on love, 50, 116–163, 208; on mass psy-
    chology, *see* group psychology; on the
    myth of the hero, 139–140, 170–172,
    187, 213; on object-choice, 118, 120, 130,
    135, 140–142, 152; on object-libido, *see*
    object-love; on object-love, 117–118,
    121, 136–137, 140–141, 144, 149, 153;
    on the oceanic feeling, 126, 145–146,
    162; on overvaluation, 117, 119–120,
    122–123, 125, 134–136, 140, 144–145,
    163; on panic, 131, 136; on the pleasure
    principle, 26–28, 32, 147, 154–158, 159;
    poet, 139, 213; on the reality principle,
    27; on the role of the father, 123, 129–
    130, 132, 136–137, 141, 146, 148, 155,
    157, 159–163, 188–192, 210, 211, 212;
    on the role of mothers, 51, 139–141, 146,
    155, 160–162, 188–192; on the scientific
    myth of the primal horde, 123, 137, 150–
    151, 160, 186, 188; on seduction, 32, 43,
    51–52; on sexual bondage, 172; on the
    social bond, 124, 125, 134–136, 148, 153,
    155, 159, 162; on sublimation, 41–55; on
    transference, 48, 162; on war, 30–33
Fuchs, Eduard, 20–21

Gaze, 14, 56–57, 62, 70, 72, 77, 80–81,
    83–88, 100, 103–104, 110, 167, 184,
    186, 200–202, 215
Girard, René, 210
Group Psychology and the Analysis of the Ego
    (Freud), 116–117, 124–146, 152–153,
    155, 161, 208, 209, 213
Guilt, 25, 28, 49, 102, 105, 108–109, 111,
    153, 155–156, 158, 192–193, 209. *See also*
    masochism guilt, and guilt

Habermas, Jürgen, 210–211
Hartmann, Eduard von, 23
H.D., 162
Heine, Heinrich, 1
Hoffmann, E. T. A., 205
Hunt, Lynn, 209
Hysteria, 25, 142–143, 191

Id, 29–30, 34, 145, 193
Idealization, 5, 125, 136
Identification, 4, 38, 97, 99, 104, 106, 109,
    111–112, 117–122, 130–132, 136–137,
    140–144, 152–153, 158–160, 170, 180,
    203, 204, 206, 209, 210, 211
Ideology, 4, 34–35, 93, 112, 181, 185,
    203
Impotence, 93, 103, 104, 208
Incest, 3, 39, 115, 152, 188, 209
Interpellation, 97, 102, 106, 112, 203

CPSIA information can be obtained at www.ICGtesting.com
Printed in the USA
LVOW072008141211

259483LV00001B/47/P